Madre and I

WRITING IN LATINIDAD

Autobiographical Voices of U.S. Latinos/as

SERIES EDITORS

Susana Chávez-Silverman
Paul Allatson
Silvia D. Spitta
Rafael Campo

Madre and I

A Memoir
of Our Immigrant Lives

Guillermo Reyes

The University of Wisconsin Press

Publication of this volume has been made possible, in part,
through support from the
SCHOOL OF THEATRE AND FILM AT ARIZONA STATE UNIVERSITY.

The University of Wisconsin Press
1930 Monroe Street, 3rd Floor
Madison, Wisconsin 53711-2059
uwpress.wisc.edu

3 Henrietta Street
London WCE 8LU, England
eurospanbookstore.com

1   3   5   4   2

Printed in the United States of America

Library of Congress Cataloging-in-Publication Data
Reyes, Guillermo A.
Madre and I: a memoir of our immigrant lives / Guillermo Reyes.
p.   cm. — (Writing in Latinidad: autobiographical voices of U.S. Latinos/as)
ISBN 978-0-299-23624-3 (pbk.: alk. paper)
ISBN 978-0-299-23623-6 (e-book)
1. Reyes, Guillermo A.   2. Hispanic American gays — Biography.
3. Immigrants — United States — Biography.
I. Title.   II. Series: Writing in Latinidad.
PS3568.E8834Z46   2010
818'.603 — dc22
2009041310

The names of the principal families have been left intact—the Reyes, Cáceres, and Bravo families, in particular. Some names have been changed to protect people's privacy, my cousin "Catalina" in particular, and a few others. My friend Eugene chose to have his first name mentioned but not his last. The youthful obsession "Santos" is definitely a pseudonym, along with other lovers.

To

MARÍA CÁCERES

and

GUILLERMO E. REYES

Contents

Acknowledgments

Special thanks:

To the Virginia Piper Center for Creative Writing at Arizona State University for grants administered under Jewell Parker Rhodes that allowed me to travel to Chile and interview relatives.

To the School of Theatre and Film at Arizona State University for its support and that of its director, Linda Essig.

To my various students through the years. I hope this explains a few things.

To friends Daniel and Trino. They would know why. To Eugene, who was there when most of it happened. So were Gordon and Sean, and a few others.

To the Villar sisters—Amparo, Isabel, Carmen—for providing sisterhood to my mother in her time of need, and to Amparo's daughter, Rosemary, for providing sisterhood toward me.

In Chile, there are still all those aunts—Gladys and Nelly, in particular—and Teresa and her children.

To the Reyes family who became part of my life recently, and will add to it from now on.

Madre and I

Prologue

La tristeza más grande que tengo ...

"My saddest regret is that I won't be leaving you money," my mother wrote down on a piece of paper the day her cancer was diagnosed in Portland, Oregon, "like other mothers would have done." She repeated this confession over the phone with a nervous laugh. "I'm just not a responsible mother," she said. I couldn't help but feel a wistful longing for times when a smile was better justified—although a smile broke out of me nonetheless, quite defiantly of the situation. What was I smiling at exactly? At my mother's uncanny ability for making me slip into nervous laughter at the worst possible moments. Recall President Reagan's reaction to being shot in a nearly successful assassination attempt: "I forgot to duck," he tells Nancy as she runs to his side that spring day in 1981. My mother gasped in delight to hear the newsman quote the injured president precisely at a moment when she thought she might cry, and managed to like Mr. Reagan for the first time. As a Chilean immigrant, and a progressive-minded person, and mostly a low-wage earner, she had never empathized with a man who "worked for the rich," as she might have claimed once, but nonetheless, his sense of humor proved disarming. Mother voted for his re-election in 1984, the only time she voted for a Republican. In spite of my own battles with my mother, I became used to the same baffling energy of unlikely gaiety even in times of extreme sadness. The letter was one of regrets and apologies, and yet one of her most cherished examples of singing was Edith Piaf's "No Regrets—*Je ne regrette rien.*" Always disarmed, always courted by her insane banter, I am an admirer of her *esprit* of alacrity, my one true

3

form of "inheritance," if such things truly matter. At times, they do, of course. I have despaired all my life over our humble background and our lowly immigrant status, and all those things that have ensured the marginality that one inherits in lieu of hard cash. But oftentimes, I forgot about them, even ignored them. I wanted to be a writer at the age of ten, but as it would turn out, writing as a career would prove elusive. I wrote plays: too marginal. Playwriting continues to evolve into the same status as poetry: lofty and out of touch with the masses, therefore inconsequential and, in some cases, elitist. But if I write screenplays that feature Latino immigrants, the Hollywood agents still complain. "You're not writing for real Americans." That's an actual quote from a prominent agent in Los Angeles. That was America in the 1990s, and we immigrants were blamed for California's ills, crowded freeways, riots, even the quakes. We consumed public resources, we were leading the state downhill, and we were mostly nonwhite. I have a few off-Broadway credits by now, and Arizona State University hired me to helm their playwriting program. I am on an academic track. Same goes for the rest of my life. I have gotten a private life of sorts, but I get the feeling my mother always wondered when I'd get a real one. I concluded early on in my pessimistic youth that life was something that happened to others. I would just sit by on the sidelines and inertly watch it pass me by like a parade. I have nonetheless aged well, reversed my youthful pessimism, and struggled against passivity, seeking to take the initiative and put my life in motion. Still, often I fear the cancer has moved in, made a home of our genes, first claiming my father, then my mother, and eventually settled somewhere in the recesses of my own body. I won't get out of this alive, I realize, but that's also worth a laugh. It's a riot. I hear a great poet in the back of my mind urging me to rage against the dawning of the light. I'm too quiet and unassuming to actually *rage*, but I am inclined to agree that that's what I should do. I agree that one day I will find a way to rage, maybe just vent, and use anger to extricate some meaning out of this life, and yet I can't bring myself to cry. The aesthetics of a quiet person is to find a smile. I forgot to duck. My mother understood all this. Don't look back in anger, she might have said or thought, and sorry about the life insurance thing. I forgot to open the account.

Your mother is in the hospital" was the first message I heard in my office in the Department of Theatre at Arizona State University. One of her employers who had hired her as a nanny in Portland found her in her apartment, conscious but unable to move. A crippling pain emanating from deep in her spine had brought her mercilessly down on the pristine rug of the living room. She was taken to the E.R. and from there diagnosed with an advanced metastasized cancer that had apparently originated in her breast. Mammograms had never caught the original cancer, and in the first days of her diagnosis, the doctors couldn't decide where the cancer originated, and were only in agreement that it had spread.

I flew into Portland a day after her diagnosis, and, at first, she avoided talking about cancer. She wanted to talk about herself as a mother. "What about the time I slapped you really hard when you were six? I was afraid you'd turn out *con defectos.*" Defective, or literally, with defects. She said this, too, with a smile. What defects could she possibly mean? My writing career, my single status, my marginal sexuality? All of the above? Mother was the class clown, the rebel, the Chilean immigrant lady with a big mouth and the instinct to entertain. Children loved her, mostly because they sensed she was one of them, a child with wrinkles and graying hair. She was a professional nanny, having initiated her career as a Hollywood maid, and she was also my own caretaker, the adult role model, a single mother with a bastard kid and plenty of secrets that I've had to unearth gradually through a lifetime. Mother didn't talk much about her past. When asked uncomfortable questions about my father, the married Chilean teacher who'd left her pregnant in Santiago nearly forty years previously, she became uncomfortable: "Why all these questions? Just make something up." I could choose to write a book of fiction. It would make things easier certainly, but that isn't the point of memory—a memoir should be lucid, introspective, candid, not a mystery of the missing father and the evasive mother. My work gets a little harder without her cooperation, but nonetheless I manage to uncover a few truths. The rest goes unspoken.

Mother was also wrong to assume she'd left me with plenty of nothing.

She's left me with a wealth of images to endure this sweet agonizing curse of a mostly sound memory—my own, that is, not hers, which hesitates and blacks out at convenient moments in the narrative.

Before going too far back in time, if I have to choose, I'll say the most entertaining image I can remember is Mother holding the Best Picture Oscar in 1978. Not hers, certainly, but nonetheless the real thing. A Chilean immigrant with a thick accent, Mother was never employed by the entertainment industry—except of course in that one area relegated to the immigrant: maintenance, naturally.

"The Best Picture Award goes to . . . *Annie Hall.*" It's Oscar time in 1978, for films released in 1977. Up on the small screen, two middle-aged men make their way to the podium to accept the much coveted, but also hyped, award. We were in the living room of our one bedroom apartment on Sunset/Formosa in Hollywood. Mother shared the costs with a long-time friend, Carmen, another Chilean woman approximately her age, around forty at the time. They slept in cheap hotel-style single beds in their diminutive room. I camped out in the living room on the couch with a teenage attitude of ownership and defiance. The TV was clearly mine, and I called the shots before we ever owned a remote. Nonetheless, it didn't take a fight to convince Mother to watch the Oscars. We had driven to Hollywood from Arlington, Virginia. She, Carmen, and a nagging kid on the back seat had made the long haul through the heartland; two Chilean, unmarried, man-less immigrant women and one bastard kid making their way west without a guiding principle other than movement. We were errant, aimless in our wandering path, but in search at least for something concrete, such as change and adventure. The road to Hollywood seemed to be the best route. We knew no better. Mother had grown tired of the sedate Virginia suburb across the Potomac from the Watergate, and her job as a file clerk seemed to be the dead end of the American dream. She didn't emigrate from Chile to get stuck filing claims for GEICO. In Hollywood, she hadn't had much luck in landing anything glamorous, but ultimately maintenance for the Bel Air and Beverly Hills crowd came close to glamour and grandeur for someone foreign and unemployed and with a limited command of the English language.

"That's Mr. Yaffee," Mother said of the gentleman holding the Oscar. She was referring to Charles H. Joffe, one of the producers of *Annie Hall.* "I clean home for him."

"No way!" I said in that youthful American expression.

"No, *I* work for him!" Carmen spoke up to claim the rightful credit. "You just help!"

"The two of you? No way!" I tended to answer in English, though my Spanish was still functional, not forgotten, just unused. I tended to live in my own teenage sphere of influence, and the choice of language was my own. I spoke like teenagers did, preferably on television, since they spoke better than the sorry-ass kids at Fairfax High in the Jewish District populated by immigrants from all over the world, including Russian Jews, Koreans, Mexicans, Armenians, even a few other Chileans like ourselves. TV shows hired writers who came up with cool dialogue. I was Ritchie Cunningham and the Fonz combined. I spoke, in other words, in the English of acceptability around a high school, not that I was easily accepted, but a kid can only hope. Another fact: I had never heard much about Mother's work. I rarely paid attention to María's maintenance gigs, but on Oscar night, it dawned upon me that my mother might lead a more interesting life than I had dared imagine. At that age, ignoring one's parents and rebelling against their less than average lives seemed an important modus operandi. But today I heard her say she worked for one of Woody Allen's producers.

"I show you," she added, defiantly. The next day she took her modest Instamatic camera and had her friend Carmen take a picture of herself holding Mr. Joffe's Oscar at his home. Then María surrendered the statuette to Carmen, who dutifully posed for her own picture. All in a day's work. To this day, I doubt Mr. Joffe remembers briefly employing those Chilean immigrants with an Oscar fetish. But his patio's in the background.

I asked her many years later, as her body lay on a bed in a Portland hospice recovering from the aftereffects of chemotherapy, about this Oscar night. "*Voy a tener que admitir*—I must admit," she began. "Carmen was right . . . no, I didn't work for Mr. *Yaffee*, not directly. Carmen worked for him. I went in to help her sometimes, but when I saw him on TV, I grabbed the spotlight. From then on, I told everyone I worked for him and I had the picture of me and the Oscar to prove it. Carmen took her own picture of herself with the Oscar, but it was my idea. I treated it like my Oscar. I held it in my hands and thanked the Academy until Mr. *Yaffee* came home and I quickly put it back."

I hold on to the picture for dear life along with my other important documents such as my passport and condominium papers. I study it, I admire it. The sun endows the Oscar with a surreal glint. One can almost hear the magic tinkle in it. But then the shadows in the patio descend upon María's face, giving my mother's nose an unusually large protrusion, making it seem she's wearing something bought at a fun store. Her own was never that big, but the sun gives off that illusion. It's beauty and the nose, a perfectly tailored comedic effect that shows off the clown in my mother's personality. She's having fun, that Chilean Groucho woman, an immigrant in the United States. Who let her in? Somebody, hide the Oscars.

I feel estranged from her final days. I live in Arizona, she lives in Portland, and I fly in when I can and slowly notice that I'm losing her. She's no longer the charming, debonair, spirited woman who left everything behind, first in Chile, then in Arlington, Virginia, then in Los Angeles, dragging me along on her fabulous adventure, I, her one illegitimate son, nothing too unusual in her working-class Chilean family. I was only one in a family beset by the problem of the elusive male. I had come to terms with the often disconcerting facts of our family history. We ranged from the many devout *católicos* in the family who actually married, had kids, and dwelt among the faithful, and those like us who were born out of wedlock but raised among the "legits," lived in their midst, did our first communions and confirmations without a hint of our deviance. We were forgiven, blended into the family fold, and we rarely had to talk, if at all, about our condition as the bastards. In the United States we not only were confronted with the need to make a living for ourselves in a sink-and-swim society far away from our family, but we also became social experiments—the new immigrant masses in the aftermath of a new wave of immigrants, from Latin America and Asia particularly, who have transformed the American heartland in the aftermath of the 1965 immigrant law reform that allowed non-Europeans to immigrate more freely into the nation.

We can only succeed at one or two things. Mother bought the American Dream in full but later realized, with her limited English yet boundless energy, that her accomplishments in the consumerist, competitive American tradition would be "limited" to being a good mother, but she was imperfect as well and concluded in her last note that she lacked responsibility. She was impulsive and had gambled part of her wealth in Indian casinos and in her favorite city, Las Vegas. I was her only son and inherited her yearning to have it all. I have failed at most of my yearnings, of course. I can only take on so many issues, as the heir of this much energy, drive, and dysfunction, and can barely work through the limitations in my own character, especially the other black mark upon my character aside from my illegitimacy, which is my queerness, a source of pride for some, but a burden nonetheless that requires the clearing of yet another set of hurdles, not to mention the clearing of throats among more conservative observers—bastard, queer, foreign. Three strikes and you're out.

This is the story of all the burdens of filial duty and pain, but also a celebration of the misadventures—and some actual adventures—of one mother and one son, and the legacy of a struggle we each brought with us to our adopted country, the United States. I hope to honor that struggle, expose its failings, celebrate some of its achievements, and, more importantly, feel free to remember without fear or constraint.

A Memory: Playing with One Doll

Every Sunday, a ritual. *La feria* arrives. It's not a fair most people in the U.S. might imagine. The farmers who live on the outskirts of Santiago descend upon the city to sell vegetables and fruits, and local merchants follow with cheap wares, toys, and even chicks and ducklings. My grandmother steers me away constantly because one day I'll ask for a bunny, then a puppy, and I haven't learned to accept no for an answer. Soon, I would ask for a doll.

The farmers install themselves on Pedro Fontova Blvd., which crisscrosses the neighborhood of La Palmilla. They line up, hundreds of them, selling ripening vegetables and juicy fruits, mostly oranges and apples. It's not a tropical country. Bananas have to be imported. No mangos, no guavas, just the basics for a country best known for wines. But when they offer grapes, I have to wonder: Who doesn't have grapes at home? Who buys them? Vines have become trusted companions in the average Chilean home, living things with arms that stretch out to hug the children, and almost every backyard's obliged by custom to grow one as part of our heritage. So I can't imagine a home without a vine, but obviously somebody out there is lacking one. Perhaps it's the unfortunate dwellers of new box-like apartment buildings in which there's no space to grow anything; still, apartment buildings haven't entirely swallowed up our neighborhood yet, which is mostly made up of quaint colorful homes, compact, intimate, sometimes even a bit wretched, housing generations of us. We live in such close proximity that the grapes appear to grow out of our limbs. The farmers and merchants park their buggies in front of our home and the street fills up with horse dung. The merchants don't clean up after themselves. The city sometimes comes around with a truck to scoop it all up; sometimes it all rots until a rain might sweep it away, but there are no guarantees, from the weather or from the city. Horse dung may fertilize the earth, but it can't do the same to the pavement. There are days when the neighborhood just plainly stinks.

I follow my grandmother to *la feria*, where I find the ducklings, tiny recently born ones that I hold in my own small hand, as they struggle to get up on my palm and waddle. We used to grow our own vegetables, but now our garden grows only flowers, daffodils and calla lilies. My grandparents have left the country life behind. No farming for them—they are now city consumers. Grandma carries a wicker basket that I watched her brother-in-law in the countryside make in less than ten minutes. His hands adroitly picked up long, thin, pliable sticks and tightened them into a firm fit like the morbid embrace of the branches off a dead tree. It's a revered gift, this wicker basket, and I—as a child—treat it like a member of the family because I saw it being born. Grandmother moved into the city where she worked as a cook for a wealthy family, and they hired, in turn, a French cook to mentor her in the making of finer delicacies, from Mille Feuille pastries to onion soup and coq au vin. As a child, I grew up benefiting from her culinary expertise, meals made from scratch. This was one child who had no trouble eating. My mother even refused to cook unless Grandma was indisposed or away on a trip. "Who'll appreciate my cooking?" my mother said, only half-jokingly, and her complaint was real enough. Grandma held sway over the kitchen and didn't even teach her own daughter how to make French pastries, not out of selfishness, as my mother herself became a city woman interested in cosmopolitan fashions and international films. She never pressed the matter. She was never that interested in cooking. Grandma's a hefty, short lady who carries the basket on her hips on our trips to *la feria*. She won't let me keep the ducklings. We don't raise ducks or chickens; we're city folk now. My grandmother puts the ducklings away and rushes me along. We have to choose among a well-arranged mountain of ripe, red, juicy tomatoes in the stand across. Sellers shout, "This way, *casera*." I never knew what that word meant until I had to put two and two together. *Casa*, the word for house. A *casera* is someone who takes care of it, but it's not the Spanish word for housewife—*ama de casa*—and in some countries, *casera* means landlady or housekeeper. At *la feria*, all the women are called *caseras*, an odd word that country people have adopted, which rings well as a jingle that sells. Those country people. We had moved away into the city, and we didn't use their words, at least not any longer.

Grandma will spend her Sunday afternoon in the warmth of a kitchen, baking some delicacy or other, this time Chilean cuisine. She spends the same time with her Chilean empanada as she might with a French soufflé. She kneads dough at a calm, cool pace as if she massages a dear client, as a pot slowly cooks the meat with raisins, olives, eggs, and spices, which she will then stuff into the dough. That one day, I am working around her. I am a musketeer fighting my exotic enemies like pirates or Indians, aiming my plastic musket at the wind when suddenly the earth moves beneath us. The spices fall on the ground, and spill on my face; it looks like I'm bleeding. My grandmother sweeps me into her arms and pulls me outside onto the patio. My mother comes running and, at the first sight of me, screams. She also thinks I'm bleeding, but instead, my eyes are aching with chili sauce as the earth continues to shake and roll, and I feel a vibration and a roaring of the plates beneath as they shift and push up against each other. We hold on to one another, as I hold my grandmother's hand with my left and my mother's with my right. We are lined up as if expecting the earth to open beneath us, and we'll be able to hold on to another's hand to prevent it from swallowing us up. But the swaying begins to abate, and then the earth stands still again. My grandmother reassures us all; it's passed, it was a small one, perhaps 4.5 on the Richter scale, so back to the kitchen. She uses her apron to wipe my face. My mother breathes a sigh of relief as she takes me to the bathroom to wash sauce off my eyes, which are still stinging.

Our world is warm and tasty, and the spices in Grandma's empanadas create a hearty appetite as my mouth waters in expectation. No eating disorders in this family. We eat, we nourish the soul. The relatives arrive, and there's exultation throughout, hugs and kisses, and comparing notes, as in: where were you when the quake started? A child is required to kiss every single aunt, uncle, godparent, distant relative, and neighbor who comes to visit. A boy will do so until his teens, girls are stuck for life performing the same duty kissing everybody, and even a grownup man is expected to kiss all the ladies on the cheek, also for life. Chileans touch each other lightly, but warmly, and personal space is defined quite differently than for Americans.

People arrive, almost every day, sometimes unannounced, and Grandmother is always ready to greet them with cakes and tea. The children are summoned to greet the guests with our hugs and kisses. I recall this childhood of intimacy, even of physical touch. In my adulthood, one hears stories of Americans confessing about inappropriate touching from adults, celebrities denouncing their own parents of molestation, an odd thing for us brought up by family members who were always kissing and hugging us. I remember the comfort of aunts' and uncles' kisses, and I wonder how many of them would be denounced on American television nowadays. The American concept of personal space deteriorates—in my opinion—to psychoanalysis in which people recall all childhood as violation, even at the cradle, as Americans denounce not just their parents, but their priests, teachers, and scoutmasters for inappropriate behavior, recalled thanks to "flashbacks." Chilean childhood would be, by American standards, all about perverse acts of illicit touching. Yet, all I can recall is warmth and comfort in the embrace of adults.

One day, not long after the earth shook on that one Sunday, I followed Grandma to *la feria* again. This time, I didn't fixate on the ducklings or little chicks or bunnies and parakeets. This time I became enamored of a doll. I had never played with dolls before, but somehow I became fascinated by this one, a cuddly bundle with blonde curls. I picked it up and asked my grandmother to get it for me. I was a bossy child; I demanded it. She looked at me aghast, mortified, even embarrassed. The woman seller with orange-tinted hair beamed back a look of perplexity, even disdain. Where was her selling instinct? She agreed with my grandmother; it was time to shoo me along like a stray dog. She wouldn't sell a doll to a boy.

"You have plenty of toys back home," said my grandmother.

"But I like this one."

"All right, let's just go."

I must have been five years old. I owned my share of toy soldiers, Indians in head gear, American cavalry, World War II airmen with adjoining planes, policemen, firemen, and other manly weapons such as the modern fighter jets like the ones that policed the airways of Santiago. I would stage my share of world conflicts using all of them, bringing them to a full boil of face-to-face conflict until, shortly before lunch, they would explode into a conflagration of mass destruction. In a few years, Santiago would be invaded by a fleet of Hawker Hunter jets, unloading bombs on the presidential palace, but that was in the future. Up until then, war was only a boy's game, and Chileans spoke of their—our—country as an idyllic land where conflicts were settled at the ballot box. Our military obey civilian orders. We are a modern country, unlike those other Latin American countries, and we don't harbor dictators and other signs of Third World decrepitude; we are a Latin American Switzerland. There was no concern for the manly games of our military. In fact, more adults were concerned at that particular time with my insistence on wanting a doll than they seemed to care about a military uprising. Augusto Pinochet was an obscure colonel somewhere in the Santiago garrison. One day he'd be a general, later the dictator, but that was in the future.

"How come I can't get that doll?" I asked at the lunch table that day. My mother joined my grandparents, and my uncle, the teenager José Luís, in their ridicule of such a notion. Rather embarrassed, the adults pleaded with me: boys don't play with dolls; boys don't grow up to care for babies. That's what girls do; dolls prepare them for motherhood. It seemed rational enough except that once I had seen that doll, I'd grown obsessed with her face and with her smile and the thought that I could hold her in my arms and make her fall asleep.

"Now, stop that!" my mother shouted. "We're not buying you a doll!"

Tears began to flow down my cheeks. I let out a hysterical cry that might have shattered more than crystal, as in ear drums perhaps.

"Go to the bedroom right now!"

My mother drew the line, but the crying seemed to soften up my grandmother, who said she could always make me a doll out of rags. Absolutely not, Mother said, stopping that notion.

"I only want the one I saw at *la feria!*" I shouted.

But my mother wasn't having any more of that. I reluctantly went off take a nap, resenting the punishment of isolation. When I woke up, however, my grandmother was standing by the bed. She was holding the doll, the same one we saw at *la feria*, and then, with some reluctance on her part, as if hoping she'd done the right thing, she handed it to me.

"I don't know why you'd want this," she said. "But here it is, and God help you. If boys make fun of you, just don't come crying to me."

Overjoyed, I hugged the doll lovingly, then held it in my arms, rocked her, and turned her sideways to burp her and calm her down, and prevent her from crying. My mother walked in and her face turned beet red.

"Where the hell did you get that?"

Prologue

She was rushing to grab it from hands, but my grandmother intervened.

"*Ya déjalo*—Just leave him be!"

"Mother, we can't do that!"

"He'll grow tired of it; you'll see."

"I'm never getting rid of her!" I cried out. "I'll take care of her for the rest of her life."

"Oh, great!" My mother was a young woman, thin, on some sort of diet mostly made up of substituting saccharine for sugar, and she got jittery whenever she was nervous, and this situation clearly ruined her day. But I wasn't budging. My uncle José Luís came in and broke into a fit of laughter. My mother chased him out the door. Grandpa got lured in by the commotion, but one look at my arms bearing the doll, and he shook his head as if to say: what is this world coming to? Cousins arrived, and they marveled at the sight. The girls appeared envious at the sight of a brand-new doll. My male cousins just ran away, finding the sight of me with the doll rather frightful. They grabbed pebbles from the backyard, found a way to make a hopscotch game out of it, and ignored me the rest of the day.

A few days passed, and I woke up one morning without understanding what had happened, as if it had all been a dream, and normalcy was restored. The doll had disappeared in the middle of the night, and I didn't appear to miss it. I was back at work on the toy soldiers creating havoc and world conflict, a ruckus that everyone admired as cute, lovable behavior for a boy. Less than a decade later, General Pinochet assaulted the presidential palace with toys that were real and killed actual fellow citizens, and he became, for some in our family, a hero. I would never play with dolls again, and I would remember from a distance, from the United States, this once peaceful country of Chile now redefined by the manhood of its fellow men in arms, the ones who defy communism and liberate the country, and leave, in the wake of their actions, mass graves, raped women, fellow Chileans in exile, and many other dead or missing. I look back, but learn to look forward as well, as I become a U.S. citizen. My attempt to play with a doll, even just one, affronted the sensibilities of my family, and yet for some members of it, my grandfather in particular, the subsequent blitzkrieg of our own armed forces against alleged enemies of the state became a glorious act, a restoration of manhood, patriotism, and stability in our lives. I was too young to have understood the alarm and the shock to a boy's enthusiasm for a doll, but I will have an entire lifetime ahead to calculate my manhood in the

Prologue

wake of the knowledge I began to absorb at the time. Something, including military resistance, was in the air, constantly demanding rigid conformity and loyalty. Something would have to give. Only now as an adult would I begin to realize it all started at *la feria* with one doll.

1

Love Child

I am not, by my family's standards, illegitimate. But, really now, what are the standards? Whose standards anyway? I bear my father's last name, and this fact, my mother convinced me once, pulls me up a notch or two in the hierarchy of bastardom. I may know nothing about my father's family and can only imagine vague scenarios inspired by Leo Tolstoy's dictum that "every unhappy family is unhappy in its own way." I wish them luck. My birth rankled some nerves, or so I am told, but since then, it's all been silence. Dead silence of past sins unspoken. The main players are by now dead, and only the product of such a sin—well, myself—lives. Geography plays a part—and proves a formidable barrier—in my current state of ignorance, but in the eight years I lived in Santiago as a child, in the same city and a short bus ride from him, I never met my father. If I was spared the sibling rivalries and the posturing for paternal attention along with the weddings, baptisms, and inevitable marital strife, I was also not expected at my father's funeral. I was not exactly invited. But to be fair, I was in the United States by then.

In retrospect, the fact that I never saw my father wither away in his early fifties of leukemia left me unprepared to confront my mother's cancer later in life. I was spared the pain, but was robbed of the grieving process. I was informed of my father's death long after the fact. I stumbled into it due to complications with Chilean bureaucracy that allowed me to obtain, if little else from my father, a death certificate (more on this amusingly morbid matter later).

Love Child

Unbeknownst to the paternal branch of the family, an offshoot of them has established roots in the United States, but does it matter to those folks at all? I could be one of many of such children, and who would know? The legitimate branch of the family does not owe me any favors, and I don't owe them mine. I lived in the United States with my mother more than three decades. I sit here as a more or less well-adjusted adult in the office that houses my Arizona State University professorship, writing in an adopted language that, for the most part, obeys my inclination toward rhetorical overkill. My native tongue appears to have exiled me along with my native country. I can express myself in Spanish to a certain extent, but it's a childhood language, monosyllables and childhood rhymes, all innocence and no technique, no rhetorical flourishes, just the facts ma'am, and the bare sounds of the child, the moo-cow of a Joycean infanthood. I've no patience with Romance language accents, and I don't buy the Latin American proclivity toward heavily formal diction that hides bureaucratic insincerity. I like the modern, journalistic clarity of the contemporary Yankee idiom. The grammar in all my rejection letters as a writer has been plain and dry, nothing fancy and overworked. I've known rejection, but at least I've gotten it straight. Perhaps I've attempted too hard to shed my background and adopt that tilt of the head of the San Fernando Valley dude while speaking in a lingo that has become, like, a joke to most people, but which is for me part of the acculturation process. I was—I've been—that Valley dude who says "you know" a lot and who could converse in that "gag me with a spoon" type of redundancy. It is one of my masks, one of my many rhetorical skills. Overkill, as well. I can be an excessive personality, even when I strike people as "reserved." An excessive man trapped in a reserved personality? How have I managed that? A paradox, and a mystery, the legacy of a murky background I can't easily explain.

In the United States, my mother and I became, for lack of a better word, middle class. For at least a while anyway, before our debts caught up with us. Mother kept up her mortgage payments for her house in the San Fernando Valley and held out until 1998, when she could no longer pay them. Her life as a Valley nanny had started with a successful transition from low-paid immigrant to home ownership and small businesswoman. But the center couldn't hold. The home demanded upkeep, and any extra income was sucked into an insatiably hungry money pit. I was incapable of helping my mother out of this quagmire. I was, 'nough said, a writer. I couldn't contribute to the mortgage. I was offered a position at Arizona State University, and I took it. I arrived in Arizona without a car and with a hundred dollars in my savings account and an overdraft in my checking. Mother was forced to foreclose and move on to Portland, Oregon, where a new life awaited her—a private nanny, but not a homeowner, and that was at least a much-needed escape from the obligations of bourgeois responsibility. We nonetheless had managed for a while to flourish away from the respectable legitimate branches of our "Old World" family. We built a life in the United States for ourselves, which, on the surface, attempted a suburban homogeneity of home, car, cable, and credit card debt, and marked a radical break from the type of life our Chilean relatives currently lead. The home had been bought with the help of my mother's official husband—that is, the Chilean undocumented immigrant who married her to straighten out his papers. Before the tragic end to that relationship in Los Angeles, this husband helped fill out the papers that ensured my mother would get the bank's loan to buy her home. It seemed fitting that, as illegitimate children that my mother and I both were, we would be helped into home ownership by a false marriage. Our induction into the middle class was accomplished by a series of moves, on the undocumented man's part to gain legality, and on my mother's part to obtain his help in moving up a notch or two out of our stagnant renters' status.

Still, the legitimate Reyes family lives on in Chile, oblivious of our moves in the United States. We are separate entities, castaways, exiles, from the family life that our very existence once threatened when it was revealed, with my mother branded "the other woman," and I the "bastard." My father's marriage was threatened, but not dissolved. We disappeared into that vast world of Immigrant America never to be heard from again. We went away; his family life thrived thereafter. Mother and I may have fit into the vast, anonymous landscape of the San Fernando Valley in California, and yet we lived on without the privileges of home. My looking back even betrays a cop-out in me as if I were yearning for belonging—as if in spite of a progressive public face that eschews patriarchal lifestyles, I would rather be inheriting land or getting appointed to the presidency through nepotism like other straight, privileged people do. Failing that, an invitation to my father's funeral would have allayed my youthful fears that I didn't really matter much in the scheme of things. That's too much to ask of respectable people, however, and as Eva Peron discovered in her own bastardry, the only way to catch the attention of legitimate folks is to rise above them, preferably by taking over a nation, and then eventually banishing them all. Very diva-like, but I'd only wish. I lack the dictatorial instinct, let alone the diva-dom (except in my plays, perhaps, where any posture is possible). I've become a creative writer instead to compound my lowly standing in this world. I do carry, however, my father's actual name, and this, I've discovered, sets me apart from the many bastards that came before me in my mother's family.

So what's in a name? My mother, María Graciela Cáceres, knew from experience the significance of one. Born out of wedlock herself, María Graciela bears my grandmother María's maiden name of Cáceres. My grandmother, in turn, was born equally fatherless and inherited her name from her mother, Natalia Cáceres. I became an exception to a family tradition that bore the signs of matriarchy by default, maiden names carrying the family forward in the absence of the male willing to donate a name while so eager to leave behind his seed.

My great-grandmother Natalia never spoke of illegitimacy, certainly not that of her own children. Natalia was more than reticent, more than just the discreet eighty-plus-year-old matriarch with bobby pins in her glowing grey hair. She maintained the family secrets with the tenacity of a Chilean branch of the secret police. And what about all those missing branches in the family tree? One was supposed to act as if they stood, firmly and visibly, connecting us to the past, and if she were to die leaving behind nothing but a ransacked skeleton of a tree, at least the secrets would die with her. But not without a struggle. I was nine years old when I learned to make my great-grandmother suspect I was the enemy. The entire family had begun to make no sense to me, I told her in Mulchén, her hometown in southern Chile, and the town where I was born. I had reviewed her list of children, many of whom bore contrasting last names. It made no sense that one pair of daughters there should carry her surname, and these other daughters here yet another one. What exactly was going on? Natalia pulled down her pince-nez, reached for the Bible on the lamp table by her bed, and placed it in my hands as if she'd placed burning coal in them. "*Ay, tantas preguntas!* Read this," she said, "and learn!" She went back to her knitting, feeling safe I was under the care of the right guardian, which would explain it all for me without having to get specific about us.

Love Child

She didn't realize I had won first place in my class in Santiago. Reading was clearly my strength. Soon enough, I was making my way through Genesis and arrived at the point in which Lot's daughters get their father drunk and lure him into bed to have him impregnate them. I pointed this out to her and asked if there really hadn't been any other men in town available. I'd obviously missed the point, too. Lot's daughters were clearly not about to marry their own father, of course, and after he'd unceremoniously offered them to the Sodomites because their virginity did not seem as valuable as that of the male visiting angels whose favors were (apparently) being solicited, the whole thing struck me as an act of revenge.

"Grandma, I think the daughters must hate Lot, don't you?"

"Why? What are you talking about? What do you know about these things anyway? You're a kid."

"Lot tried to sacrifice them to the Sodomites. What type of father does that? And then, they get him drunk and everything, and next they're going to have his baby. It's like they used him and then, after that, they'll have God punish him or something for raping his own daughters. If God punished Sodom and Gomorrah, then Lot needs to be punished, too, because he's such a jerk."

Natalia had never quite met a child like me, I now suspect. I doubt she'd ever asked her own grandmother to explain incest, sodomy, and rape in one request alone.

"*Ay, pero qué horror!* This chapter is not for children." She snatched the book away from my hands and locked it up in her armoire for the remainder of my visit. The Bible had proved too scandalous, a good reason to read it, I should think. But if it was such a Holy Book, why did it become off limits? That summer, I realized that catechism had taught me a filtered version of the Bible and that the real thing held more interesting tales that made adults blush. It's a great discovery about faith, that it's not all about holiness and purity, but about sin, and that was titillating. The story of my family would prove more palatable that way, really.

That same summer I spent unsettling Natalia, I also figured out that the man I called my grandfather was not my mother's biological father. Surely, Tata (as I called him) behaved like a grandfather. He was the only one I'd ever known since an eerie silence worse than death suffused all conversation related to my father's side of the family. I'd been taught to tell kids in school that my father had died a victim of a plane crash while flying over the Andes. Who'd said that and when? I can't recall. But that was the story I was supposed to tell when and if kids asked. This didn't explain why his entire family, including my paternal grandparents, appeared to be equally missing. If your father died, wouldn't his parents—your grandparents—rush to be by your side along with his brothers and sisters in a time of need? Had the entire Reyes family disappeared in one vast apocalyptic event? Had they all crashed together? It'd be a couple of years later when I'd hear about the Uruguayan rugby team whose plane crashed in the Andes—my neighborhood essentially—and who'd been forced to eat the dead in order to survive. In my childhood, I had already imagined the entire Reyes family living in the Andes, cannibalizing each other, which would have explained their absence in my life. Strange thoughts for a kid, but as the Uruguayan team discovered, these things did happen, and call me prescient because I had somehow imagined the crash first like the Hollywood movie the story would eventually become. All because somebody had fed me that story as an answer to my question about my father.

"*Te armas toda una película*," my mother once told me about what I did with a simple tale. I regurgitated it back as a movie with big stars, a large budget, and Cinemascope. I would keep up strange tales late into my teens, even in the United States, where I was supposedly the son of a Chilean diplomat.

In 1970 my mother came to the United States to work as a nanny for an American family in Bethesda, Maryland. I'd been left in the care of Tata and Grandma and the many extended family members around them. But my grandmother's health deteriorated. Pancreatic cancer quickly tore through her, and she died a month after my mother's departure. A war of words ensued between Tata and my mother through international mail, and I was in the middle of it. That was one of the reasons I was hounding my great-grandmother Natalia that summer. I'd been sent to stay with her and her granddaughter, also named Natalia, or Nati for short, and they and several family members had to cope with my growing curiosity about everything.

No need to buy this child puzzles. He had an entire family to unscramble and put back together.

Tata grieved my grandmother's death in the most peculiar way, by planning to remarry almost immediately. During the wake, his best friend, Don Elmer, stepped up to him in front of my great-grandmother and great-aunt Tecla and offered his unmarried daughter, Teresa, as Tata's new wife.

Love Child

"Teresa, come here," said Don Elmer, at least according to my vociferous aunt Tecla, who remembered this too vividly. His daughter, in her thirties, came forth toward the dining table, looking apprehensive as if she knew what was to come. She had come to the wake at my grandfather's house to mourn his wife's death. She didn't expect her father to tell her, "Don't you want to marry Don José now?" It sounded more like a command than a question. She blushed, smiled, and could only politely say, "If he'll have me."

The scandal tore through the family and isolated my grandfather immediately. First, my great-grandmother Natalia left town, then her two granddaughters, Eva and Nati, taking me along with them. My grandfather felt the loss so tremendously and the emptiness in his bed and his home so intensely that the grieving process became about filling the void as soon as possible. This widower's grief wasn't paralyzing, but, conversely, it became a call to action. He announced an engagement in less than a month and married within three. And, no, this was not a Chilean custom. It was not a "cultural thing." This was a bizarre personal call on his part, which would cost him dearly in family ties and in sympathy. My grandmother's family thought his actions inconsiderate and plainly shocking. I became torn between the Cáceres family and my grandfather, who felt the need to stand up to the family alone. If my great-grandmother considered his actions madness, even lust for a younger woman, I also understood his sense of abandonment. My grandmother was dead, and my mother had left for the United States. I shared the feeling, too.

I know that Tata did make an attempt—no matter how futile—to put the happy family we'd known back together again without having to marry. He wanted my mother back, to begin with, and at least this would have delayed the need to find a new wife, and my grandmother's family would have been mollified and less inclined to denounce him as a scoundrel. Tata could barely write full sentences so instead he dictated his letters to me. I wrote them down like a faithful scribe. I was nine years old, felt extremely useful to be writing down Grandpa's thoughts, and I couldn't help but feel the excitement as I became caught up in a grand epistolary struggle between my mother and my grandfather.

Tata demanded that my mother renounce all her U.S. "pretenses," as he saw them, and return to Chile to take over household duties, which meant Mother would need to return to take care of him and the house, cook, clean, and sew and all the stuff that was expected of her as a woman. Of course, I missed my mother, but I couldn't help cheer for her as she wrote back angrily, dismissing his taunts and threats. I knew a raw deal when I saw one, and I believed she was doing much better in the United States, earning "big bucks" by Chilean standards and having a good time with her cousin, Nelly, who'd been the first to leave for the United States. They were single girls out on the town in Washington, D.C., and they were far from home and on their own. They considered it a privilege to live and work in the United States, even if they were doing "only" domestic duties. Poor people have their logic, and that was theirs. They were grateful to be in the United States, because, ultimately, they felt that was their start to do something venturesome with their lives. The United States provided a break for what they considered to be a provincial or unpromising way of life in Chile. It made no sense to my grandfather, however, why any Chilean woman would risk her pride to work as a nanny or a maid in the United States. We were supposedly above such things. We were lower middle class really, but a notch above the masses. It seemed to matter to some people, like my conservative and himself peasant-bred Tata.

My mother resisted. Her letters proved unfriendly. So that's when I started wondering. Her attitude appeared disrespectful—and I had to read the letters out loud to him with the flair a hyper, dramatically inclined child like me could give it. *No puedo volver y prefiero traerme a mi hijo lo más pronto posible.* "I can't go back, and I'd prefer to bring my son over to the U.S. as soon as possible." Talk about *armar toda una película.* I didn't have to film the movie of these events. She won me over immediately because I also sought to travel, and it would be a true adventure, not a fantasy. Grandpa had to accept the fact that Mother not only wasn't coming back but now also threatened to take me along with her. She never called Tata "Querido Padre" in her letters. She addressed him as "Estimado Don José," as if he'd been the local landowner somewhere. He was a retired policeman, and a man who'd never been without a woman in his house. This type of treatment hurt. I felt for him as well. I read the letters to him, and I watched his reaction, which brought him to tears every time. I felt like the midget who humors the king, and this king was turning into Lear.

Tata finally and with great trepidation accepted my mother's decision, and immediately determined—as if to do it hastily before he could change his mind—to marry the youthful and pretty Teresa. They held a wedding party barely three months after my grandmother died. It made sense to him. My mother's own decision to stay in the United States had pushed him into it, and he claimed to be the victim here. He was alone; he needed a woman. It seemed logical to him to marry immediately. Some—I would say most—of the Cáceres family would refuse to speak to him for the rest of his life. First of all, Teresa had been a childhood friend of my mother. They'd grown up together, become teenagers, and had flirted with the same young men at dances and at the beach together. And now she had become, practically overnight, my mother's stepmother. Her father, Don Elmer, was my grandfather's buddy from the days he'd spent in the *carabineros*, the Chilean military police, which would soon help rule the entire country through a military putsch, which my grandfather stubbornly supported. Don Elmer's attitude toward his own daughter was one of possessiveness, even jealousy. Many years later, Teresa would tell me: "My father would not approve of any suitor for me. I brought home men my age, and he would find fault with each and every one of them. But when your grandmother died, he thought his buddy, your Tata, or Don José, as I knew him, would make a good husband. I said yes. At the time, I even had a job in an office that I enjoyed, but they made me quit immediately. I was given no choice." My grandmother's family was too busy maligning Teresa as a ruthless conspirator. She had planned it this way, they said, to immediately move in after my grandmother's death. My mother observed the events from Washington, D.C., with some wicked bemusement. Teresa pairs up with my stepfather? she wondered. What a joke.

Teresa was married to my grandfather for nearly twenty-seven years until he passed away. She bore him two children, a boy and a girl, who themselves are now adults. These are the Bravo family, not a blood-related family, but nonetheless a product of one of those arrangements that most young people today in Chile would consider bizarre, even alien. At the time, Teresa bore the brunt of people's disdain. I was the only one on my mother's side of the family who spoke to her and treated her with respect. Even as a child, I understood her dilemma. She was only allowed to marry an older man, and now the Cáceres family maligned *her* for it, without taking into account that she had little to say in this arrangement between the older men.

This period was an odd one in my life as well. My mother, in the United States, had put into motion the paperwork needed to obtain a visa for me while I was in the midst of this major family struggle. With my grandfather rushing into a quick marriage, I was being taken care of by female cousins, Eva and Nati at times, other times by my great-grandmother Natalia. But the cousins decided to follow Natalia out of our Santiago home after my grandfather made his fateful decision to marry. One morning I woke up, and the two sisters were packing my things along with theirs. You're coming with us, they let me know. You're not going to some stupid wedding.

I ended up with my great-grandmother Natalia in the south: in Mulchén to be exact, a cool, thickly forested town that leads into the heart of Chile's Lake District, where my great-grandmother Natalia had lived since childhood. Natalia had, of course, also chosen to boycott the wedding. She called Teresa *la otra*, which is something you would call a mistress. She theorized that Teresa had conspired to be first in line to marry my grandfather to gain access to his military pension as soon as my grandmother died. "We're a poor country," she said. "People will do anything for a pension. We need security, and we need men to survive in this country. This woman. She was waiting in the wings, waiting for your grandmother to die. Her parents proposed the day of the funeral. I was there; I heard it all. The mourning wasn't over, and they were already telling your grandpa to marry their Little Teresa. I wouldn't be surprised if she'd been his mistress before my daughter died."

I fought back, however, as a loquacious and oppositional nine-year-old was wont to do. "She didn't do anything wrong," I told Natalia. "She just needed to get married because she was getting too old!"

"But why wouldn't men marry her to begin with?" My great-grandmother insisted on following her line of reasoning. "They didn't want used goods."

"But I like her!"

"You would!"

This entire summer, the south-of-the-equator summer of December–March, was spent in a battle of wills between an eighty-year-old woman and a loquacious kid. I was an *atrevido*, a loud-mouthed disrespectful child, and I must admit, without my mother's powers of persuasion and discipline, I was a contentious child, but for a good cause, or so I thought.

It angered me to know there was so much ill will in our family, which led me to naturally question the family's history and its secrets, particularly as I began to discover the issues of bastardry, related to signs of cruelty throughout the family. I didn't have the wherewithal as a nine-year-old to provide intellectual perspective into illegitimacy, but even at that age I seemed to be trying hard to get to know the facts. First of all, I resented plenty of things and said so. The dismissal of Teresa as the evil other one (*la otra*) struck me as extremely unfair, and it led to plenty of fights. But I also had to call into question Natalia's treatment of her granddaughter Nati, who told me her story that summer with a casual tone, a matter-of-factness that seemed resigned to her fate at the time. Young Natalia, in her late teens by then, had gone to Santiago as a little girl to take care of her grandmother. She was basically the sacrifice of a large poor family born to Uncle Ismael, my grandmother's (also illegitimate) brother, who lived with his family in a poor, working-class neighborhood in Santiago. Grandmother Natalia had visited one day and had set her sights on Little Natalia. She will take care of me, the older woman decided, and took her back home to Mulchén with her as a prize, separating her from the rest of her family when she was six years old.

"I cried for days on end," Little Natalia eventually told me much later as a fifty-year-old adult. "I didn't know where they were taking me. I wanted to be with my mother, not my grandmother. She took me back home and taught me how to cook, make breakfast, clean up, make beds, and all sorts of other things, such as buy charcoal and warm up the place in a small coal brazier. I actually loved my grandmother, but I didn't think that I should be taking care of her alone. A year later, I was allowed to visit my family in Santiago. When I entered my parents' home, my sister Eva came out and looked at me as if I'd been a complete stranger. 'I'm here to see my mother,' I said. 'She's *my* mother,' said Eva and ran inside, afraid I'd take away her mother. My own little sister had forgotten me!"

This same shuffling of women that had made Teresa marry my older grandfather had also affected the Younger Natalia, and it made me aware as a child that there was cruelty in all these arrangements, products of poverty perhaps, but which threatened us all with a certain imposition of authority, making us all feel like bastard children. We certainly had plenty of those. Even legitimate children had reasons to fear. They could be taken from their immediate families at any time to fulfill some larger family duty.

But I still had one form of privilege and I sensed it: my mother was in the United States, and she would send modest amounts of cash that looked hefty in a child's hand and—more importantly—she also sent down promises to take me with her. I clearly had something—big travel and adventure—to look forward to, and during this summer that I spent away from her, I had time to form my impressions of this rather bizarre society of intricate family entanglements, which often grew into scandals. I kept a record of impressions in a series of notebooks, which my stern great-grandma called "nonsense" when she flipped through them, because I would draw family portraits, along with those of sports figures, politicians, and mostly American movie stars, and it became a rather surreal world of images without much of a narrative (an early style had been born).

I lived in Natalia's house, a noisy box of creaky wood that dried up in the summer and emitted noises that Natalia attributed to the insistent *penando*, the haunting of troubled souls, in the outskirts of a small town with streets that were only slowly being paved. Natalia's street of Villa Alegre was now partially covered with gravel leading into a dirt road that took you officially into *el campo*. We were on the edge, within walking distance from a downtown in which one single movie theater in a neatly kept plaza of benches and fountains kept the town feeling connected to civilization. On the other side stood the wilderness from which our family had emerged like savages. We still lived one step away from such a life. I waited every day for the one mailman to bring me news from my mother, but I wasn't counting the days to leave either. Plenty of stimuli kept me entertained. A constant flow of people—cousins and aunts from the city—would come to stay with us, and they brought with them the gossip about *la otra*. Somebody had visited and heard Teresa tell my grandfather she wanted new furniture, a new washing machine, and silverware. The gossiping aunt found these demands horrendous, opportunistic, materialistic, and, more unforgivable than anything else, disrespectful to the dead. Only four months had passed, the gossipy aunt would remind us, four short months after your grandma's death, and they're already married and talking about new furniture.

Gossip nourishes a child's imagination. I had grown curious about my family's other historical outbreaks of scandal. At that point, I still believed my father had died in a plane crash in the Andes, that my grandfather was my mother's biological father, and that my family was otherwise entirely legitimate. This latest outrage, my grandfather's hasty wedding and the reaction of the Cáceres—my grandmother's—family, made me start wondering about the entire picture, and the pieces were coming together gradually.

Love Child

For instance, in Mulchén, I sat down next to my teenage cousin Eva and started to describe my strange position as a scribe and go-between during my mother's and grandfather's struggle over whether she'd come back from the United States. Eva flipped through her movie magazine that one afternoon, and said, "Why should he be bossing her around? Really, who does he think he is?" She went back to her magazine, not realizing how quickly I was putting two and two together.

Her odd dismissal of my grandfather made me bring up the subject around the much more direct aunt Tecla, who lived in the downtown part of Mulchén and whom I visited every other day. She was my grandmother's younger sister, and one of the sisters with a different last name, not Cáceres, but Almazabar, yet another confusing fact. Sisters whose last names would not match—this nine-year-old had noticed that, too. Aunt Tecla was a lively, spirited woman in her fifties with a need to converse about all sorts of intimacies even with a child over a formal tea hour of bread, cheese, and jam, and a lovely presentation of old but well-maintained tea cups. It was another cool afternoon in the Chilean south, a rainy, forested region that stood as a barrier to Chile's subpolar winds as they moved north. At four o'clock, we promptly sat down for the tea hour. That's when the truth would sieve out of Aunt Tecla, as she poured boiling water from a kettle: Tata was not my mother's actual father!

"Children are told so many lies!" she proclaimed. I had realized it by then, too. I wasn't surprised. But I was fascinated to hear it directly from an authority figure, casually, over tea. "Why can't they just come out and tell them, 'You were born out of wedlock.' There! I mean you, too! Don't think you escape from that predicament! It's not that unusual in our family, so why lie about it? But it's not about protecting the children, is it now? It's about protecting them—the parents themselves—as if revealing they sinned like any other mortals were such a shameful thing. We're afraid of what the children might say! Then you grow up to be afraid of what everyone else might think, what society might say or do. All these fears are ridiculous! It's a country full of *acomplejados*." This word loses its bite in translation. *Acomplejados*, people with complexes, suggests a bigger, more intractable aspect of the human condition, a piercing stigma that afflicts people who become so paralyzed by societal attitudes to the point of becoming inert and ineffectual in life altogether. Coming from Tecla's forceful mouth, it suggested condemnation beyond what one simple word could do. *Acomplejados*. It made sense. It described my family. It would describe me growing up as well. An exquisite word, as searing as a hot iron on the skin.

It all made sense now. With my father not a victim of some fabled plane accident that I no longer believed anyway, my grandfather not really my genetic grandfather, my father's branch of the family altogether missing, my great-grandmother not bothering to discuss Lot's scandalous daughters, I understood too well that adults couldn't exactly be trusted with either their own history or with scandals out of the Bible. I had easily grasped matters of conception, within marriage or otherwise, so that the technical aspects of my birth seemed to square with the facts. Everything else about my family, however, defied the norm. We were by all purposes more mysterious than the stork herself, and at least that story made sense.

The great aunt Tecla, who'd revealed my step-grandfather's real status in the family, and who'd been one of the first to rat on him when he started discussing his need to remarry during my grandmother's funeral, had many more stories to tell. Aunt Tecla spoke in a rush as if eager to let it all be told before the family censors overheard. Yes, her mother Natalia had borne one daughter and two sons out of wedlock as products of a complicated amorous liaison with a wandering gentleman that never ended up with marriage. No shotgun weddings for Natalia's lover. He was gone, or at least banished in a collective case of amnesia from family memory. Not much else was known about him. A traveling salesman perhaps with a wife in another town? These children carried Natalia's last name for that reason. When Natalia later met a man willing to marry her, the potential groom demanded that the three bastards—*los guachos*, as they were called—be sent away. And they were. Shortly before the wedding, Natalia shipped her illegitimate children, among them my grandmother, María, to relatives willing to take them in. I suspect Natalia learned to perfect her reticence then, her regrets expressed privately in deference to the children she needed to calmly put on a train and banish. We'll still see each other, I hear her saying, every year for Saint Carmen's Day, her patron saint's day. For the rest of their lives, the children would come back home to Mulchén to visit her at least once a year on Saint Carmen's Day, her exiled, cast-away children remaining faithful, eager to be reunited, never to discuss publicly their dispersion through the nation. The youngest, Uncle Alipio, eventually died while a teenager, knifed down, Tecla said, in a brawl. Uncle Ismael ran away from the care of aunts and lived among a family of Mapuche Indians. "Horse meat!" he always told me as if sharing a favorite recipe. "The Indians, they taught me that horse meat makes your teeth stronger and pearly white." Yet, his own smile was prominently toothless by then, so go figure. I never got the point until I figured it out: his teeth had lasted longer than that of the average impoverished adults whose teeth sometimes barely lasted through their thirties. But horse meat? Never went near it myself, choosing to believe in fluoridation, part of the Communist conspiracy, I was later taught in the United States. Every country honors an urban myth or two.

In her teens, my grandmother María Jerny Cáceres left her aunt's house where she'd been sent to live as an unwanted *guacha* and became a live-in maid for a prominent landowning family in the small town of Coelemu. In this household, she met the man who'd become my actual biological grandfather. I know him today as Biological Grandfather. No name was ever recorded. My mother also bears her mother's maiden name, Cáceres. This forgotten gentleman worked as an accountant in the service of the prominent family. My grandmother became pregnant, and the gentleman in question not only refused to take responsibility for the child but would not consent to allowing my mother to carry his name. The patriarch of the prominent family had to make a decision about whom to believe: his accountant or one of several peasant maids? No contest. My grandmother was asked to leave the premises.

They meant to call my grandmother "Jenny," an English-language name popular at the time, even in a Spanish-speaking country like Chile, but Natalia arrived at the town clerk's office not knowing how to spell it. When she asked the town clerk, he took a guess and helped her fill out the form, spelling it as "Jerny." My grandmother ended up being nicknamed "La Jerny," pronounced "Herr-knee." La Jerny, they called her, a nickname people always asked to hear again to make sure they got it right. Who on earth chooses to be called "herr-knee"? Yet, she lived and died with the name. My great-grandmother Natalia at least admitted it that summer: "That stupid name was a mistake, but it stuck."

María "La Jerny" headed for Santiago with her one fatherless child, my mother. In the nation's bustling capital, she readily found employment as a live-in maid for yet another prominent family that kept a cadre of servants to maintain the house in immaculate order down to its minutest details. Opulence, high walls and columns, Persian rugs and shiny silver and crystal: all betrayed a Chilean yearning for an aristocratic lifestyle that included tea time, scones and crumpets, and fine teacups. My grandmother learned the epicurean art of cooking there from a professional French chef. I still recall sumptuous meals at the dinner table in the otherwise humbler surroundings of our Santiago home. Quail's heads stuck out of crusted cups filled with pureed vegetables. I poked the birds' beaks with my fingers. They looked less like food than toys for children to play with. Unfortunately, this same prominent, respectable family willing to train my grandmother in culinary skills, presentations, and overall manners grew weary of Jerny's bastard child as she grew up. There was little time to supervise her. The Gentleman of the House didn't want the servant's child running loose among his own children. "La Chela," they called her, a nickname for Graciela. La Chela even got into fights with some of these children. She was out of control. She had to be punished.

Grandmother interned my mother in a school for girls run by German nuns.

"They ruined my life," La Chela would tell me. "Those nuns thought they taught me discipline, but what they really taught me is resentment and hatred. At first, I thought I'd grow up and become a novice. I thought of the calling as devotion to God and purity. I would save myself for Christ, and I would grow up thinking in terms of purity. Yet, the nuns taught me to hate myself, and since I couldn't obey all their rules because I was rebellious, I just ended up hating nuns like them. Why would God condemn me to something only mildly more pleasant than a concentration camp? No insult meant for Germans, just those fucking nuns. They were Nazis. Some of them literally had swastikas in their bedroom next to their rosaries, at a time when German immigrants in Chile supported the Nazi cause. Chile remained neutral during the war until the very last minute because of the pressure of German-Chileans to remain isolationists. I hated these nuns and I associated them with Hitler."

La Jerny would visit her daughter once a week with packages of fruits, breads, and candies. But during the war, shortages of food compelled the nuns to seize all packages, claiming a need for war-time generosity with European orphans.

"If only those orphans had seen our stuff!" my mother complained, still angry in her sixties. "The nuns confiscated them for themselves, those greedy Nazi bitches!"

She recalled digging through trash cans and eating banana peels or just about anything that looked edible.

"There I was eating ants," she continued, "catching them with a stick. The ants would climb onto it and then I'd lick the stick clean like an armadillo. They tasted crunchy and stung like hot sauce. The Nazi nuns ate our food. We licked ants." Years later, on a black-and-white television in Bethesda, Maryland, the glaring images of the child actress Elizabeth Taylor in *Jane Eyre* suffering through mistreatment at a girl's school made my mother pay attention. "There I am," she said, pointing to the poor, decrepit Liz and Little Jane Eyre. "That's what it was like."

Fortunately, back at the wealthy family's mansion, La Jerny became the sidekick and companion to the butler, José Bravo, a handsome country man, a newcomer to the city uncomfortable in the butler's starchy uniform he was required to wear. He was a spirited creature, who humored her and sang Mexican *rancheras* to her, and was eager—like the rest of the country folk who comprised the servant class in Santiago—to make it in the big city. They became a couple, an odd one in her eyes. He was a tall, broad-shouldered man with a day laborer's physique. She was short, in turn, stocky, even plain-looking in her eyes, and some seven years older. I remember digging through picture albums and being surprised by pictures of my grandmother with missing heads.

"What is wrong with this picture?" I asked.

"Too ugly, that's all," she responded. It didn't make sense to me. Half of her pictures were mutilated.

My grandmother decided at one point in her life she could no longer bear to see herself in pictures she considered unflattering, and she removed her face from them while leaving the rest of the picture untouched. Eventually, with time, she either accepted her looks or simply gave up on them as most of her surviving pictures seem to be from "old age," her later fifties, when she no longer cared.

"The only important thing that happened to your grandma at that age was that José fell in love with her," said Aunt Tecla. "And I'm not sure why. She wasn't a great beauty. She was, perhaps, lively. That must have been enough for a country lout like him." It made sense, then, the missing faces on the picture. La Jerny didn't think herself beautiful enough to attract the handsome, younger man, but nonetheless she did, and married him before the opportunity ran out. That's how he became Tata.

Aunt Tecla was entitled to her opinion of Tata, but what mattered most was that my grandmother saw him not as a lout, but as a sexy country bumpkin with all the attributes of naïveté, innocence, and virility. He became a stepfather to my mother and a kind one at that. He was not about to demand that the bastard—my mother—be sent away, as had Natalia's husband a generation earlier. A man could still demand that of his wife, if necessary, but he chose not to. He and my grandmother married and made plans to leave the house of wealthy socialites in which they served and strike out on their own. My mother eventually stopped living under the watchful eye of the Nazi nuns and moved into a house in the mushrooming suburbs of Santiago, fully furnished with dogs, appliances, and, for once, a family, one that sustained an actual living father. That was a sign of prosperity for our family, to gain and maintain an actual father, not simply a father figure. The two bastard children, the two Marías, formed a family that became middle class, *católica*, and respectable. That's why talking about the past was mostly forbidden, or at best embroidered with stories about the father who supposedly died in a plane accident.

I was born, therefore, into a household that included what seemed to be the commanding authority of a real grandfather. José Bravo, or Tata, behaved as one, and nothing at that early age led me to suspect otherwise. I had to wonder, of course, in my childish curiosity why I could not carry his name, that vivid, intrepid exclamation of a name. Nothing in his attitude betrayed the fact that I would never be entitled to it. I was not a Bravo, but even today I envy the rhythmical, lively name that I'm not privileged enough to carry. Bravo. In all likelihood, it would have made better sense for me to carry the matrilineal name, Cáceres. It had been good enough for the previous children born out of wedlock, but the ability to carry my father's name must have been a singular prize for my mother. Bravo would have been, however, a more dramatic name for me, the playwright. We dramatists enjoy names with applause built into them.

The legitimization of the family came at a price. My mother dropped out of school to work and to help finance the family's lower-middle-class lifestyle on an empty patch of land in Conchalí, on the northern outskirts of the city. María spoke of doing time in various factories of a growing industrial base that lured people to the city in the late 1950s, turning Santiago into an overnight megalopolis with shantytowns springing up overnight and earning their name of *callampas* or mushrooms. The Bravos were not about to live in a *callampa*, however. They built their house brick by brick, wall by wall, in the gradual course of ten years. The government had sold the land in hectares small enough so that, overnight, houses sprang up, one followed by another with shared walls like a stacking of the cards, row after row without that detached, private, to-each-his-own look of Eisenhower's suburbia. The Chilean equivalent could never boast green lawns, garages, or white picket fences. All the fences that sprang up in our neighborhood were of a multitude of colors with sometimes unbecoming barbed-wire fence around them to keep out thieves. The area became crime-ridden. Youth gangs from even poorer neighborhoods would be known to rob homes sometimes for simple bread, maybe cash, what I call the Jean Valjean type of banditry: thieves who simply needed to eat, not the more highly armed gang-ridden type of crime that besets that part of the city today. But at least a dreary look of sameness could be avoided. There was no grand design, no master plan. Bricks, mortar, pieces of wood, tin cans, whatever the residents could afford, went up in uneven structures. Government services weren't readily forthcoming either. Residents drilled wells and outhouses until the mid-1960s, when finally sewer lines were gradually built, roads paved, with phone lines springing forth from downtown Santiago to reach us mile by mile, block by block, until we got our own phone in 1969. The outhouse became obsolete. Modern plumbing made our punctured tin can of a shower with a hose stuck inside it seem embarrassing, if somewhat ingenious, in retrospect. Tata tore down the chicken coop, and we didn't raise chickens or grow vegetables anymore; we grew flowers instead. We had a dog for a few years, then a cat, but no edible animals. The grapevines were obligatory as well as decorative. They were part of the culture. Every year the grapes arrived promptly by February, and we'd let them ripen before taking them down—and one year the fall storms of March came too early, and I woke up to find my grandfather struggling to save bunches of grapes from a torrential downpour that threatened to sweep them away. We had to eat grapes the entire week, make juice and fruit salad out of them, put them out as obligatory snacks, or give them away. Those were the remnants of our humbler rural background. We were city folks now; we bought our poultry at a local *avícola*, a place that sold dead birds kept half-fresh, sometimes rancid, in a faulty refrigerator whose overheated motor sometimes fumed and shook. That was the price of progress.

Once covered in dirt, our kitchen floor was spruced up with genuine tile. Parquet wood covered the temporary concrete that had lasted on the dining room floor for about a decade. Add the electricity and the phone, and the new, modern house was just about complete. The family was settled, the accommodations modest, but nonetheless urban and comfortable. A boy was born to my grandparents, whom they called José Luís, and he would become my mother's one legitimate brother. A child born within wedlock also signaled a form of progress.

My mother, María Graciela, had begun to entertain higher aspirations. She worked for a couple of years at a pharmaceutical factory stuffing painkillers into plastic bottles. By the time she'd turned twenty-one, she had had enough. She enrolled in night school and showed up on her first day of class eager to get started on something, anything, new.

"At first, I studied to get a degree in accounting, but then I couldn't continue. Numbers bored me. I thought I could benefit from more language skills—grammar, literature. I enrolled in Spanish because I thought I needed to be able to express myself somehow, and to read and write something other than a simple document. I thought I could become a little more cultured and sophisticated. I watched foreign movies and read the subtitles, but eventually, I wanted to understand American, French, and Italian movies without the subtitles, and in Santiago, there was always a young man you met at a party who spoke about Fellini and Bergman, and I wanted to be able to say, 'Yes, I saw *La Dolce Vita*, and here's what I think.' All I could say was 'wonderful, terrific, very moving,' 'it made me cry,' or 'she wore a wonderful dress in that scene,' that type of thing. It was getting to be embarrassing. My cousins were meeting men who were poets and musicians and could quote Neruda and Mistral, and I felt embarrassed around them. I went back to school to avoid becoming one of those silly girls who has nothing to say."

Her Spanish teacher turned out to be the youthful Mr. Reyes, fresh off a university training program as a Spanish major, assigned to night school on his way to a full-time teaching assignment. He was also married, as she would eventually discover, but by then the teacher and the student had become a couple, and that is how, in her attempts to escape the effects of illegitimacy by gaining an education, María returned to it: she gave birth to the teacher's child. In spite of some noble attempts in the United States, she would never complete formal schooling. She, like many women before her in her family, would dedicate her life to rearing her only child.

"But at least he did teach me about literature. I wouldn't have read *Anna Karenina* without Guillermo staring over my shoulder. It was slow reading, and it was almost a thousand pages, and I must have slept through half of it because I don't remember it. If it weren't for the Greta Garbo movie, I wouldn't have known she threw herself in the path of a moving train, and not a moment too soon. But at least I could say I read Tolstoy. I never claimed to finish it, but it was good enough for me. I was a woman of culture now."

They were in love, my mother claimed much later, and I took her at her word. To even suggest that I was merely a conceptive accident in a Catholic society that discouraged prophylactics and banned abortion would be unkind. An annulment of his marriage was possible, but also taboo. He was the father of several children by then (exact numbers are unclear since this family is still a mystery to me, made up of people I've never met), legitimate ones at least—who knew if there were other children out there like me, and who could prove it? María Graciela decided she'd give birth to the teacher's child as a form of romantic retribution for her own status as La Otra. The birth was planned, she claims. It was designed to leave her with a certain satisfaction denied to her mother and her grandmother before her. The illegitimate child became *el hijo natural*, a linguistic improvement, a child born of nature. My father did not skip town. My mother made this quite clear to me in my teenage years, to set the record straight. She didn't want me to think of my father like those men out there who leave women behind. My father considered himself a Socialist in a reactionary country barely awakening and eager to confront a power structure in which divorce and abortion were illegal. He did not wish to contribute to the manly pursuit of impregnating women and leaving them to fend for themselves. This may have been the unofficial pastime of conservative gentlemen in Chile. She reminded me the father of the nation himself, Bernardo O'Higgins, was born as the *hijo natural* of the Irish-born Spanish governor and his creole mistress.

"*El hijo natural es tan chileno como la empanada,*" she said, but I often wonder if other Chileans, patriotic ones especially, concurred that an out

36

of wedlock child was as Chilean as the meat pie. But she was a single mother in need of coming up with palliative words.

Still, my father realized he had made his contribution to this national legacy of bastardom and was conscientious enough to endow me with his name. Not that he also wanted me to carry his first name in addition to his last. Mother and he argued over it. My father was on an "El Cid kick," naming his children after characters from the classic poem about the Spanish national hero, Rodrigo Díaz de Vivar, who fought against the Moors. One of his daughters had already been named after Rodrigo's wife, Ximena. Rodrigo was his first choice for a boy's name. But my mother didn't buy literary allusions. He was the Spanish teacher. She wasn't. She preferred to think of herself in terms of instinct and passion, and she was more possessive of him, a man she would ultimately never keep to herself. She demanded use of his full name, first and last, and that's what she got. *El Cid* ended up on the screen that year with Charlton Heston and Sophia Loren, a grand, colorful spectacle, something the couple would see together. The romance off screen, however, would dissipate soon enough, and what was left, at least, was something more solid than a myth, the small triumph of a woman who secured her child the full recognition of his father.

I met my father only once. I was fourteen. My mother sent me to Santiago upon the recommendation of an analyst in Silver Spring, Maryland, who theorized that, as an alienated immigrant teenager, I yearned for the contact of a complex family megastructure such as ours in Santiago.

"But which family?" I asked with the same nagging tone of voice that had once compelled my great-grandmother Natalia to snatch the Bible from my hands—the Bravos or the Cácereses? Or maybe the Reyeses, who probably spoke of me in whispers? The Bravos had given me a grandfather, who then went on to remarry too quickly for the Cáceres family's comfort, and he was out. The Reyes branch had never played a role in my upbringing, and, by default, the Cáceres family, mostly the women, provided the actual rearing, nurturing, and support.

The analyst had her work cut out for her. She was Cuban American and was expected to preside over the needs of the entire D.C.-area Spanish-speaking immigrant community of troubled kids. She looked exasperated, perhaps burdened by my inquisitive, puny little presence. I asked more questions of her than she of me: What's it like to talk to so many people in one day? You speak only to kids or to adults as well? Are adults more difficult? If so, why? Do you specialize in the Latino community only or do you treat other Americans, too? Are their problems different from ours?

"Are you in denial about your family?" she finally asked.

"No, why? Are you?"

"Don't answer with a question. Just answer."

"I don't know what you mean."

"Are you ashamed to talk about your family?"

"But I've told you everything about my family!" I raised my voice. It was true. She had even made a chart, trying to keep up with the various names—Bravo, Cáceres, Reyes. I had spared her several others. "Why would I be in denial?"

"You talk about them as if they were strangers."

"They're in Chile. They practically are, aren't they?"

"But you're ashamed that you've made a better life for yourself among others like this Bravo family. They're not your blood family, and you correspond with Teresa."

That was true. My letters to Chile were more likely to be sent to La Otra, the woman my family had disparaged and called names when she married my grandfather. She had become a Bravo by marriage. And she was a Castro, and I had made a home for myself among her sisters and her nephews in the months before I had left. The Castros had become yet another family I appeared to have adopted to gain a sense of belonging. The fact that the Cáceres family didn't much approve of them didn't seem to faze me in the least.

"You identify with the outsider, with *la otra*."

"Aunt Teresa was nice to me. She was funny and made me laugh. Why shouldn't I be part of her life?"

"You call her aunt, but she's not an aunt."

"I know. What difference does it make?"

"You see yourself as a guest in other people's families because you don't have to belong, you don't want the responsibility of having an actual family. Perhaps you don't want a family."

"No, maybe I want more than one! Is that a bad thing?"

"I told you to stop answering with questions."

"Why am I even here?"

Love Child

The analyst didn't have much patience with me after this. "Send him to Chile," she ordered my mother, "the sooner the better. He needs to reconnect to those people back there. He clearly doesn't connect to anyone here, including me." In school, I'd already perplexed counselors by being a well-behaved student who could skip class at the least expected moment. Other kids smoked in the bathroom, but I was the straight-A student. When I ditched a course and spent periods in the bathroom, I did it in an exemplary manner: reading biographies of people who overcame adversity, such as Helen Keller and Frederick Douglass. When I showed up to class, I boasted a new lexicon: "I have a query," I would say. "I beseech you to answer my questions." A classmate once swung a fist at me after class and fractured my nose for using too many words he hadn't heard of. My English teacher appeared to agree with him: "You can be annoying sometimes. Why can't you just use 'question' instead of 'query'?" I was learning the English language, but some words made me appear fanciful, and even the English teachers feared I was turning into William Safire or, worse yet, another erudite William, William Buckley. I didn't know then that learning an excess of English verbiage was considered dangerous and even offensive to some native-born Americans, and that as a child you risked not only censure from the teachers but a punch in the face from your peers. These Americans demanded that immigrants learn English, but not improve upon their limited vocabulary.

Our apartment in Silver Spring, Maryland, was robbed once—for reasons other than my lexical violations, I would assume. Thieves broke a window in the middle of the day when I was at school, and my mother and aunt were at work. Neighbors claimed to have heard nothing. The thieves got away with two old stereos, a portable radio, my aunt's new color television set, and some jewelry, but left my prized possession, my own color TV, my portal into American culture. We felt the need to move across the Potomac from the seedy, crime-ridden Silver Spring neighborhood into the better trafficked, better maintained suburbs of Arlington, Virginia. I made a break from the past then. I walked into my new school having suddenly gained a father. I made one up, that is. My English teacher praised my "autobiography" in which I revealed my father worked for the Chilean Embassy and wrote propaganda for the Pinochet dictatorship. Good liar or good thespian? You be the judge. I filled the new role with great aplomb. I kept up the pretense for years. Nobody in my school seemed to know who

Pinochet was anyway, and it seemed fitting somehow, living in Washington, D.C., that I should be a diplomat's son. The pretense abetted my position at the top of the student heap as a straight-A student, which was real enough. The moment I was able to avoid the truth about being some bastard son with a fractured family, I was able to step into the shoes of people who mattered. I pretended to be a big shot's son from Santiago, and, therefore, I became one. The truth will set you free, the Bible says, but in my case it became a burden. The Big Lie initiated my theatrical ambitions and made me, I think, live out the necessary self-delusion necessary to survive poverty and bastardom. Besides, it was fun while it lasted.

The analyst and the counselors who knew the real story, however, still insisted on sending me to Chile for the summer. I did not resist. But she didn't count on me going to Chile unsupervised. My mother couldn't afford to go with me. She took out a personal loan to pay for my round-trip ticket to Santiago and had to stick around to pay for it in installments. This was therapy, after all, my therapy, and my mother paid for it out of her meager clerk's wages at GEICO Insurance. I was put on a plane. My summer turned cold in the tempestuous Santiago winter right in the midst of the Pinochet dictatorship. A fourteen-year-old boy let loose upon Santiago with American dollars could act up a storm of brattiness. I experienced a period of sudden personal freedom in the midst of a sullen, deadly dictatorship.

The year was 1975. Generalissimo Augusto Pinochet reigned with an iron grip and was at the height of his power and, I should add, his popularity. Most reports one read in the United States portrayed a despot who ruled over the oppressed, browbeaten masses—except that in this case the dictator managed to draw the admiration of some of his subjects, sometimes with great zeal. My own Tata, I learned upon arrival, had become an ardent supporter of Augusto Pinochet, and he and other supporters considered this a period of great "freedom from communism." The general, Tata claimed, had saved the nation from the Cubans and Soviets who'd arrived in the early 1970s to promote the Socialist government of the late Salvador Allende. I'd heard the usual rumors of Pinochet's human rights violations, torture, arrest of political opponents, all easily silenced by a wave of self-congratulatory boosterism that credited the dictator with millenarian powers of salvation. I was fourteen, and I tended to nod at everything adults had to say about politics. I kept them happy this way. I had my opinions, and I knew how to keep them to myself. I also had three hundred dollars in spending money in my pocket, which, thanks to a favorable exchange rate, went a long way that summer (or southern hemispheric winter). Spending money kept me satisfied and oblivious to the reality of Chile during one of its worst recessions since the 1930s. The dictatorship appeared to have brought, on the surface, peace and tranquility to the nation after years of chaos. I told my grandfather I was a Pinochet supporter, and he hugged me. He wept. I stood with limp arms on my side, feeling stupid. I went to my Marxist aunt's house next and declared I had serious reservations about the dictator's human rights record. She saw right through me, however. "*Ay, por favor, otro día,*" she said. "Get back to me." I also knew (as my mother had revealed a few details about his personality) that my father was a Socialist, and that I would have to approach him, if I were to do so at all that year, with great care. But the thought of calling on him, a man I'd never met, intimidated me. I spent the entire summer vacation in Santiago not once making contact with him until I felt compelled to try only because the Chilean bureaucracy coerced me into it.

September came around, and I was already a week late for school back in Washington. My mother somehow let me get away with being gone that long—perhaps she needed the break from me as well. September also marks the Chilean spring, highlighted traditionally by Independence Day celebrations. In better times, national elections were also held in September to equate democracy with the birth of the nation. Students got at least two weeks off, for which we were deliriously grateful. In our family, Saint Mary's Day also merited a rambunctious fiesta that reunited all branches of the party because my grandmother was otherwise too self-conscious or even self-hating about her age and her looks to celebrate her birthday. Instead she celebrated her namesake patron saint's day. It was a party that celebrated not so much the Virgin Mary, but all the women who were her proud *tocayas,* her namesakes. But the memory of those loud, festive celebrations had passed on. Grandmother was dead, and the military had imposed their will on the country on September 11, 1973, turning it into their own day of celebration conveniently attached to the September 18 Independence Day celebration. Moreover, the country was living under a curfew, so any parties had to lower the music and keep the guests inside all night, if necessary, because they couldn't re-emerge into the streets until six a.m. A party that celebrated a saint's day ended up like an all-night vigil. Something was lost when the partying had to be kept at a minimum noise level, and the guests were told to refrain from even peeking out the window. During curfew, the guards had authority to shoot any strangers in self-defense. That year, the military and its supporters prepared to celebrate two years of dictatorship. I had grown weary of Santiago. I wanted out, and I needed to get back to my glamorous life as a high-achieving diplomat's son.

I wore a tie and jacket to walk into Braniff International to book my flight like any other adult traveler. I aroused suspicion, naturally. The clerk asked me about a paternal consent to travel. Not parental, but paternal. I looked perplexed. Under Chilean law, I could not travel outside the country without my father's consent. Instead, I had on me a notarized note written by my mother in case of any bureaucratic eventuality, but to the patriarchal authorities of Chile, María was only the woman who'd given birth to me. While the father was alive, whether legitimate or not, a minor was required to obtain his father's consent to leave the country. That meant I really had to contact my father. The teenage capacity to catastrophize came into full view: *The embarrassment of it all!*

I tried to work through my panic. I thought I could get the consent through the mail. Surely father would be discreet. I wouldn't even have to talk to him, nor would he have to bother meeting me. I asked one of my aunts to call on my behalf. She refused, saying I should be man enough to deal with it. Man enough? What did this mean? I resented the insinuation. But she was right; I was terrified. I had never spoken to my father, let alone met him. Why go through this burden at all? Since I wasn't man enough, I was *female enough* to disguise my voice and pretend that I was an aunt, any aunt, calling on my behalf.

"Your son needs a notarized consent to let him travel back to Washington," I said in a high-pitched voice similar to the voice of one of my aunts. My thespian skills, learned in a class at the Maryland Academy of Dramatic Arts, had finally begun to pay off. Just as I'd earlier gained assertiveness as a diplomat's son, I found myself in complete control in a woman's voice. It was an old trick. When I called the Maryland Academy to enroll in a drama class, I told the owner I wanted drama lessons "for my son." Later, I told my mother I had been accepted to the Maryland Academy of Dramatic Arts and would she please pay for my lessons. My mother consented, gave me a check, and she never even had to talk to anyone.

Besides, I had saved her from the embarrassment of having to use imperfect English.

"Would you please mail the said document to such-and-such an address?" I asked, hoping the man would be discreet enough to mail it, no questions asked; but to my surprise he said he'd come over to my grandfather's house the next day to deliver it himself. He said he was looking forward to meeting his son. He even said he wanted to meet this new aunt he'd never heard of. Time to panic!

What am I going to do? I didn't tell anyone about my impersonations of some fictional aunt. I was too embarrassed at the success of my thespian dare, but even more embarrassed that my father had bought my voice as a woman. Even then I couldn't bear the queer implications of such a thing. I had to keep the entire matter to myself. I announced to my grandfather and his still maligned younger wife, Teresa, that my father was coming over. Teresa made a sumptuous tea-time presentation, the cakes, the little sandwiches, the odorous sensation of a perfumed tea in the air. But I needed to produce an aunt. I didn't know how to explain that my father expected to meet this unknown aunt. I thought I could get somebody from the neighborhood to impersonate such a woman, but to no avail. My time ran out.

When my father arrived and asked to meet the aunt I'd impersonated, I let it be known she was gone for the day, and he left it at that, thank God. That was my first conversation with my father. Face to face, man to man, I avoided talk of my female Other. A few years later, in my twenties, I would write a short story based on this incident of impersonation. A too-clever editor from an obscure Colorado literary magazine scrawled a note in his rejection letter: "It's too Oscar Wilde for my taste." At fourteen, I didn't know and had never read the venerable sodomite/martyr, but how fitting that my disguise should have been taken as an artifice comparable to an Oscar Wilde play, one worth rejecting since no serious piece of fiction could possibly feature such an unlikely incident? I had enacted a scene from Wilde's play *The Importance of Being Earnest* in my real life before I had even heard of the play. The title of this story later became, naturally, "The Importance of Aunt Augusta," and this was not the first time that my real life should be condemned for its fictional preposterousness. At that age, I had already managed to create farce, and I was already getting rejected for it.

Love Child

My father arrived at Tata's house and appeared to take it over with a wave of a cigarette in his hand.

"I'm here to see my son," he told Tata, who answered the door. The older man complained to me later that my father hadn't even greeted him properly. He simply expected to be let in. My grandfather often did this with guests, complained that they didn't pay sufficient homage, so it was often difficult to figure out who to believe. I didn't need that type of bother that afternoon. My grandfather made me more nervous than I needed to be with his own insecurities.

My father did seem to have a direct and to-the-point manner about him. He was there to deliver the document and then to leave as quickly as he could. But my grandfather's wife, Teresa, served tea and bid him to stay. My father obliged, at a time when I didn't particularly care to sit down and talk to him. He was a short, pudgy man, much darker than I'd expected, with a brown tinge on his skin that appeared Polynesian. I could live with illegitimacy, but at the time, it seemed a greater shock to me that my father had turned out to be nonwhite. Having inherited part of my mother's relative lightness, her Spanish blood, I had not counted on this particular discomfort. It bothered me, and it silenced me. It seemed like a strange thing to discover, since I'd never seen a picture of my father, and my mother had never described his looks. Chileans have a peculiar attitude about race, shared by many Latin Americans who are partly European. They consider themselves white if they are only partly white. If you behave and act white, and claim a Spanish or European ancestor or two, you're white in Chile regardless of your looks or your background. My mother, like many people of Spanish descent, often spoke condescendingly of Indians, blacks, and other people of non-European background, but on the other hand, she had no problem falling in love with a man as dark as my father—except that she never called him a dark man, and probably never considered him such because he was educated, well spoken, and he "acted white." Perplexed as to what all this made me, I let my so-called nonwhite father do most of the talking. It was, to say the least, with my inclination for passing as Aunt Augusta over the phone, a day for disguises.

Mr. Reyes spent over an hour lecturing me on the destruction of Chilean socialism and the defilement of the nation by the military. He taught at a public high school where he could be held liable for any anti-government graffiti on the wall. He and his fellow teachers had to go around spray painting or scrubbing over it every single day before going home, fearing they'd be arrested for subversive activities. One of his female colleagues had been raped by a group of soldiers when held as a political prisoner. She ended up pregnant and would soon be giving birth to a child of rape, a child of General Pinochet himself, he said. What would she do with this child? he wondered; what could she do if abortion was not an option because the same fascist government that had allowed for the violent implantation of a child in her womb wouldn't let her get rid of it? To protect the sanctity of the Catholic family, I would assume. I never found out what became of this child. Later, as a student, I wrote a play about a child of rape, and his return as a terrorist who hounds his father, a Chilean general. My playwriting professors at UC San Diego accused me of writing unlikely and "melodramatic" scenarios for the stage. The history of Latin America, especially in the 1970s, comprised one preposterous event after another. The Chilean truth would prove bizarre for American sensibilities, adding great stumbling blocks to my artistic, dramaturgical, and literary ambitions. My inclination for Wildesque exaggerations annoyed my teachers as much as they did that editor in the literary magazine, but I was too diffident to just tell them this really happened. I didn't know how to close this gap between the precious dictum that creative writing teachers repeat as a mantra, to write what you know, and then their tendency to tell you they don't believe it because they haven't experienced it. The stories I heard from my father that one day fall into that chasm. It was "realism," but my teachers dismissed it as melodrama, or worse.

I was distracted by conflicting thoughts that afternoon; while Father drank tea in my grandfather's house and casually talked about atrocities with a matter-of-fact tone made all the more macabre for its simplicity and truth, I yearned to be back in white suburbia, in Arlington, Virginia, where life seemed simpler and slower. In one rash decision, I might have chosen to erase the entire memory of Chile itself from my mind. I wanted to be a U.S. citizen, the whiter the better. The Chilean tragedy had begun to do more than disturb my spoiled adolescence. It had touched the lives of actual people. Surely I already knew this, but under the influence of my grandfather and his right-wing friends, I went about remarkably carefree in Chile, under the illusion that perhaps General Pinochet had been a savior from Communist totalitarianism, a necessary evil to forestall communism. Yet, my father firmly believed that the coup had been an excuse to clamp down on progressive thought. The Communists had been nowhere near taking over the country, and the hysteria had been planted by the CIA and their right-wing collaborators to help justify a violent overthrow. I have come to the conclusion that Father was partly right, though I hold no illusions about Soviet/Cuban aims for the country either. The Socialists, however, seemed to be unfairly associated with Communist totalitarianism and paid the price for it. But at the time, I was a kid, and I thought Father talked way too much about politics while I yearned to be listening to KC and the Sunshine Band in my comfortable apartment across the Potomac. It seemed comforting to think I would soon be back in Arlington talking to my classmates about the top forty countdown delivered on a weekly basis over the radio by Casey Kasem.

Father left the signed document on the table. It was a rolled-up piece of paper tied up with a string, resembling a diploma. He drank the last sip of his tea, shook my hand, and, realizing I hadn't said much and only nodded compliantly, he wished me luck. I walked him to the bus station, and he waved goodbye from the window of the bus. He was this underpaid high school teacher who apparently couldn't afford a car, and he was constantly threatened with political imprisonment by a fascist government. He had plenty on his mind. My own fate seemed like a side diversion. I was something that had happened briefly years earlier in his wilder youth, and he'd been man enough to admit it, and that was the end of that. One last wave, and a very wan little smile, and he was gone. I would never see him again.

Five years later, I returned to Chile. I was nineteen, still a minor under Chilean law and still a Chilean citizen thanks to the bungling of my papers by the Immigration and Naturalization Service. My native country was still under the firm stronghold of dictatorship. I was even eligible for Chilean military service, which I hadn't been aware of until I arrived in Santiago. I feared being held at the airport, inducted immediately into the army to become one of Pinochet's soldiers. If I wanted to leave the country, which I clearly did not want to serve under the circumstances, I still needed to contact my father once again to get his signature and his consent. This time I figured I was wiser, more mature, and that I should offer some opinions worthy of a prospective U.S. citizen. I'd become, of course, an opponent of the dictatorship and thought that would please my father. Furthermore, I would talk this time. I'd be assertive. I wanted to prove that

Love Child

I wasn't just any bastard, but a more enlightened, more civilized one not unlike the Irish-Chilean hero Bernardo O'Higgins. He would then attempt to take me one step further: to recruit me into socialism. I would resist, show independence, stay firmly within the solid, bourgeois reformist tradition of the U.S. Democratic Party. I'd campaigned for Senator Kennedy in the 1980 election, in my first year at UCLA, while still a noncitizen (I didn't know that legal residents are not allowed to be involved in partisan activities). Nobody asked or checked. I attended fundraisers and drank wine with the adults. I appeared, at least, to be an adult. In Chile, that summer, I was ready to impress my father. I was eager, in fact, to have an intense conversation with him about issues that mattered deeply to him. I made the phone call. No disguises were necessary this time. I did not pretend to be anyone other than myself. Aunt Augusta had been retired, and I no longer pretended to be a diplomat's son. A woman answered the phone. She didn't identify herself. She announced tersely that Father was dead. He'd succumbed a year earlier to a rare form of leukemia after a long struggle. She then told me, firmly and rudely, that if I called again I would be shot. "*Te llega un tiro por la cabeza*" is how she put it, with even a little bit of a laugh behind it. Under the circumstances, I didn't think it was funny. Perhaps she feared that, like the plot of any Latin American telenovela, the bastard child was calling to make a claim on the inheritance. Father was a teacher, and I doubt he left much of an inheritance. Years later, my half-sister Ximena would say she never spoke to me at the time and didn't believe her mother would have said this to anyone. If my only concern had been to obtain that dreaded piece of paper the government required for me to leave the country, now I didn't need it. The authorities would finally recognize my mother's notarized permission allowing me to travel.

I felt only a vague sensation of sadness over Father's death. So much time and distance had passed. I never mourned for him, and his family didn't seem to want me to. Here was a situation none of my middle-class friends back in Arlington and Los Angeles would understand, I figured. I'd barely gotten the courage to lie about my parents being divorced, something my American friends could relate to, but I realized at this moment I could no longer keep up that facade. My father was dead. He'd never been a diplomat in the service of General Pinochet—as I'd led my classmates and teachers to believe—and he would surely have taken exception to being cast in that role. The teenager in me still lamented the embarrassment of it all.

Meanwhile, I needed to get out of Chile. I lined up at the Santiago registrar's office to get an official death certificate that would prove to the authorities my father was dead. With that certificate in hand, I could then show my mother's notarized consent to travel and, yes, prove to General Pinochet's tyrannical authorities that she, even though a woman, had become my legal guardian. I for once felt completely free from Chile, detached entirely, all ties severed. I would not return to Chile for another twenty-three years.

2

A Santiago Education

At school, violence erupts and becomes part of my life. At home, there's a contrast, a refuge, a calm afternoon in which Grandmother and Great-Grandmother drink tea, listen to a soap opera on the radio, and work at adjusting seams or making new dresses on hire for women in the neighborhood.

Great-Grandma Natalia utters in cranky disdain about these modern women who can't make their own dresses as she cuts cloth and wonders why she has to do this—for a few extra *escudos*, was the answer. My grandmother is more tolerant: city women work and still have to take care of the home and the children, so give them a break, she argues with her mother; we provide a service for these women and use the money for summer vacations.

It's a small world of work and duty, and long-term planning. But at my school, the aggression, masculine bravado, and sportsmanship of hunting down the faggot fall exclusively upon me, and I am left to fend for myself. At home, my mother opens up a store, and we trade used magazines and books to a neighborhood in need of a little culture, if only pop culture, comics, and illustrated romances. A cartoon version of *Don Quixote* might get passed around, along with a couple of non-illustrated Agatha Christies, the only books even aspiring to high culture. Reading is still reading. Words become real. My life at home opens up my eyes to the world. But at school, it becomes about learning survival strategies.

My early education is a world in conflict.

I was sent to school to be battered, harassed, sometimes injured. That's what boys did. It was natural. I wasn't supposed to complain. If I cried, I was a sissy. But I was a sissy anyway, which was one of the reasons I was beaten up to begin with, and if I cried, I became more of one—sissier and sissiest—and then netted further abuse. I also got perfect scores in most of my assignments, another reason to receive severe beatings. A know-it-all is even more dangerous than being a sissy. When I placed first in the class for four years in a row, I must have unleashed other resentments on top of homophobia. I came to associate school with a jungle that I would one day escape—and yet I did well in school because I absorbed learning from every other aspect of life around me. My mother felt torn. She contributed to the acceleration of my learning, but that also contributed to the resentment at school. She wanted to protect me from abuse, but she often succumbed to the cultural pressure of letting boys be boys.

"Boys are supposed to play rough," one of my Socialist aunts told her. She might have been expected to stand up for the downtrodden, but she didn't defend me. "If you protect him all the time, how's he going to grow up and protect himself?"

This aunt—and I had my share of them—bitterly opposed the dog-eat-dog world of our capitalist society. She romanticized the saintly proletariat, the oppressed masses, but with me (and apparently just for me), she was laissez-faire all the way, baby. Darwin meets Spencer meets Pinochet, and may the best man win. She was not really my "aunt," but all women that age who were cousins qualified as part of a sisterhood. She was an aunt, but she consistently sized me up from the eyes of a masculine world. She seemed to be horrified by my femininity.

"My boys are tough," she constantly repeated. "My boys know how to fight."

I could see my mother turn away, intimidated by her and feeling a sense of deference. She looked up to this slightly older cousin, an assertive woman in an admirable, stable marriage to a young man from our hometown of Mulchén. Association with this aunt appeared to make a difference. My mother felt compelled afterward to tell me I just needed to be tougher. I needed to fight back. Yet, I didn't know how. My idea of being tougher was to get more perfect scores, but then almost everybody, including the girls, would resent me. My mother wouldn't accept less than perfect scores, but this also set me apart. My uncle and my grandfather were immersed in their own lives. My grandfather enjoyed his retirement by fixing up houses for people in the neighborhood, doing small paint jobs or often transforming chicken coops into guest houses. My teenage uncle chased girls early on in adolescence and wasn't particularly interested in fighting, though he certainly knew how. He was tough and followed the ethos of boys in the neighborhood, which was to hang out, whistle at women from a corner bar, and make obnoxious comments about women's behinds. My Socialist aunt came home feeling flattered.

"I like it when they whistle at me," she said. She had reached her thirties and felt rejuvenated by a whistle. She continued to talk about the proletariat and the movement to liberate Chile, but boys being boys appealed to her. My mother seemed more skeptical. If any men whistled at her, she tended to turn around and give them a dirty look. But nonetheless my mother followed the advice not just of cousins but of any other people who warned her of the consequences of my apparent femininity.

I didn't want to learn how to fight. Fighting back seemed alien to my character. At school I had to grin and bear it, and even today I don't get much sympathy from this tale. People who knew me then seem to imply I asked for it. As a child, I was expected to take up arms and defeat the enemy without weapons training. If I bled, I had a handkerchief to stem the blood from the nose, and bruises one learned to take for granted. Things began to get cruel at home, too. My mother showed me an illustrated book of Roman times. Soldiers were throwing a man down a cliff.

"That's what they used to do to faggots once," she said, the implication being that they could again if I didn't straighten out my act.

It was an uncharacteristic moment of cruelty. I believe she thought she could "cure" my condition by scaring me straight. I had no allies left in the fight. Even my mother seemed to be threatening violence.

At school I formulated my own rules: be careful whom you talk to. An amicable new boy in school began by talking to me about his family, his hobbies, the music he listened to, what he did on weekends, and so on. I imagined I was making a friend, at last. But once the other boys got a sight of this, the pressure began: what are you doing talking to him? He's a faggot. You need to stay away from him. The next time he saw me, he walked away quickly, or to prove himself worthy of the other boys, he pushed me out of the way. "I'm not talking to you, faggot," he shouted. "Get the fuck out of here."

I was apparently not allowed to have any friends among the boys. As a result, I often played with the girls, which only compounded the problem.

A Santiago Education

My schooling became an education in a caste system, proving that people did their best to make themselves feel superior to others. I contributed to it by declaring myself more intelligent. I was the teacher's pet, and I deserved what I got because of my condescension, but it was often hard to tell which was which. The boys found plenty of excuses for making me a target everywhere I went regardless of what I did.

In my neighborhood the people who were literally excluded from society were not simply the sissies, but the gypsies. They lived in tents along the path of the main street on Pedro Fontova Boulevard. The women wore loose satin robes draped around them, as if clothed in the seven biblical veils of Salome. The gypsy boys wore simple cotton pants, with shirts that opened up around the chest, making them look like pirates, and sometimes sexy and exotic. Their golden locks made them look even more alluring. They were from Hungary, people told me. They speak "Hungarian," but really what did anybody know? I was a child and accepted what I heard. They were more likely to speak the gypsy language, Roma. Their often striking blond looks made the mestizos among us jealous. We were supposed to prize white, European looks, especially among our own locally admired stock of German Chileans, but if these blonds were gypsies, it was as if they had to be hated and marginalized, often beaten, for having wrested control of a prized genetic attribute such as blondness, which didn't belong to them. How come they were whiter than us when they were supposed to be our country's n———s?

Their kids were not even enrolled in school. Their parents didn't want them to learn, people say, but I doubt that any of the gypsies would survive a day in our school, which was ruled not by the teachers but by the bullies.

A gypsy woman stopped me on my way to school one day, in winter 1968. With her odd loose garments, and a withered look and wild curly hair, she looked frightful, like a witch ready to sell a poisoned apple. She wanted to read my fortune. I told her I didn't have any money, which wasn't true. I carried a little pocket money to buy roasted chestnuts from a vendor. She wanted to talk, however, and said her parents came from *muy lejos*, but she was actually born in Chile. She claimed a passion for Sandro, the gypsy showman who had become a popular pop singer throughout Latin America and a heartthrob in movies in which no one mentioned his gypsy background.

"I like Sandro, too," I responded with some enthusiasm, but I had to watch it. I had been warned many times not to mention I "loved" a male singer, no matter how crazy I was for any of them. Girls screamed when any popular song came on the radio, and I wasn't allowed to scream with them. I had to temper my enthusiasm. Liking was strong enough, and suspicious for a boy.

She touched the leather bag in which I carried my books.

"I wanted to go to school once," she said. She could have been in her late twenties, or maybe older, prematurely gray. Age wasn't something I estimated well at that time. On a wintry day, she had stopped me close to the entrance of the school, next to a rail where usually vendors gathered to sell candy to the children during breaks. No vendors were to be found on that dark, gloomy day. Fog that enveloped the city during the night had begun to clear slowly, but it still lingered, clouding up the road. Bus drivers kept their lights on. The gypsy woman had emerged from this fog, but the initial fear in me had begun to dissipate. I grew more comfortable around her.

"Why didn't you go to school?" I asked, naively.

"You people don't want us to learn," she said. I had never thought of that. I didn't think there was an official policy preventing gypsies from enrolling in school. But it seemed true enough, because no gypsy children were enrolled in our school, or were some enrolled and managed to hide their identity? How did one hide one's identity? I thought of Margarita, the curly red-haired girl who sat in the last seat in the back of the class because she was the tallest. She looked "exotic" enough to us but never admitted to gypsy ancestry when kids teased her. We thought of her as "Spanish," which was foreign, but nonetheless still part of our ancestry. The idea of hiding one's background hadn't occurred to me at that point. I would use hiding or disguise later in an American school. "My father said one day gypsies would start our own schools, but then we moved into another neighborhood, and every year it's a new place for us. And they never got around to enrolling me. . . . I still want to learn to read and write."

"I'll teach you," I volunteered. A smile sparked up on her face, but then just as quickly, it dissipated.

"Oh, no, no, no," she said. "There's always trouble."

At that age, I only felt a mild disappointment, as if somebody didn't want to play with me. But it began to dawn on my young mind that some people weren't wanted, or felt unwanted, or had been made to feel that way. One day at the local movie theater my mother made a point of moving out of her seat when a gypsy woman sat next to her. "They're thieves," she said. I didn't question her choice and moved with her. I never connected the dots. My mother, who was warm, loving, and caring, made a hateful comment, but I didn't see her as the same mother who also claimed faggots could be thrown down the cliff. It's just the way things were.

The woman decided to move on that day, realizing she was not about to score some pocket money from a child who insisted he didn't have any.

"Sometimes little kids with money want their fortunes read just like their parents," she told me. "That's really the only time you people let us into your homes," she added, "because you think we have magic powers."

"Well, don't you?"

"We must have some sort of power that you people believe us. . . . Yes, so I suppose we do."

I only heard the last part. They did have power, I thought. My eyes brightened up, and I decided to go running, as if scared that she would cast a spell over me. I looked back, and she was waving at me, laughing as well.

That was my only conversation with one of the people who lived in the colorful tents. From then on I would hear rumors, for example of a cousin attending a picturesque, extravagant, gypsy wedding that turned to tragedy when a jealous lover killed the groom. I would later discover that the highly charged scenario actually came from a play by Lorca, *Blood Wedding*, but my relatives in Chile seemed to get their stories from anywhere they could find them.

I would never see a gypsy student in my school, though years later another cousin claimed one enrolled in his school, and that the kids stared at him as if he'd been a Martian. By then, I knew the feeling. School was the place where one trained in the skills of condescension, hatred, and worse, but attitude came from home as well. For me, the bullying finally became too much, even for my mother. She finally broke down and lodged a complaint—for very specific, limited reasons, but it was something. Not only were my peers pushing me around in the third grade, which was of course considered natural, but now older boys began to get into the act. A group of boys from the sixth grade were coming up to me during recess and pushing me around, stealing my snacks, and unleashing a wave of punches and kicks on me. The boys from my class looked on in disbelief, and probably some resentment. He's our faggot, let us take care of him, was the apparent response, but they weren't about to defend me in front of older boys. I began to arrive home with more severe bruises all over my body (the earlier bruises had never really shocked anyone).

My mother walked me to school one day and demanded to talk to the school principal about this new group of older bullies. The principal came up to me and made me tell her everything I knew, everything I'd told my mother. She actually looked shocked. How can that be? Such things shouldn't be happening at our school! Where is the pride of being a good citizen and a good Christian? She seemed sincere, if naive, as if she really couldn't believe such things went on around her. It wasn't an act. The principal told my mother she'd take care of it. I was suspicious at first. When my mother left, I thought: There she goes, leaving me in this nest of vipers again. But the principal was a woman of her word: she walked me into the one classroom of sixth graders and made me stand in front of the class. The sixth-grade teacher then told me to point to the boys who'd been bullying me. I felt like a traitor, but I did it anyway. I pointed the finger at all five of them. They looked horrified, as if they feared being sent to some detention camp in Patagonia. Alas, humiliation would be strong enough to get the message across.

Their teacher made them get up, and in front of the class, she went up to each and every one of them. "You ought to be ashamed of pushing around a smaller boy like that!"

The boys looked down at the floor, their faces blushing in embarrassment, and tears were falling from their faces. The shame of having to stand in front of their class and be accused of beating up on a smaller boy worked wonders. They never bothered me again. But the ethics of bullying were limited to this one phenomenon, this one unscripted rule: you may not bully boys who are smaller. Bullying boys your own size and age, however, was allowed. My mother never lodged that other complaint and seemed to fear that I would come across even more of a sissy if she—mommy—were to come to school to denounce those boys as well. I was on my own. Much later in life, she'd say she feared I would not grow up to be a man if she were always protecting me. Sending me off to a school every day where I'd be harassed and walk around in fear was supposed to make me a man.

At home the world created by the tightly knit Bravo family created a completely different structure. I was lucky that school was simply a four-hour ordeal, from eight a.m. till noon. The Chilean school system couldn't afford an all-day shift. The schools had two shifts, two separate classes. Afternoon victims populated the school from noon to four, and I would spend the rest of my day at home, where safety and comfort reigned.

My enterprising mother quit her job in the assembly line of a vitamin factory and opened up a used magazine and book store. The commuting to and from work had become monotonous. Two buses in the morning and then back made the whole thing a waste of time. Having my mother running a business from home seemed ideal. This new business allowed her the freedom to run it as she pleased and to control her own hours. My grandfather knocked down a wall in the one bedroom facing the street, and this became the store where I spent afternoons reading everything I could lay my hands on. Our neighborhood was by no means wealthy, but it was enterprising and populated by the country folk who had gone into the city to make their mark on the world. We were all settlers in the area. We couldn't afford to open up an actual book store, and most people in our neighborhood couldn't afford to buy books. So we did not sell them; we traded them. That's why it was called a *cambio de revistas*, a magazine exchange, which also became a book exchange. People would bring used books or magazines and trade them for a minimal fee. My mother also added candies, which attracted children and were an extra source of revenue. Every penny counted; they added up to savings and greater financial independence.

Imagine the traffic of a small neighborhood shop where people came to get their magazines. The latest *Superman*, or *Batman*, *Lone Ranger*, the *Archies*, or *Little Lulu*. Adults had their own magazines—romances for women, girlie magazines for men—although naked centerfolds were unheard of yet. In a few years, they'd take over. Meanwhile, a woman in a tight swimsuit kept the gentlemen looking satisfied and coming back for more. Women preferred illustrated romances and specifically the novels of the Spanish author Corín Tellado, a phenomenal raconteur who sold millions of books depicting and revealing the love fantasies of young and older women alike. I was a fan of the superheroes myself, but an occasional new magazine would catch my attention and imagination, such as an illustrated import from Mexico about the adventures of Aztec Gods. The popular Chilean cartoon the Little Condor, or *Condorito*, would also be exported to Mexico and other parts of Latin America, and the pop culture weekly *Ritmo* revealed the latest showbiz gossip that alerted us to the latest scandals, Elvis's wedding to Priscilla, the Supremes touring the world, a Jackie Onassis sighting, Julie Christie winning her Oscar for *Darling*, Liz Taylor for *Who's Afraid of Virginia Woolf?*

"That was my husband and me," commented a friend of my mother who dropped by to talk about the movies and trade a copy of *Ritmo* for another. Like Martha and George in Edward Albee's play of marital discord and existential delusions, filmed with Liz and her husband Richard Burton, this friend smoked and drank late into the night. She wasn't a drunk, she made sure to emphasize, but when she and her husband got into it, things got nasty. "Maybe I don't start making out with the young guest, but we often throw things against the wall. It's about getting it all out, and then making up afterwards. That movie was about us."

People dropped by and shared these tidbits with my mother, who listened patiently and soothed them whenever she could by offering a cup of tea. I would listen in on these conversations, while pretending to read my comic books. At other times my mother withstood the assault of vendors who showed up carrying eggs, homemade bread, churros, German pastries (*el berlín* in particular, a donut look-alike minus the hole, with a creamy filling), and countless other concoctions we couldn't buy all day without losing our appetite for dinner. My mother politely turned down the various offers, such as shoe shine and housecleaning services and whatever else people cared to offer.

None of these people sparked the children's imagination quite the same way as did the homeless El Falabella, a local man with mental disabilities who slept in alleys until the neighbors built him a wooden shack that looked like a dog house. There was no such thing as a NIMBY (not in my backyard) movement in our neighborhood. These people actually built the shack in between two front yards, facing the traffic of the streets and quite visible to everyone. Falabella would crawl into the space and sleep because it was too small for him to actually stand up inside it. The same people would allow him to use their facilities, and neighbors took turns feeding him. When a gang of hooligans attacked him one night, men from the neighborhood ran out to chase after them and later to soothe him with a glass of wine. The police came and took away a couple of teenagers who had mistakenly imagined this man had money in his shack. El Falabella survived through handouts. He did not live in a cash economy.

He had been named after the most elegant clothing store, Falabella, in downtown Santiago. His own clothes were hand-me-downs, which he wore until they were in tatters and somebody else in the neighborhood came along to replace his raggedy sweater or his torn pants. El Falabella wore his rags and accepted his name without ever signaling he understood the irony. He spoke like a little child, and he often came to sit at the doorstep of our store until he would tire and return to wandering the streets. But if anything appeared sad to him, one would find him in a corner crying like a five-year-old.

"Why are you crying?" I asked him once, surrounded by other children who gathered around him looking curious. He reached into his pocket and showed us the lifeless remains of a pigeon he had found by the road.

"*'Ta muerto*," he said.

He stood soothing the head of the dead bird with loving care. The children told him to bury it. He allegedly carried it until it disintegrated in his pocket.

It occurred one day to the local movie owner to put El Falabella to work, to join the market economy and thrive. He made El Falabella sweep the entire theater with a broom every morning after a long night of triple features. One day in winter, storms brought a violent downpour into the city, which flooded part of the theater. El Falabella came out screaming, "*Es el diluvio.*" El Falabella knew enough about the Bible to think it was a sign of the end of times. He broke out into tears again until the children consoled him that this was an average winter flood, which had damaged at most the interior of an old movie theater, but was not the end of times.

Many years later, El Falabella was found dead inside his shack, and his body was laid to rest at a local cemetery with the help of a priest and a couple of neighborhood men who were the pallbearers. Nobody else showed up. No one knew where he'd come from, or how he'd gotten there. The priest threw away the countless Nescafé containers that he used as plates for his daily meals, and which were his only possessions.

My mother's shop helped open up the neighborhood to me in ways I would not have experienced behind the safety of our home. In that comfortable world, my grandparents carried on as if living in a garden, watering plants and looking over our vines year after year to point out the annual blossoming of buds into grapes in various colors—shades of black, red, and rosé—which would hang from everywhere in our patio, looking sumptuous. My grandfather's rule was not to touch them until they were ripe and ready to be eaten. The store, however, brought the public further into what had once been a bedroom. Into it poured fellow citizens, some genuine eccentrics, and also the vendors and beggars, and it was a new education for me as well. The rest of the world opened up, too, now that we had access to countless books and magazines.

My mother supplemented my initial reading of cartoons and children's books with specific choices she made on my behalf. She started to bring home one by one the issues of an encyclopedia called *El Monitor*. Once you owned all the issues with the letter A, you then bought a cover that bound all of them together, and it created a piecemeal encyclopedia. Unfortunately, my mother left for the United States as we were completing the D's, and because the collection stalled at that letter, today I have the habit of saying, "I learned everything in Chile from A to D." In the United States, one would have access to encyclopedias at a public library.

The popular magazines also sponsored contests, and stores like ours sold the coupons necessary to enter them. Participants bought an album made up of categories, such as singers, movie actors, the seven wonders of the world, or famous landmarks such as the Empire State Building, the Eiffel Tower, or the Sistine Chapel. The pictures came in tiny envelopes, which I opened with anticipation to fill up the album. But the business of selling them required the publishers to try everyone's patience. Some of the pictures were not released till the last weeks of the competition. Our store became the crossroads for the trading of the repeat pictures. Once the album was filled up, the participants entered the drawing held at the end of that trading season. We attended a concert by well-known Chileans singers, and that's when the announcements were made. Top prizes included a trip to Disneyland and a French Citröen. Smaller prizes would have to make do when the bigger ones proved more elusive. A neighborhood woman, in her late fifties or so and not exactly an athlete, had her picture featured in the latest issue of *Ritmo*, as she proudly held her prize: a soccer ball. We had a good laugh with that one, as we imagined the tiny woman going home to put her ball on top of a trophy case and exhibit it to all her friends and relatives as her prize in the contest, not letting anyone play with it.

The woman who won the trip to Disneyland was featured in another issue of *Ritmo* after she traveled to Anaheim, California. She went into a store where she found a Chilean woman working her shift. The Chilean woman, an immigrant herself, is said to have broken down in tears to have found a fellow Chilean so far from home, and the two women were pictured in the magazine embracing. An old lady read the article and started to cry in front of my mother, who soothed her, as she did so many others, with a cup of tea. Other *comadres* came around to read about the woman who'd gone to Disneyland. My mother got sick of the weeping women and put away the issue. "*Ya basta con el lloriqueo, por favor,*" she said.

What type of education was this? Few children in my neighborhood had access to the information I was privy to, for better or for worse. It was a pop culture bonanza. Surely, Ariel Dorfman, the Chilean writer/novelist who later wrote an entire book (*How to Read Donald Duck*) denouncing the protocapitalist propaganda found in cartoons such as the Disney ones, especially Donald Duck, would—I'm certain—denounce my education as the brainwashing of a child that enabled his participation in the excesses of the market. Mr. Dorfman's book reveals an aspect of my childhood to the world. At least in the Western democracies, of which Chile was one, popular culture would compete with the local parish, or temples, or the various other faiths struggling for one's attention. Ours was not a monolithic culture. Chile boasted a range of political parties, from conservative and Christian Democratic to Socialist and Communist. Ideologies ranged from extreme right to extreme left, and the country had not yet succumbed to a dictatorship of either political persuasion that would limit points of view to one chosen ideology—as would happen in Chile on the right, as it happened in Cuba on the left. To blame Donald Duck (or actually Disney) for the brainwashing would be to ignore that Ariel Dorfman, a leftist, himself lived in Chile and contributed to the competing ideologies of that period. Somebody in Chile—or at least books by foreign writers allowed to be read in a permissible cultural climate—had clearly contributed to shaping the ideological fervor needed to turn against Donald Duck. In his memoir, *Looking South, Headed North*, Dorfman narrates how children marched outside his home denouncing his anti–Donald Duck book. It's possible, had I known about such a march, that I might have joined them, although today I understand Mr. Dorfman's contribution to the debate and would avoid this march as being against my own Voltairian principle of defending freedom of speech for points of view I don't share. Dorfman also valiantly admits his own ideological excesses at the time that made him write a book denouncing Donald Duck, helping him come to terms, one would think, with the duck.

My mother felt so strongly about learning that she couldn't rely on the magazines at our store alone. She bought me illustrated books on the history of Chile as well as world history, technological innovations, the making of cars and planes, flora and fauna, and geographical landmarks. The first book I read was, clearly, a Marxist's worst nightmare: *Cinco centavos para gastar*, or *How to Spend Five Cents*. A child gets coins from his family, and he goes around comparing prices, to see how best to spend them. Nobody warned me about credit cards at that time, which would have been a real service considering my future dependence on them, but no one owned a credit card in my family until we moved to the United States, where we would pick up such a ghastly habit. In comparison, a child learning how to best allocate his five cents now appears quaint by comparison, even economically sound.

Then came the fairy tales—Little Red Riding Hood, Snow White, Sleeping Beauty—with the obligatory Disney tie-ins. Hours were spent learning the basic story, then singing with the songs that played on our record player. The soundtracks and the illustrated books—all contributed to that whole new world of unrelenting sweetness and wonder that Mr. Disney advocated, as long as one wasn't a unionized worker in Anaheim. The illustrated biblical tales came next, in the form of an album in which I would collect pictures of all the Bible's heroes and heroines, including the semi-clad Samson and Delilah. The Bible held an alluring sway for a child like me, not simply for its religion, but for its sensual delights. Pictures of biblical heroes in loincloths did not help abet modesty and innocent thoughts. And albums on national and international soccer teams did not simply make me aware of the national pastime. Soccer was something in which I wasn't normally included, since boys wouldn't play with me, and I in turn never learned how to play. But the pictures of soccer players in shorts kindled a mild sensation I couldn't define at the time, attraction for the forbidden male.

Next came acceptance into the Disney Club. I never knew if Mr. Disney owned the local branch of his office, or some enterprising local businessman opened this up as a chain store of sorts. We collected "points" for the Disney magazines we bought. We sent in our points, and the club honored us with military designation, a rather creepy practice in a country in which the military would eventually depose the constitutionally elected president. Since we owned a magazine store, we had obvious access to this privilege. My mother sent in the coupons to prove our devotion to the Disney cult, and we would get in the mail a pin labeling the lucky child a "sergeant" or a "captain." I eventually earned enough points to be declared a Disney "general," and then I showed up at the Disney office downtown for a special tea service with all the other little "officers" from throughout the city. I wore my general stripes, and I was one of the few, one of the brave. This was clearly the type of education Dorfman railed against. I was a proud Chilean general, fighting for the international nation-state of Disneyland.

My mother paid for private English lessons. We couldn't afford a private American or British Academy, so we had to make do with an eccentric, bizarre old lady tutor who once showed up at our school calling herself an expert. Several parents took her up on her offer, and on Saturday afternoons, the school would lend her space for private lessons. This old woman, dressed up in a delicate gray suit with the reddest face I'd ever seen, a product of overdone makeup and powder gone wrong, or perhaps just plain alcoholism, stood in front of the class, making us repeat words. Behind that look of austerity and sternness, I came to sense desperation. She wore the same suit every week, and she hardly ever smiled, as if life had been rough on her. Why wasn't she in a regular teaching job? Had they eliminated English teachers from the schools? Or just her? I felt her pain, but I didn't like her. My grandmother and other elderly women were warm and friendly, loving, and eager to touch and hug. This lady kept us away with generous dabs of cologne that assaulted our senses and made us keep our distance just to avoid fainting. This sad little woman had no lesson plans other than lists of words meant to be repeated over and over again. I had no idea whether her pronunciation was English or American, or anything Americans or English would recognize as their own. I fear today that she was a charlatan soaking money out of parents who wanted their children to gain the distinction of speaking English. Repetition of words is all we did for eight weeks until my mother put a stop to the whole thing. She didn't have to go to class to see the debacle for herself. I came home with the list of words that we repeated in class, badly pronounced at that, and that was it.

"I could have done that," my mother said, and stopped paying for the lessons.

Learning English was eventually accomplished the hard way, in the sink-or-swim policy of language immersion a few years later in the United States.

Most important for my education, however, and above all the decisions that she might have made on my behalf, was my mother's enthusiastic, restless need to simply get away from the house and the neighborhood whenever she could. She left my grandparents in charge of the store, and we would go off into downtown Santiago to explore a new facet of the city, eager to learn what was new, or whatever would stir our imagination. My mother needed to see it for herself—the latest hit film, the latest art exhibit, an international exposition, a troupe of Russian ballet dancers on a goodwill tour. A visit to relatives would also do. My aunt Gladys (another cousin) ran races, and we would go see her train. Sometimes, we joined her for laps around the National Stadium. She and her equally athletic husband, Hernán, were artisans who made copper figures they sold to tourists, and they would take them to expositions that showcased the work of local artisans. I would sit watching customers ogle at their products, and the money—always modest, but an income nonetheless—begin to pile up. Artisans held parties, too, along with poetry readings, theater skits, and dance, with their children making circles around the adults. These children, including the boys, miraculously, appeared too busy enjoying themselves to dedicate their time to beat up on me. I met cousins who actually talked about arts or were learning themselves to make pottery vases and copper figures, and who showed me how figures got made. Thanks to these excursions, I learned that children did more with their time than think up ways to hurt the local sissy.

My mother's constant and insistent practice of taking me out of the neighborhood whenever possible was one of the most enduring memories of those earlier years. Mother was the prototype of the exuberant nanny, the Maria von Trapp of the Andes instead of the Alps. This exuberant young woman made us children run through the streets of Santiago singing Chilean songs—all that was missing was the Rodgers and Hammerstein soundtrack. The kids often complained that their parents didn't take them anywhere, mostly citing lack of money. My mother showed that it didn't take great amounts of money to attend an exhibit or hike up the hill of Santa Lucía. A short bus ride away, in downtown Santiago, a big city could be explored, taking one away from TV sets and, more importantly, from the dreary sameness that our impoverished neighborhoods often created. My mother excelled at fulfilling a child's curiosity. From the national museum to the former Spanish fort of Santa Lucía, she provided the field trips necessary to make me yearn to know more. She also knew how to back up a field trip with an illustrated children's book—the Spanish Conquest illustrated. Stories of Indian warriors, Lautaro and Caupolicán, the Spanish conquistador Pedro de Valdivia, whose portraits hang in the national gallery, and the hero of Chilean independence, Bernardo O'Higgins.

An international exposition would open downtown, and Mother would find a way to be there. Exhibits of world cultures, pictures of people living in China, in Russia, in Europe or Africa with demonstrations of dress, music, and food made for fascinating viewing. My mother would scour the papers for announcements of these events, and the moment she found one, we got dressed up. The idea was to look one's best. Mother wore a distinct dress sewn by my grandmother with a movie star in mind, an elegant riff on an Audrey Hepburn outfit in *Breakfast at Tiffany's*, perhaps with a bit of cleavage and leg showing. I would have on a white shirt, with a jacket, sometimes a bowtie. When we visited downtown, we were expected to show class, no matter how poor we might be. Lower-middle-class people especially seemed eager to show good taste and manners.

Then my theatrical ambitions got an inauspicious start when my mother told me we were going to see a Disney film. It turned out she had lied. She couldn't find a babysitter, and she had tickets to go see a play instead. When the curtain went up in a darkened theater, I didn't see any animation, no talking or singing animals, no flying elephants with long ears. Instead, a live human being was talking, a young woman in a party dress mouthing off some adult dialogue about relationships. It couldn't be! I began to protest, to cry, loudly kicking the seats in front. We were sitting on the last seats up against the wall. In order to get this crying child out of the theater, my mother had to make the entire row of patrons stand up, as I continued to wrestle in her arms, rebelling against the idea of live theater. Fortunately, my mother found a better way to get me to see a play—one with puppets, which drew my attention and made me feel the theater was something I could enjoy, and even participate in.

She bought me an entire set of puppets of the Red Riding Hood saga, which included the title heroine, the wolf, the grandma, and the woodsman. She bought the plastic heads, to be exact, and my grandmother sewed cloth onto them to give them a body. My hand would slip into the cloth, and I manipulated the heads with my fingers. After a while, I started playing all the characters myself. "Fine. If you're going to play all the characters," my mother said, "then let's put on a puppet show."

"A puppet show. Sure, let's do it," I said.

In our store, she passed the word around to all the mothers in the neighborhood. Puppet show on Saturday at three p.m. My grandfather nailed together a frame for my puppet theater, and I set it up in our magazine store.

That Saturday, we filled up the store with children who bought up all the candy, an early lesson in commercial tie-ins, and then out came Little Red Riding Hood inside the frame box where I hid below manipulating the puppets. With the help of a little cousin, who was my "backstage" assistant, I played all the characters' voices while he held the opposing character— Red Riding Hood vs. the Wolf, the Wolf vs. Grandma, the Hunter vs. the Wolf.

We were the only spectacle anywhere in that vicinity. Puppet shows often came with traveling fairs. Otherwise, locals just didn't do such a thing. The puppet show became an addition to Saturday afternoons, except that my mother couldn't afford to buy more figures. There were only so many kids wanting to watch "Riding Hood" over and over again. The puppet show, repeated too many times, predictably had a limited run, and my mother began to prepare for her radical departure for the United States. At this age, however, I felt the stir of theatrical frenzy—I wanted to put on more shows. One afternoon, a throng of relatives and neighbors' kids gathered to celebrate a cousin's birthday party. I decided then I would re-enact Zeffirelli's film version of *Romeo and Juliet*, which had stirred enthusiasm for the stage and for the sensuality of the love story, but, of course, I didn't have the script, and I had no idea where one could locate such a thing. Stay put, I told the other kids, I'll write a new script based on what I could remember from the movie, so I went off into a bedroom with paper and pen and isolated myself, thinking that in fifteen minutes I could pen the dialogue needed to at least re-enact a scene. But the words wouldn't come. The simplest scenario, even when borrowed from somebody else, required language, which failed me. The parents came to pick up their children, and still I hadn't written a word. The cousins came to stare at the sight of an eight-year-old writer suffering from a major case of the Block. They left looking disappointed since I'd stirred up their enthusiasm for spectacle and then couldn't deliver.

But I did manage to stage a beauty pageant. My mother had recently left for the United States, and I doubt she would have approved of such a thing (there was also the stigma of a boy getting too enthusiastic about such a feminine enterprise). I was left to the care of my grandmother, who died within a month of my mother's departure. My grandfather became immediately preoccupied with marrying the younger woman, Teresa, and the other relatives taking care of me were obliging and busy enough to let me go ahead with my strange scheme to honor local beauty. I chose to crown a proud Miss La Palmilla, a junior one. But I didn't have time to actually to draw up elaborate rules and judge contestants. I chose the next-door neighbor, Charo, to be Miss La Palmilla, by proclamation, and then two more girlfriends from the neighborhood who didn't mind being declared the runners-up, or the "princesses," as we called them. I set up a podium in the backyard, and I invited a set of curious kids from the neighborhood, bribing them in with soda and cake. My grandfather readily handed over the money for the treats, and I even went shopping by myself and set up the snacks on a table in the backyard. The girls used their white communion dresses to play the part, and my great-grandmother Natalia made the sashes for the three winners. It was a good distraction for an eighty-year-old woman who'd come to Santiago to see one of her daughters convalesce and die. It was a case of a child keeping adults distracted and occupied. I played the host in our backyard beneath the grape vines, which were beginning to flourish in the late spring. I invited the contestants to stand in front of the crowd and revealed, in ascending order, the first runner-up, the second runner-up, and then . . . there she is . . . the winner, Miss La Palmilla herself.

Charo took her victory seriously. She shed tears as she waved at the kids applauding her with a somewhat lame, bored look. Charo had been a neighbor ever since I could remember. Her slanted eyes made people rudely call her "la china." She was pretty and, yes, exotic looking. She was my playmate for years, and people predicted we would grow up to marry. In fact, when I went to visit in 1975 in the full blossom of the teenage years, she taught me the delicate craft of French kissing. She declared her love, but I simply took her technique and, eventually, rather shyly, applied it to a few young men later in life. My eagerness to crown her queen, however, was interpreted as love and conviction.

That afternoon, knowing the party would end quickly after the crowning, I determined we would then parade the queen and her two princesses around the neighborhood. We should walk, I told my gathering of curious kids who had never been involved in a beauty pageant before, and then the queen and the princesses can wave at everybody. One of the princesses had a better idea.

"My dad owns a pick-up truck," Princess 1 said. "We can ride in the back and wave at the people from above, like a carriage." She went to fetch her dad, who arrived looking perplexed, even dizzy. He'd been drinking at a local bar. He was perfectly game, even enthusiastic about our idea—but he was also dangerously drunk. We didn't care; we wanted spectacle. The kids piled up in the back of the truck. I set up the queen and her princesses on their own chairs. Where was my liability insurance for such a thing? In Chile, nobody in our neighborhood talked about such a thing as insurance. Our lives were a game that destiny played, and there was no point worrying about it. The drunken father drove us around the neighborhood slowly and at an even pace in order to allow curious passersby to stare at the spectacle.

A bunch of boys ran behind us. "What's going on?"

"It's the queen," I told them. "Behold the queen!"

"What an idiot! What a faggot!" was their typical response, but the rest of the neighbors seemed eager to play along.

"Wave at the queen," a mother told her little children, and then a whole bunch of other children came by to wave along. "Look, she's so pretty in that dress! Look how pretty!"

"How can I become queen?" one of the girls shouted at the truck.

"It's a privilege," I told her. "Many will try, but only one will make it."

"But I want to be queen!"

"Try next year!" I told her. One of the princesses stuck her tongue out at her.

The truck went around the neighborhood once, which must have taken half an hour or so. We had managed to attract the attention of all the children, who came running to stare at the strange spectacle. Some of the boys waved obscene gestures, but most of them appeared genuinely in awe.

When we got back to our house, the mother of Princess 1 was waiting, looking upset.

"You're drunk!" she shouted at her husband. "You're driving these kids around the neighborhood and putting them all at risk."

"Mommy, he was driving slowly!" The little girl came to defend her father. "Nothing happened!"

"We just wanted to exhibit the queen," I told her.

"Oh, what queen?" She took one glance at the sensitive Charo, who still had tears in her eyes and who seemed to think this woman was ruining her day. "Who chose her queen?"

"I choose the queen!" I shouted back.

"Who says?"

"I say! It's my pageant!"

"That's right," said the driver. "He's the master of ceremonies, more respect for the boy. But hey," he turned to me, "next time, you make my daughter the queen, you hear?"

"Of course," I said, making promises I'd never keep.

"All right, we're all going home!" announced the mother. "Get these kids off the truck. No more beauty pageants for any of you."

Thus began my career in theatrical spectacles . . . of some kind or other, and the reviews that go with them.

At school, the usual bullying, pushing, and pulling continued unabated for the remaining time of my residence. At first, my mother's personal tutoring appeared to complement whatever I learned at school, but in reality, it was school that ended complementing, if barely, everything my mother taught me at home. Whatever the teacher tried at school, my mother did better, including reading, writing, and arithmetic. Her tutoring ensured I got perfect scores. But my local school would remain an unhappy place for most of the children. Poverty—and the poverty of imagination among most parents and teachers—seemed to ensure failure. I don't remember these children talking about the future except to dread it. I sensed the sadness and the frustration in my peers' lives, and I felt distinctly set apart. My mother made it clear I was destined for greater things, and my ego was swollen enough in this one aspect of my life to make me feel that attitude. I refuse to believe I was haughty and condescending toward the rest of the students, but I simply felt that with better grades, I would get out of such an environment. I at least held on to the hope that being different would make me special, a cut above, even though paradoxically I was a sissy, not quite a man, not quite human. I made the best of my distinction nonetheless. I knew I had it better than most of these kids. My mother's imagination—her unique enthusiasm and curiosity for everything—allowed her to stir up mine. Imagination was the one resource we had plenty of. But it was difficult to share it with children in my school, a place most went to fail.

Another important difference, which worked in my favor for once, was that my mother was single and felt no qualms about leaving everything behind and going to the United States. This aspiration began early enough for me to sense hope during all those years of attending the same school. I had reasons to believe I would one day leave my abusive peers behind and start a new life far away.

The first glimpse of this life was the announcement that my aunt Nelly had landed in Valparaíso on a ship in the middle of the winter in 1968. She was making her way back to Santiago, and we would catch a glimpse of this traveler at her sister's—Aunt Gladys's—house. It meant taking a bus downtown and dressing up, which was part of the event. She had returned, this much-vaunted, talked-about cousin who had left to go work in the United States. She already inhabited a special place in my imagination. I imagined her as one did a foreign visitor, an adventurer, or a worldly traveler, someone with stories to tell and maybe gifts. She had flown away to the United States once, and now she had returned in an ocean liner. I remembered her vaguely as a figure from earlier in my childhood, mostly a plump woman with small eyelids and a big infectious grin. She had been one of us, a commoner. But years had passed, and my grandmother said everything changes about you once you travel abroad. Some grand transformation would bring her back to us in some charmed new form. I expected a leaner, taller woman looking like a dancer from one of the Elvis Presley movies, dancing the go-go while wearing miniskirts, boots up to her knees, and a fat ribbon to keep her long hair away from her forehead.

I was wrong about the look. She still looked like the aunt Nelly I remembered, but the changes were in her attitude, her smile, the way she could answer questions about Washington, D.C. She had walked the streets and seen the monuments, and yet her work was altogether humble. The disparity between what a maid could expect in Chile—mostly abuse, poor wages, and a classist condescension verging on disdain—and this maid from the

United States made the jobs seem like worlds apart. She was the live-in maid for a Bethesda, Maryland, couple, and yet she could somehow afford international travel. Aunt Nelly had just landed on a Chilean commercial ship, not a cruise liner. She and a Chilean friend (a lovely, humorous, warm, older lady, La Chepita, who also worked in the D.C. area as a live-in maid) had managed to get a cabin on a ship that normally didn't carry passengers. It was bringing back auto parts from Detroit and other American exports. La Chepita was blessed with contacts, one of whom happened to get a friend to grease the wheels, and they were allowed to ride with Chilean merchant mariners who serenaded them as the only women on the ship.

My mother explained it this way: "La Chepita has a son who's now a lawyer, and he knows people." That was it. That was supposed to explain it all. But what was odd to me was that a lawyer in Chile was considered a prestigious position, and yet it was no secret that his studies were paid for by the hard-working woman who spent considerable time working as a maid in the United States. And now these two women had undertaken a virtual cruise that allowed them to visit their family in Chile. They crossed the Panama Canal and arrived in Valparaíso, Chile, rested, tanned, and full of life. A country that allowed the domestic help enough leisure time to undertake such an adventure seemed miraculous. Aunt Nelly was still the plump, lively, woman in her thirties, but she showed the stamina and spark of Nell Carter singing "The Joint Is Jumping" in *Ain't Misbehavin'*, a monolith of a hard-drinking, hard-partying woman during the Harlem Renaissance. Nell and Nelly became one person in my imagination.

During this get-together, I noticed Aunt Nelly approach my mother and, handing her an envelope, say, "My boss sent you this letter." Why would the boss do that? Correspond with my mother? I discovered that Aunt Nelly had been planning to bring somebody to the United States to work alongside her. She had been alone for a long time in a neighborhood in which nobody else spoke Spanish. Her boss, a matronly woman with a protective, motherly attitude, had advised her, through a translator, "Stop crying, Nelly, I'll bring you one of your sisters to the U.S. so you won't be so alone." None of her sisters was available. They were married or had some other commitment that prevented them from coming. Instead, they found a cousin, my mother, eager, willing, ready to undertake the adventure. That evening the two women conferred about future plans. I didn't know my mother was preparing to go to the United States. "I didn't want to disappoint you," my mother told me years later. "If things didn't come through, it would have seemed premature to get you all excited beforehand."

For at least two more years, I heard my mother talk about her visits to the U.S. Embassy in Santiago. After the passage of the 1965 Immigration and Nationality Act, Chile got its quota of resident alien visas, and my mother had been among the first to apply. Knowing her, she was probably the first in line. With the sponsorship of Aunt Nelly's boss, my mother was offered a job in the United States. Some time in June 1970, my mother went to another routine meeting with the embassy people, who had been holding her off for nearly two years. To her surprise, she was presented with the paperwork that would later finalize the steps to get her an official green card at a time when such cards were still green. She had become a legal, fully documented immigrant to the United States.

One reason to hesitate was that my grandmother had become gravely ill. She had undergone gall bladder surgery and suffered cardiac arrest during the operation. The doctors revived her, yet she was left in a critical state. She gradually recovered during that winter but spent most of her time in bed. My mother decided that my grandmother was dying of "cancer of the pancreas," but the doctors never confirmed that. They could never point at anything other than gastrointestinal difficulties. My mother's diagnosis was based on symptoms she had read in a book. A Chilean doctor, el Doctor Elizalde, had written a best-selling book about the vegetarian lifestyle that also prescribed a specific diet for every malady one could imagine. Fruits, whole grains, and vegetables would cure just about everything. (That was the general thrust of his argument.) But my grandmother was too far along in a diet that included red meat and animal fats to be resuscitated with a change to vegetarianism. Nor did she make an effort to stop eating meats. My mother's diagnosis ended up being just as good as anybody else's because the doctors had no clear answers either.

Whatever her malady, it was killing her. With an ailing mother and a child who was to be left to the care of a public school system that horrified him, María could have been easily persuaded not to go, but my grandmother herself spoke out against changing her mind.

"My mother didn't want to hear me complaining that I had a great opportunity and didn't take it because of her," María said, decades later. "She didn't have long to live, and she knew it. There was no point in me passing up this sudden chance to work abroad and do something different with my life. She herself had left the countryside to go settle in a new life in Santiago. Unlike my stepfather, she didn't beg me to change my mind, and instead encouraged me to take the plunge, so I did."

During an evening in late September 1970, a few weeks after the historic election of the Socialist president Salvador Allende, a flock of Cáceres family members and friends accompanied my mother to the airport for some history making of her own. Today's Santiago doesn't allow for family members to watch a plane pull away and then take off. Security concerns prevent one from walking a member to the actual gate of departure, and one has to watch behind a glass panel where no one will hear a bon voyage shout. Back then, Mother left the gate on a bus that transported her and other passengers to the plane. She gave us a final wave before boarding, and then she was off. We were like a fan club—a crowd of twenty-five or so— waving and applauding, creating a ruckus that people associated with celebrities. The plane disappeared into the darkness. My mother was gone to the other edge of the world.

My mother would not have left me alone, however, without knowing I was well accompanied. An entire family, of aunts, cousins, even my great-grandmother, would contribute their share of coping with a difficult, moody kid such as myself. The family was already rallying around my ailing grandmother, known to everyone as "La Jerny." A death watch began as soon as my mother left. Visitors invaded the house from every corner of the country. There was no time to be alone. La Jerny held on for an entire month and got a chance to receive one of her daughter's vivid, detailed letters, revealing the long plane ride to Miami, where she changed planes for Washington, D.C., the taxi drive to the house in Bethesda, Maryland, where Aunt Nelly worked, and then her introduction into a house where she had been set up to work for another family. My mother fulfilled the purpose of keeping Aunt Nelly company, but another cycle of preparations would begin. My mother intended to bring me along.

A month after my mother's departure, La Jerny died. Her prolonged ailment had slowly taken the light out of her. She kept her daughter's letter nearby on her lamp table and made me read it out loud every night before she went to bed. Then one morning in October she did not wake up.

A Santiago Education

Shadowing these circumstances, at the school—the prison, as I had begun to call it—a small miracle occurred during my final year. Our teacher, a severe, regal, thin, but pretty woman, Señora Arriagada, had fallen ill and required an operation. She was gone for the rest of the year. A substitute arrived, briefly, who added to the usual horror with his bullying and humiliation of students. On the first day he decided discipline would be his theme. Every question that was answered badly netted a slap on the palm of the hand with a ruler—for just about everyone except me. I would pay for that in the schoolyard, but by then I was used to it. This gentleman, rather pudgy and red faced, lasted only a few days. For some inexplicable and merciful reason, he was reassigned to another classroom. And the next day, into our classroom of nearly thirty students, both male and female, walked a certain Mr. Mendoza. He was a short, dark-looking gentleman with a thin moustache. He entered smiling with a comfortable stride, which already revealed a different disposition. A sincere, warm smile went a long way to pacify a classroom.

He initiated his lesson plan by writing out some words on the entire chalkboard. We thought: Oh no, homework of some kind, words to memorize, and whoever gets it wrong would be severely beaten. Instead, he made us get up and sing the words. What he had written down were simply lyrics to some folkloric song about Chilean heroes. It didn't matter really what the song was. He made us get up, to sing loud and proud. What a concept! From then on, Mr. Mendoza began the day's lesson with two or three songs, sometimes repeating ones we'd already learned just to get them right. He created, of all things, a chorus out of us. But more importantly, he created, for the first time, a contented class. I didn't think my schoolmates would ever walk around looking cheerful or generous. I remember that year—even as my mother left and my grandmother was ill—as a time of contentedness, at least at school. The songs we learned woke us up for the first hour, and then we would happily work with Mr. Mendoza on the inevitable math assignments or the memorization of vocabulary. Whatever he cared to address, he had our attention. He had earned it. We knew the reward would be one more song at the end of the school session. We sang about everything—about waking up in the morning to plough the fields (a Victor Jara song, most likely), or some distant heroic battle, or a religious song about brotherhood. Somehow, this incredible teacher managed to salvage school for us all. For the first time, I believed my peers were beginning to learn, and I would not have to stand out and be punished for it.

Mr. Mendoza prepared us for a presentation in front of the entire school, songs about the heroes we were supposed to remember from the fight for Chilean independence. He chose me to deliver a eulogy. I read the words from some book, about two heroic brothers who martyred their lives in the struggle against Spanish oppression. The words hardly mattered. The fact that we created a spectacle, did it in an organized manner, rehearsed meticulously, and then presented it to the rest of the school, which applauded us, seemed miraculous to me. That he chose me to deliver the words was also flattering, but what was more important was the teamwork that went into making this event.

I left for the United States not long after. Visiting Chile in September 1980, barely nine years later, I spotted Mr. Mendoza in downtown Santiago as he rushed to catch his bus. I thought about catching up with him and letting him know that he had saved my public schooling from the daily session of abuse it had become. I would have liked to explain the importance of finding a teacher like him at a time when my mother—my real teacher—had left, and I was in need of mentoring. But the bus whisked him away, and I never saw him again.

3

Comadres

Mother was drowning in Ensenada, Mexico. Her arms were tired of waving, and there was no lifeguard in sight. The sun was setting, the beach isolated, and a few fishermen sailed somewhere in the distance too far for them to see her. Only a few seconds before, she had turned around to say something to Mario, the companion who swam by her side. He disappeared behind her.

My mother, her best friend Carmen, and her Chilean *comadre* Sara, along with Sara's husband, Mario, and their teenage daughter, had formed their weekend caravan and headed south to Mexico. They formed a small but thriving Chilean-American community that often gathered in the only Chilean restaurant at the time, El Rincón Chileno, on Melrose and Heliotrope near the Los Angeles City College.

The *comadres* and *compadres* enjoyed crossing the border to Mexico, speaking Spanish, shopping for tourist trinkets, and eating *pan dulce*. They were a tight-knit, unified, lively crowd. I avoided them like the plague, as I did with most adults, along with their family units, values, and familial bonding. I was an American teenager, I thought, more grownup than teenager actually since I was going off to college in the fall, and I would no longer be treated like a youngster. I had little use for the immigrant experience and preferred to stay home reading some cruel Nietzsche tirade, excerpts of which had been assigned by my Advanced Placement English teacher Mr. Battaglia once, but I had taken to reading it for pleasure. Morbid pleasure. Some antisocial habits, alienation, even rudeness, must have rubbed off from *Ecce Homo* or was it *Twilight of the Gods*? I did not want to be seen with my mother and her Chilean friends.

That afternoon Mario and my mother ran into the water for a final swim before hitting the road back to Los Angeles. They swam away from the beach, toward a comfortable spot where the water reached up to their chests. Mother had visited the beach before several times, but Mario was unfamiliar with it. He usually swam in his pool back in Los Angeles. Mother said later that Mario didn't know the Pacific Ocean the way she'd always known it like a seagull, from Chile to California, and down to Baja. She felt at home there and quoted a Neruda poem about finding one's way back to the sea.

"I want my ashes to be spread there," she once said. "I will go back to the sea."

"We're getting fancy," I teased. "Quoting Neruda and all."

"It's no laughing matter. All creatures emerged from the sea. That's where I want to be put to rest."

It almost happened that summer.

Mother felt a strange sensation, water tickling at her feet like an eel passing through and then suddenly tugging away at her leg. She couldn't move forward. She couldn't swim out. She turned and saw Mario struggling with the same forces. "*Sabes qué?*" she asked, keeping it casual. "It feels like I'm drowning."

"Well, me too," he answered with a nervous smile. The two of them locked eyes with an intensity that signaled it was time to panic—and to make others know it. Hey, we *are* drowning. They began screaming, waving their arms. "Help!" She did not remember noticing she was splattering water and howling all by herself. She waved her hands toward shore, but nobody could see, and nobody heard her pleas. I've had it, she thought. She started praying, saying her goodbyes to the world, accepting the inevitable and surrendering to fate gracefully and compliantly. Then it occurred to her, of all revelations to have: the image of the brat, the boy she called "Willy."

I have a teenage son back home in Los Angeles, my only son. All he has in the U.S. is me, a mother; the rest of the extended family lives across the continent in Chile. I'm not leaving him like this, el pobre Willy.

The water kept pulling her back in, but she insisted on swimming forward. She was making little progress, and realized her energies would be expended any second. It occurred to her to stop trying to swim. She lowered her leg, figuring she had nothing to lose, and she might as well try to get a firm footing on the sand. To her surprise, she touched ground. She took one small step, and then another, and started walking forward. She began to make headway. The intensity of the tide began to lessen. She had swallowed water and was afraid she would throw up, lose her balance, and sink. The waves were breaking on her head. She was afraid of being rolled over, but she remained standing. She breathed in, and then her body began to emerge from the water, slowly, gradually. She arrived at the nearly isolated beach, fell on the ground, and then, with relief, threw up on firm ground. She looked up and saw the face of a beaming little Mexican girl looking at her in wonderment and awe, and then she remembered Mario. She got up, startling the girl, and stumbled forward, weakly and feebly trying to move, but nonetheless she gathered the energy to suddenly run with greater purpose in search of Mario's wife, Sara.

"Sara! Sara! I was drowning!" she shouted as she reached the spot on the beach where Carmen, Sara, and Mario's daughter stared back at her, horrified. "We were both drowning!" Her friend bolted out of her place in the sand and went screaming in a desperate search for her husband. Fishermen, docking nearby, heard her cries of help and ran forward. They got back on their boats and went searching for him as the sun had nearly set. They found Mario's lifeless body floating nearby. A trucker volunteered to drive them to the morgue in what Mother called the longest ride of her life. A Mexican blanket covered Mario's rigid, pale body, and his wife and daughter stood incredulously by, holding on to the side of the truck as it hit potholes and crushed their bodies together.

Mother didn't find a public phone inside the morgue, and found an assistant too rude to let her use hers because she said she was keeping the line open for an important phone call. Outside the morgue she found a diminutive old lady who barely reached up to her chest. She led her to a Mexican public phone. María's hand shook uncontrollably now, and she didn't know the number to make a collect call to Los Angeles. This old woman stepped forward to help her. In L.A., I heard the ring in the middle of the night and answered the phone. I had gone to bed after a rerun of *Saturday Night Live*.

"We lost Mario," she told me.

"What? What do you mean, Mother?" I remember the call despite the haze of sleep.

"I was drowning with him," she added, "but I thought of you back in L.A. reading your books. I couldn't let go."

I was stunned into silence. I finally blurted out some words about taking care, driving back carefully. I failed to ask for details. I am still amazed that my curiosity didn't kick in till much later.

When she arrived at our apartment in Hollywood the next morning, Mother gave me a long hug. "I just didn't want you to be an orphan. Being a bastard is hard enough," she added, this time laughing nervously. She actually used the Spanish word *hijo natural.*

I was eighteen and about to start my first year of college at UCLA. I was relieved Mother had survived, but astounded to feel a touch of guilt, the audacity of this poor woman who couldn't let go of life because of her only son. I must be such a burden to her, I thought. She has no other life but me. How could I ever match this act of bravery and leave home for college, and return only rarely and begrudgingly, as other normal young people are supposed to do? This time was supposed to be about my rite of passage. Not just a rite, but a right. I was leaving in the fall to live at Sproul Hall, one of UCLA's dorms in Westwood. I wanted distance. I wanted to stop living in a crowded apartment like an immigrant so I could live in a crowded dorm like a happy freshman. I was self-conscious about our way of life, despondent about it. I had camped out in Mother's living room in Los Angeles for three years, and I never brought friends home to witness our tenement-style living. Sharing a room with an American student and eating dorm food sounded like an improvement over my current living arrangements in Hollywood. I wanted to experience progress and live with a sense of hope for the future. My mother's life, stuck in what appeared to be an endless parade of cleaning gigs among Bel Air patrons, left me uninspired. I was grateful for her many sacrifices on my behalf, but still I wanted out. It seemed that with this survival "act," Mother's presence would remain engraved in my imagination and my conscience forever. There was no letting go of her even as I planned to put her life behind me. She *would* think of me as she was drowning, and say so afterward. I was either a terrible son or a typical teenager, or both. She had bought me an expensive watch for my birthday that year, and I had immediately sent it back. "I am not interested in the materialist/consumerist nature of society," I told her. She sold the watch to a friend and gave me a cheaper Timex bought at the local Thrifty's. My hair was long, and I was listening to Bob Dylan and Janis Joplin, pretending to be in the 1960s a decade too late.

Aside from disdaining our poverty, I was repelled by the spectacle of watching poor people such as my mother and her roommate Carmen pursuing property in wild consumerist abandon. Mother's life and that of her immigrant friends was spent comparing notes on their employers, their wages and treatment, and the various goods bought, consumed, and discarded. Poor people glowing in gratefulness for domestic labor struck me as pathetic. Yet, compared to the dismal standards set back in our civil war–ridden countries, or dictator-afflicted ones, life was good. Life was prosperous, even promising. We could afford the stereo, the color TV, or the rugs on the floor, once a sign of luxury for us in our neighborhood in Santiago. I bought myself books and blank paper for my electric typewriter, and I could afford the bus ride to Westwood to watch first-run movies on the weekend. It was all I really needed out of life.

On the stereo, Janis Joplin sang, "Lord, won't you buy me a Mercedes Benz," the wailing of a country woman praying for the Lord to provide the American lifestyle most of us couldn't afford. Yet for us, the purchase of an old battered model of a car was a cause for celebration. Our prayers were answered. Joplin's song was written in jest, as social satire, but these were our lives she was mocking. Mother constantly turned down the volume on Joplin's husky voice. She failed to understand the lyrics, not simply because of her difficulties with English but because irony landed in her ears like a foreign language, and perhaps at that junction in life she could not afford to laugh at herself. I was disappointed at not being able to share rock 'n' roll music with her. She preferred the playful lyrics written by the late Chilean folk singer Violeta Parra. I tried to point out the best I could that one could find wit in a song such as "Mercedes Benz" just as one could appreciate Violeta.

"Janis Joplin's lyrics can be witty, too."

"Her voice is loud," she said quite dismissively, "and it's raspy, and she's going to lose it if she keeps abusing it that way."

"Well, she's dead now and burned the candle at both ends, biographers say."

"She was loud; that's all I know. My ears hurt when I hear your records, and same goes for that other guy, Bob Dilo."

"Dylan."

"He can't sing either."

"But if you didn't know Spanish, wouldn't you find Violeta Parra's strange, nasal voice a bizarre thing to listen to as well?"

"But at least she can write lyrics."

"And so can Bob Dylan—he writes great lyrics. You should try to read them."

"*Ay, por favor.* Who has time to figure out some hippie lyrics? You are developing strange tastes, and I'm not too surprised. You're growing up in this country, well, in this big city, and you're only young once, I guess, so you might as well listen to your records and like what you're going to like. I can't stop you. I know my mother never liked Elvis, and that hurt my feelings once. At least disco is something we can all understand."

"What's there to understand? It's just one lyric sung over and over like 'Fly, Robin, Fly.' How many times can you say that?"

"But at least the 'Fly, Robin' people are not trying to say anything. You have to go to school for years to understand the lyrics in that album, the Bob Dilo."

"It's not right that you can't appreciate Dylan. And it's Dylan, not Dilo."

"Sorry, but that's how it is, and don't play him or that Janis woman too loud, 'cause I get a headache, and don't pout; it doesn't look good in a boy."

"I'm not pouting."

"You are. You're still a little boy, and you don't see it."

I wanted out of that life, and that fall, I did get out shortly after the drowning incident. Now I was cast in the role of the ungrateful son, which I was. I recognized it even then, and yet I played it out for long periods of time in my youth. All these thoughts crowded my feverish mind even as the image of my mother, the brave survivor, lingered on ready to expunge guilt. *I thought of you as I was drowning.* You can't beat that. I was badly upstaged by an immigrant parent.

There were reasons to keep coming back to her. There was no escaping this one existence, and no inclination on my part to simply roam the world and get lost in it, though a future stint in Italy would satisfy the need for greater distance. But my mother would come join me there, too, and complete alienation was not possible. The hippie lifestyle was gone by the late 1970s, though my hair continued to insist it was possible to emulate it.

The near drowning of that summer continued to haunt my imagination and my dreams. My mother clung to life out in the middle of the ocean with sharks and other dangers and insisted on not letting go, and I could not shake that image out of my mind, whether in my dreams or in my waking thoughts. A few weeks later, instead of the initial impressions of dorm life, I was more struck by the humorous letter Mother received from a friend in Venezuela.

"Doña Norma is living in Caracas now," she told me. It was the day before I was due to check into Sproul Hall at UCLA.

Norma was another one of those unsinkable Molly Browns out there in my mother's life, a humorous clown of a woman from our neighborhood in La Palmilla. During the destructive years of the dictatorship, Chileans had left, not only as political exiles but as economic refugees as well. Norma had gone off to Venezuela with her husband to work. She corresponded with my mother, and it seemed amusing to be getting letters not only from Chile but from another South American country.

"Who the hell do you think you are?" she wrote after she heard of my mother's near disaster in Ensenada. "Esther Williams? You have to be the hero of the film—*la niña buena de la película.*"

It made sense to me. I wasn't the only one who connected the dots. We communicated in movie codes. Esther Williams, the former Olympic champion swimmer who had turned into a glamorous movie star, was the right celebrity with which to tease Mother. Her famous duet with Ricardo Montalban, singing (lip synching, I assumed) "Baby, It's Cold Outside," was also etched in my imagination. I mention it because I wasn't the only one to speak in Hollywoodese.

Doña Norma had attended the same movie theater, La Palmilla, across the street from our home in Santiago. The triple features on Sundays became a way of life for people who hadn't yet adopted the television set in droves as they would do later in the 1970s. We lived as Americans had in the 1940s, with a neighborhood bijou, supplemented by news broadcasts and radio drama. The *comadrazgo* that was born in that theater permeated conversations through long days, especially when Norma and other *comadres* showed up at our magazine stand to talk, often sitting down on the step at the entrance of the store and knitting.

"Esther Williams was from my mother's generation," my mother explained as if I wouldn't have known Esther Williams. She was explaining Norma's letter, and I didn't need the explanation. I was in on the joke.

Those Hollywood triple features had shaped us, not just Mother and me but all the residents of La Palmilla. Our theater was a cavernous place with poor maintenance, crumbling seats, and a clientele that smoked until we could see the screen only through a haze. That way of life ended when television established itself, and we were gone to the United States by then. Yet, among us few Palmillanos then living in the United States, we were the ones specifically settled in the belly of the Hollywood beast, albeit without the glamour and with the dour promise that we would be stuck in that servile mode that was our fate as immigrants. I had soured on the dream by my teenage years. I had to rebel against something, anything that might link me to my mother's generation, and clearly Hollywood was the one thing that dominated our imagination. I was headed for UCLA with a glimmer of hope for the future, but also with plenty of attitude. Mother had grown up absorbing lessons of bravery and endurance in Hollywood films, and I wasn't much different, only beginning to question that system altogether. Courage—coupled with a certain lovability and "perkiness"—was something my mother learned from the many heroines who played out their lives on celluloid: the appealing girlish Doris Day and Audrey Hepburn, the unsinkable Debbie Reynolds, the tough (though neurotic) duo of Joan Crawford and Bette Davis, and finally the ultimate martyr/heroine, Julie Andrews, aka Maria von Trapp in *The Sound of Music*.

If it weren't for a woman in Taiwan who established her fame in the Guinness Book of Records for watching the Robert Wise film hundreds of times, my mother would have gladly usurped the title. She went beyond admiration for this film. She lived in its enchantment. I, in turn, was not too far behind—until I discovered in my later teenage years the dark, hidden charms of Dostoyevsky or Friedrich Nietzsche. The *angst* in my *weltanschauung* was clearly being nurtured and established in my precarious state of mind. Up until then, I had still shared in the optimism of the American dream and could still respond to Julie Andrews with certain admiration and glee. I became much more systematic in my study of the Rodgers and Hammerstein–Robert Wise classic. I read the published script for the original musical in school, listened to the Mary Martin soundtrack, and compared it to the eventual classic film, winner of the 1965 Academy Award for Best Picture, finding it much more compelling than the critics' Best Picture favorite, *Darling*. I don't believe anybody would be entirely inspired or awed by John Schlesinger's intelligent, chic study of a bored princess. *Darling* is the type of film critics try to encourage the public to go see, and the public, for all its collective flaws as mass consumers, exhibits wisdom in not buying too much into the attitude. There's something calm, studious, and slow about *Darling*. Yet, it was the type of thing that I was connecting with in college. I watched *Darling* several times, on television or at the revival film house, the Nuart, near UCLA. One of Christie's male friends takes off with a male lover on the bike, and I found that titillating. A glimpse of a gay affair—I was in a rush to grow up and witness more of those. Another Schlesinger film, *Midnight Cowboy*, added further titillation. In *Midnight Cowboy* the hero abandons his Texas small town to become a hustler in New York City and survives under the tutelage of a street bum played by Dustin Hoffman. The film was shocking enough in its time to gather an X-rating even though there was no pornography in it, just frank talk about sex, and it became the first and only X-rated film to win the Best Picture Oscar. My rebellion entailed the contemplation of sexuality, but without the hustling. I retained wholesomeness, but kept the attitude. It was a tough balancing act to keep up through college.

Mario's funeral provoked other feelings. I attended and saw for myself that I was worried about my mother's isolation.

"I've lost my friend, and now you're leaving," she said that day as Carmen drove us to the funeral. She was beginning to plan ahead. "I want to bring José Luis to the United States."

"Why are you even thinking about that?" I asked. It was true that she had lost her friend, but I was only moving across the city. Her brother had made no effort to contact her about coming to the United States, but she believed she needed to plan ahead for that day. A one-bedroom apartment crowded with three people had become a standard way of life for her. She could not withstand the relative silence of only two people living in the limited space. We had been kicked out of our Arlington apartment for being overcrowded, but my mother was planning already to have someone take my place on the couch.

I also wasn't looking forward to this funeral. A small incident the previous day between the *comadres* had left my mother disturbed. Mother arrived with Carmen that afternoon after she had visited the widow, Sara, who had mentioned the funeral arrangements. Mother went into the bedroom to lock herself in, looking aggrieved. I figured that, finally, the shock of the accident had begun to take a toll on her normally upbeat, sweet disposition.

Carmen explained it to me, "Sara made a nasty comment."

María had gone over to Sara's to be supportive as this usually bright, rowdy, life-of-the-party *comadre* continued to cope with her husband's drowning, but she was not in the best of shape. Sara turned to Mother and said: "I don't know what you people were doing out there swimming anyway. It was getting late, and people were leaving. Why did you have to go out there and take a final swim?"

The tone was accusatory. "Your mother grew silent," said Carmen. "And Sara turned away looking angry. It was time to go. It was unfair, to accuse your mother of anything. I felt for her, too."

I didn't understand why Mother took it so personally. "But I'm sure Sara didn't mean to . . ."

"Oh, Sara sounded angry," Carmen confirmed. "Like she really blamed your mother."

At the funerary services at a local church, I got dragged into it. My mother didn't want to line up with the well-wishers at the cemetery and say comforting words to Sara.

"I just can't face her," she said. "You do it."

I was stuck with the duty of offering my condolences. I didn't know her particularly well. She was my mother's good friend. I had spent their friendship mostly avoiding them together because I was playing the alienated teenager role. I was at a loss for words. For once, I felt the weight of being far away from Chile. My mother and I had missed all sorts of family functions, from weddings to baptisms, first communions, confirmations, graduations, and, of course, funerals. Since I had withdrawn from the church altogether (and who had time to worry about my confirmation when I made an event out of the release of Ingmar Bergman's latest film, *Autumn Sonata*? And I'd also celebrated the resulting Oscar nominations that included its star Ingrid Bergman for Best Actress), I had been shielded from my father's own passing and everything else our extended family could offer up and down in Chile. I had forgotten how to mourn, to process loss, and to wish people the best.

The priest's sermon had been to the point, and affecting. I felt Mario's loss and grappled with the concept of eternity. I appreciated a note of hope, even though I wasn't particularly religious. Then, that's when my mother insisted I be the one to approach the widow.

Sara made it easy for me. She reached out to grasp my hand and, with tears in her eyes, bid me good luck. "You must take care of your mother, and hold on to her, and think about how easily we can lose everything in one instance." I shook her hand right back, gave her a light hug, and withdrew. She had managed to comfort me effectively, and I appreciated it. I wasn't much help to her, I feared.

When I repeated Sara's words to my mother, she grew silent again and didn't want to talk about it. She stopped going to Sara's place and shut her out of her life. Five years passed before my mother could bring herself to talk to this woman. By then, Sara had moved on with her life, was dating a new man, and all seemed well between them again—except the friendship had died in the meantime.

"I think I'll definitely bring my brother," she said not long after the funeral. I was at UCLA, and there was a tone of emptiness over the other end of the line. It was my mother running out of ideas for her own life, but other people's lives were something she could still help organize. "Everybody else is buying homes and new cars. I can't think about such things when my brother can't even find work back in Chile."

"Why not get married?" I said. How impertinent of me to even mention this, but my mother didn't seem taken aback.

"Oh, a woman my age," she said. She was in her early forties, still thinking like a woman in the hometown of Mulchén, where a woman that age was already dismissed as a *solterona.* Even a woman turning thirty was already suspect in Chile. "Only really old, old men might want to marry someone like me. What's the point? I'm not a gold digger. And why change the subject? I want to help my brother."

"Charity begins at home."

"When are you getting married?" she asked. It was revenge time. I was too young to get married, but I wasn't dating either. I didn't seem to have a discernible private life of any kind. I had trouble taking showers at the dorms. I was avoiding dealing with my body altogether, and only a fast metabolism kept me looking thin and boyish. Otherwise, I wasn't exercising or eating anything particularly healthy. I had the excuse of being in college. I didn't have to deal with a private life. That trauma would begin years later.

Avoidance was the lifestyle we had settled into. I couldn't argue for a choice other than my mother's need to care for others. The day care still loomed somewhere in the future, when she would save for a down payment on a home where she would set up a business. But meanwhile her brother rebuffed the plans she had made for him. He was in no rush to come to the United States. It was true he was unemployed, or underemployed, but he insisted he could get by doing something else. He went to Argentina to try his luck as a street vendor, and that was the only adventure he was in the mood for. His sister constantly miscalculated if she thought she could make choices for him. But one of those days, Mother called one of her *comadres* back in Chile. It was Aunt Chata, one of her childhood friends. I had grown up playing with her daughters, Mariela and Janet. They had kept in touch, and Aunt Chata was one of the few talented writers back home. She wrote long, descriptive letters about life with her family, little masterpieces of detail. When she had lost a child to a miscarriage, I had visualized the fetus of the child on her bed, as she described it, born dead. When the economy had forced the family to live on the tightest budget one could imagine, she described her daughter's struggle of wanting to attend a party at her school, but they couldn't put together the coins needed to pay for the bus fare. "She stayed at home," Aunt Chata wrote about her daughter. "I think she learned something about the type of world we're living in." When we drove from Arlington, Virginia, to Los Angeles, her letter put our journey in perspective: "You are charting the westward movement in the country's history." I looked forward to reading Aunt Chata's exquisite personal letters.

Mother called me up, overjoyed that day. "Your aunt Chata is coming to visit us," she said. It was a done deal. My mother had already made the arrangements. She had bought the plane fare on Chata's behalf. "She'll come with a tourist visa, but she'll work here with me, and eventually, pay me back."

Carmen was skeptical. "What if she can't earn enough to pay you back?"

"Such awful thoughts!" my mother cried over the phone while talking to me, but answering Carmen's interjections. "Carmen is always the skeptic around here. What are we going to do about her? I can't live with that type of negativity."

Aunt Chata didn't arrive alone. She brought her daughter, Mariela, and

86

I discovered later that my mother also lent her the money for that ticket. If she could afford it, I didn't see the harm in it. We welcomed this strange, impromptu reunion of the *comadres* that was the product of one long-distance call, in which Aunt Chata just said, "I'm going." It was the type of decisiveness my mother wanted to hear, and even help finance. Carmen looked on with a wait-and-see attitude. She wasn't buying it.

Aunt Chata and her daughter easily obtained the tourist visa, and within a month she was taking a bus up to Bel Air with my mother, helping her clean homes for Hollywood people. Her daughter mostly stayed behind to lounge around Mother's apartment, feeling a bit abandoned as the days went by, but at first it seemed exciting enough to be in the United States and to be watching American television. There were now four people crowded into the one-bedroom Hollywood flat, but they were having the time of their lives. I got my daily reports over the phone. The women were caught in the midst of an intense *comadrazgo* galore. Nobody seemed worried about papers at the time. It was already a given that some people came without them. It was a small miracle to have the learned, wonderful, vibrant aunt Chata in our midst, an example of that type of cultured middle-class woman from Chile who grew up fairly well-off yet was living a life in which, according to her, nothing much was happening. She was married and had three wonderful daughters, but she wanted a drastic change in her life. My mother delivered with a great flair and enthusiasm. The women would work during the week, but on weekends my mother drove her guests to the Grand Canyon, later to Las Vegas, then to the beaches of Southern California and Yellow Park. The old von Trapp spirit was back—it was María showing her charges the good time to which she felt they were entitled as her friends.

But Carmen's skeptical attitude began to become a reality. "She'll never earn enough to pay it all back."

It was true. My mother had lent her friend close to two thousand dollars, and the salaries of an average maid, shared with a helper, were not covering the debt. But my mother, at first, didn't care.

"I didn't bring them here to worry about such things," she said. "In the long run, they'll pay me. If not . . . we'll figure something out."

A long-distance phone call from her husband in Santiago caught Aunt Chata off guard one day. I had gone over to dinner. I got to see the change on her face myself. "He wants me back," she said after she hung up. "He said he'll earn back the money. He'll pay La Chela back himself." ("La Chela" was still my mother's nickname in Chile.)

There was silence. Back in Chile, men were supposed to be the wage earners, but unemployment or underemployment stirred up their pride. Chata's husband didn't have the money. Everyone knew that. Earning two thousand dollars in Chile under that type of economy was virtually impossible for someone without a major position or inheritance. My mother wanted to forget the conversation. She had planned another one of her outings, this time to San Francisco, and that's all that mattered during those intense four weeks of Aunt Chata's visit.

But Chata had her pride as well. "I said I would pay for it, so I will," she said. "When we go back, I'll wire the money, you'll see; don't anybody fret over it."

"You should stay and make your daughter work, too," said Carmen, ever so practical.

"I don't know what you're insinuating!" shouted Aunt Chata, losing her temper unexpectedly, hitting the table with her fist. "If you people care so much about money, you shouldn't have brought me here."

Mariela had tears in her eyes and turned to my mother. "We'll find a way to pay you back."

But my mother didn't want to make this about money. "Just stay, and we'll figure it out, even if you just pay a little bit. I'm really not in a rush."

"My husband wants me back!" cried Aunt Chata. "I need to get back to my family. I will pay every cent back!"

"You shouldn't go, Aunt Chata," I said. This is where I, the supposedly retro hippie, got involved. "I'll marry your daughter, and then I'll help her fix her papers."

The women looked at me with great anxiety. One didn't just get married back in Chile. One didn't do it for papers certainly. Mariela blushed. She thought of me as her friend. Marriage carried the connotation of sex. Aunt Chata looked at me as if I had said something terribly fresh.

"Nobody's marrying anybody," she said. "We're leaving. I couldn't live like this. All you people worry about in this country is money! That's all you care about."

My mother looked defiant. This is where Sara had gone wrong, too. My mother was generous and all giving, but let the *comadre* say one wrong-headed, unfair comment, and the stubbornness emerged out of her as if she'd been a debt collector. "Fine!" she said, and then turned to me. "Draw up some papers."

Papers? I looked at my mother, wondering what on earth she meant. We had my old manual typewriter back in my mother's apartment. I had taken the new electric one to UCLA, so there I sat that evening, writing some unofficial promissory note with a clunky old typewriter in which Aunt Chata agreed to make a monthly payment of fifty dollars or so for years to come, without interest. Aunt Chata had too much pride to call this crazy thing off. My mother was too incensed to stop me. I wasn't a bank. I wrote what I could in Spanish and tried to make it sound official. I left room at the bottom for signatures, and the two obstinate women, angry at one another, signed. We needed a notary public, but we didn't bother. We committed ourselves to a piece of paper that had no legal standing. It was sealed in the fury of stubborn pride.

The friendship was shattered. Aunt Chata fell sick with a psychosomatic symptom that kept her awake at night for her remaining days in Hollywood. She had kept her return ticket, and her tourist visa had not lapsed. She had kept her legality, and her pride, and she could return to her friends back home to talk about the wonderful times her friend, María, had shown her in the United States.

The truly sad thing is my mother never cared about the money. She had invested in the pure fun of sharing her life in the United States with one of her best friends. Who else would have put up two thousand dollars for that? My mother exhibited great happiness when Aunt Chata and Mariela were around. She was the hostess, and the caretaker, and the great generous fairy godmother granting her kids their wishes. She invested in that feeling, and she wanted it to last. It wouldn't have mattered how long it took for them to pay the money back. She herself had taken a couple of years to pay back Aunt Nelly for the loan that bought her ticket to the United States back in 1970. But Aunt Chata couldn't see it in that light. She felt shame in having to borrow, especially since paying back meant working in the United States as a servant. Her escape from Santiago had been a whim, the type of temporary lunacy my mother was more than glad to pay for. Aunt Chata, too, had been happy during her visit. My mother had extended the invitation for her to stay as long as she needed to. But Aunt Chata had listened to reason, or, more ominously, she had listened to her husband, who had not been happy with her sudden desertion, and what did she get in return? Her pride back, at most. Because, as she was about to leave, she confessed that all along her pride had taken a hit, even while she was having fun. She didn't believe my mother didn't want her money back right away like a normal person living in the capitalist world should. Aunt Chata's spirit of adventure was exhausted, and that practical side of her nature had been gnawing at her from the start. This was crazy, she said, and she should have never done this. She also made it very clear that she never intended to become a mere maid in the United States.

"I have my family back home," she told my mother. "I don't want to live like you."

The words hurt. Again, the accusatory words of the other *comadre*, the widow Sara, came back to haunt María. It was her fault all over again, or so said this childhood *comadre*. She would have trouble forgiving Aunt Chata for it. "My husband will pay back every cent," she insisted. "I don't want to stay here a moment longer."

Carmen drove Chata and Mariela to the airport and then walked them to the gate. But suddenly, Chata fell ill and ran to the bathroom to throw up. When she came back, she could barely walk. The airline assistant called for a wheelchair. Chata was having some sort of nervous breakdown, accompanied by a seizure or a fit, or some big dramatic mix of all these things.

"Well, postpone the trip," said Carmen. "And stay until you feel better."

"Are you kidding?" cried Chata. "I'm not going to live like this!"

That's what Carmen reported anyway: one more stab at the wound, suggesting no normal Chilean woman would live like these women did.

"That was meant for me," Mother said later.

Mariela wheeled Chata into the plane, and off they went, with the poor aggrieved aunt convulsing and crying.

"*No lo dije yo?*" Carmen was confident that she had said so. She usually was right about these things.

We didn't hear back from Aunt Chata for a long time thereafter, with one exception. My mother got wired a couple of hundred dollars from Chata's husband, and then, just as easily, the payments stopped.

"But the money wasn't the point," insisted María for years to come.

"So what was the point?" I asked.

"Sometimes, you just have to leave," she said. "It was the right impulse, but Chata didn't trust herself enough. Perhaps my niece will turn out better."

"Your niece?" I asked, my voice beginning to panic.

The cycle was starting all over again. My mother had already made the arrangements to bring her niece in the same manner, *a la mala*, with a tourist visa that would in this case lapse. Mother's savings had dwindled down to the hundreds, but it didn't matter. She trusted the impulse.

"Here we go again!" I cried in exasperation.

"*No me meto,*" said Carmen. "Keep me out of it."

But the impulse had to wait. This time her niece's parents delayed the trip, and it would be four more years before my mother would get the pleasure of playing gracious hostess once again to a fellow Chilean. Late in the summer of 1984, Catalina came to live in the United States, and this time my mother would ensure that she would stay. The girl was barely fourteen, and unlike Chata, she had no one to call her back. Somebody had to occupy that well-worn couch, and Catalina replaced me on it. I was still finishing up my undergraduate studies at UCLA, renting an apartment closer to campus, and my mother had been restless for a long time to move on to this next focus point in her life. Meanwhile, she had gotten a better job than the freelancing gigs that came her way in Bel Air. A Chilean friend—Olga, an overweight, raucous old lady with a scratchy voice—got cancer and returned to Chile to die. Mother inherited from her a reasonably appealing job, taking care of the home of the renowned designer James Galanos. She was bringing in a steady income, and Mr. Galanos was the type of caring employer who set up benefits.

"I'm a lucky woman," María said. Working for Mr. Galanos gave her status. Mr. Galanos's red dress for Nancy Reagan was photographed for the historical record when Nancy wore it to the inauguration. María felt more secure now, eager to play hostess to her niece and goddaughter, Catalina. Carmen remained the naysayer.

"I don't understand the point of asking for more trouble," said Carmen. Mother dismissed her negativity one more time. Did anybody ever listen to Carmen about anything? How many times did this woman have to be right? Mother insisted that it was somebody new and young, and a hope for the future.

"It's another mouth to feed, as I see it," said Carmen.

Catalina—or the idea of Catalina—made sense to my mother, who entertained romantic notions of providing an education for a poor young child. Unfortunately, her approach started off on the wrong side of the law, although it wasn't inconceivable for Latin Americans to bring their family members across the border or by plane as tourists. She'd find a way to get the child her papers and was confident that the move would help humanity in some way. It sounded so good, I was opposed to it just like Carmen. I thought it a distraction from Mother's idea of one day getting a degree in child development and opening up a day care center. I was all for that. But now her plans had to be suspended again on behalf of her fourteen-year-old niece from Chile. A fairly well-off friend of hers, Doña Aida, who lived next door to her family in Chile and was the owner of various businesses, helped with the inevitable bureaucratic arrangements to bring Catalina over. Doña Aida walked into the American Embassy in Santiago with her usual business acumen and loquaciousness and convinced officials that this fourteen-year-old would simply be visiting her aunt.

After our experience with Aunt Chata and her daughter, I wanted to stay away. But no, I would not be allowed to keep my distance one more time. I was inducted immediately into my mother's welcoming ceremonies. As September approached, I was assigned to enroll Catalina into high school. She would be attending my alma mater, Fairfax High, and my mother thought it made sense that I should introduce her to the campus on Melrose Avenue.

"It should warm your heart to do this, for a poor child," she said, tugging at the heart strings shamelessly. "She's your cousin. She's family."

"Send her back," Carmen insisted. "She'll have nice memories of Disneyland, and she'll be grateful for maybe ten minutes. This is Los Angeles, not Utah. The schools are not pretty."

"But Willy attended the same school," my mother told her, using me as the example, "and he turned out a responsible young man."

Carmen looked annoyed. She didn't quite know how to size me up. I wasn't trouble. I wasn't a hoodlum, but I hadn't quite turned out a doctor or a lawyer either. There was still something about me—the hair was shorter, but stylized—that bothered her. The jury was still out on what I represented, if anything. I was on my fifth year at UCLA and counting. Something hadn't fallen quite into place. She didn't like my situation. And now there was Catalina.

"It's not as if I'm going to change María's mind," she said, hoping to make the situation go away, which it wouldn't any time soon.

I complied with my mother's demand that I enroll Catalina into Fairfax High. I walked up the steps of the entrance of the building with my cousin trailing behind me during the late August registration. I approached a gentleman by the entrance who turned out to be a security guard. That was the first sign. When I attended, there were no such things as guards or locked gates. It was an open campus once, like a university. But several shootings around its perimeter had changed all that.

"Could you tell me where the registrar's office is?" I asked the guard.

The man with the sunglasses shook his head with a smirk on his face. "Young man, you need to say 'Excuse me' when you address me. You're starting high school now. You need to learn these basic things."

I realized that my low height and small boyish frame still created the illusion I was a kid, but I didn't realize that people thought I was *starting* high school. It explained why a stubborn woman at a local bar had refused me a drink after I had forgotten my ID. Another woman at a local grocery store would not sell me a lottery ticket, and you had to be eighteen to buy one of those. The guard's statement made me feel an immediate regression back to childhood. I felt as vulnerable as my cousin did. I walked her toward the registrar's office, but I realized I had to watch myself. I had to learn to say "Excuse me." I must admit that, even if I had learned some basic manners in my (by then) many years of college, I often failed to use them with any consistency. But it was my look that revealed something worse than youth: my immaturity. I was nothing more than a grown child, and a quasi virgin, and it showed.

"Excuse me, I need to register my cousin," I told one of the clerks, but I didn't even get a chance to talk to him. A female counselor, a stern Asian American woman, stopped to stare at me with suspicion. She asked me to step into her office. My cousin followed, and we both sat down in front of her desk.

"Why isn't her guardian with her?" she asked.

"She's my cousin, and she lives with my mother," I said. "I'm just helping out."

"We have had teenagers enrolled here by their pimps, and they go to school in the day and get prostituted at night," she explained to me, staring at me with disdain, sizing me up. "How old are *you*, for that matter?"

"Look, I'm at UCLA! I'm not a kid, and I'm not a pimp. My mother just wants her registered for the school year."

"Tell your mother she'll have to come in and sign the papers herself," she added. "I need to see a responsible adult."

I didn't argue. I was too depressed that my school had deteriorated to this, and one look at me, and the woman chose to treat me like a punk. I left feeling despondent of the entire situation. I was an adult, and I needed a drink.

My mother couldn't believe I wasn't able to register my cousin, and she returned a few days later with Catalina to get the task done. I should have realized then that my cousin was registering in a school that had changed remarkably since I had been a student. I should have known there was nothing but trouble ahead.

Every bit of skepticism that the prescient Carmen had expressed from the very beginning became a fulfilled prophecy. Let's just cut to the chase and say that after a few years, a boyfriend, and an abortion, Catalina left home and disappeared into the American landscape. She returned a couple of times, with two sons whom she abandoned at my mother's house, and then, as Mother lay dying in Portland, Oregon, Catalina stayed away. Her mother in Chile hasn't seen her in twenty-five years. Last time a friend of my mother ran into her in Los Angeles, she was in her thirties, allegedly living in a trailer without electricity with a new boyfriend.

What went wrong? There was clearly a clash of cultures in our home, or at least a clash of generations. We thought we knew well the environment back in Chile; Mother and I lived there ourselves. Yet, we had apparently forgotten the dysfunctions of our old neighborhood, La Palmilla. Catalina's father—my uncle—had gotten himself into trouble with the law by allegedly buying stolen goods. He was sent to prison and beaten up by guards who—he claimed—also put electric rods on his genitals to get him to talk. *La parrilla*, as it was called, or the grill, an apt symbol for the Pinochet dictatorship. Political dissidents were tortured under Pinochet's regime, but my uncle claimed that torture was readily dispensed to other prisoners, and he'd been one of them. Catalina grew up under parents who couldn't provide a stable environment, had no formal education themselves, and made their living by trying to pull deals together at a flea market. Understandably, my mother wanted to take the child away from that way of life. A small child would have been manageable, probably. A fourteen-year-old girl in Hollywood from La Palmilla was impressed instead by break dancers on Hollywood Boulevard and, more importantly, by the appealing sight of muscular black men.

Catalina had been brought up in Chile taunted by her own darkness. One look at her and another look at Janet Jackson, and one could have called them sisters. Catalina was darker than an average *mestiza*, and her schoolmates in Chile taunted her as *la negra*. I knew all about those schools. I knew that cruelty prevailed in them, and that once children found the difference in you, you'd be taunted for life. Whether you were *el negro*, the gypsy, or the faggot, it made no difference. I had barely made it out of those schools in one piece, and it didn't take much for ridicule to leave its scars on someone more vulnerable. In the United States, Catalina turned her darkness into an advantage, around black young men.

"Your cousin is pregnant," Mother called to say. I was living in West Hollywood by then, sharing an apartment with two gay roommates. I had, I thought, escaped that world and was living in another across town more befitting to my particular sexual proclivities. There was no transcending that world with a change of zip codes.

When Mother came over for a brief visit, she had thought of the solution.

"I'm paying for the abortion," she said without much emotion. It had been a long road from the girl's school run by nuns to the enchantments of *The Sound of Music* to paying for an abortion. My mother had come to support a woman's right to choose and felt Catalina had no other alternative. I agreed. I didn't think a teenage girl had any business giving birth to a child, something continues to bother me about having to impose it on her. Not that she resisted it. She behaved like a helpless child and went along with the decision. Both my mother and I were products of sexual escapades of the nonmarital kind and owed our births and upbringing to women who decided to take responsibility in having us. But the blank stare in Catalina's demeanor made me wonder what other type of problems she was having.

"*Algo le falla a esa pobre chica,*" said my mother. Her diagnosis made sense. The trauma of her Chilean experience had come back to haunt us all. The signs were there when my mother drove her niece to the abortion clinic and witnessed the young woman's strange indifference. She pretended not to care.

"She must have been dying inside," María later said. "But she wouldn't show it, not to me. I think she hated me all of a sudden for making her go through this. But I couldn't tell. She became a stranger that day, a complete mystery to me."

Catalina's behavior grew more perplexing over the next couple of months. "She now promises me to behave, to do well in school, to avoid the boys in school, especially the one who got her pregnant, and to start a new life," said my mother, who felt she was raising this child on her own. She didn't inform Catalina's parents in Chile about what happened because my mother felt that, at such distance, the most they could do was send a couple of strongly worded letters. She already realized that this child was not easily reached through language. My mother was also protective of her family in Chile and didn't want to worry them. Here was one major difference between ourselves and other Latino immigrants. Although family was important to us, ours lived in the farthest, southernmost country on the continent, and no relatives ever visited us. None could afford the plane fare, and we couldn't afford to visit frequently either. The Aunt Chata visit was a unique phenomenon with its own bizarre details. It cost my mother plenty, but she was in her own way crying out for a visit. It was one of the things she had paid for. Otherwise, distance kept us apart, and it was easier to keep our secrets than it might have been for, say, Mexican immigrants who shuttle back and forth from their native cities and towns across the border. Distance worked against us because the discipline, the family pressure, and even the shame that might have helped Catalina weren't there. We were clearly not enough for her.

"I visited the school to ask her teachers about her grades," my mother added. "I didn't mention the pregnancy or the abortion. Maybe I should have, maybe they could have counseled her, but I felt ashamed. I didn't want more trouble. I didn't want to involve the boy responsible for the pregnancy. I wanted to see what I could do to help improve things. The teachers told me the same thing. She's a quiet girl, doesn't say much in class. She doesn't turn in homework and doesn't seem motivated by school at all." The counselor told my mother she didn't expect her to graduate. She was failing. She'd have to come back in the fall to take extra classes, if she hoped to graduate at all. "When I talked to Catalina, she smiled and said she'd do anything to improve. She sounded sweet and cooperative all of a sudden. She would improve her grades, and then forget all about boys—that's what she's saying now."

A few months later, a young black man drove over to the apartment building and picked Catalina up in a limo. This was not the same man who had left her pregnant.

"I'll bring your niece back by ten, *tía*," he said, using the Spanish word for *aunt*. Rather cheeky of him. María called me up to tell me the latest news, *muy atrevido*. But he did own a limo. She didn't try to convince Catalina to stay inside that night. She knew what she was up against now. Eleven p.m. came around, and no sign of Catalina, no phone call, nothing. My mother kept up Carmen, who told her to just give up on *la pobre loca* and get to bed. María couldn't. She worried and paced around the room, feeling responsible for the latest developments. Past midnight, my mother got a phone call from the young man. Their limo had broken down on the freeway, and he promised to have the girl back by two a.m.

Mother stayed up till three, then four. Five a.m. came and went. Catalina didn't arrive till ten thirty the next morning. She came in laughing. Oh, don't worry, she insisted, they had waited for the man's sister to arrive by the freeway where the limo had broken down, and this sister didn't arrive till five, and so they spent the rest of the night at the sister's place. She wanted to sleep now. She wouldn't be going to school that day. Yes, it was her decision to make. Mother, who had barely slept that night, left Catalina sleeping, then made a quick getaway to the L.A. office of Lan-Chile Airlines.

"I just bought her a one-way ticket back to Santiago," she proudly called me the next day, borrowing the phone from the Lan-Chile office to keep me informed. "I put my money down, in cash. It was all I had in savings—first the abortion, then the plane fare. Still, it's money well spent. No more Catalina. She has a mother, and I'm only her aunt, I admit it now. I can't do much more for her. I'm going home right now to present her with my gift."

The next day, Catalina was gone. She had slipped out in the middle of the night, leaving a note behind. "Please don't call the police. I'll call to say that I'm all right. I'm going out of state with another girl with problems at home."

Mother called me again from Lan-Chile the next day to say she got the plane fare refunded minus a penalty. With the balance, she drove to Las

Vegas that weekend to try her luck. She lost $180. She called to report that, too. We wouldn't see Catalina until Thanksgiving that year, briefly picking up a paper plate of turkey and stuffing and other goods. We would see her like this, on and off for the next couple of years. She would contact us when she chose it. We didn't know where she was living or what her phone number was. She eventually disappeared altogether, but not before leaving two young boys with my mother one day.

My mother discovered the value of her own education, at least. If she couldn't raise a daughter, she would instead become a professional nanny, one with a degree. She enrolled at Los Angeles Community College, where she followed a curriculum of preparatory courses, including English. She then meticulously followed the process that led to certification in child care. The care of other people's children—infants, not teenagers preferably—became her life's work. She succeeded in doing that, as long as she didn't have to do the follow-up of helping kids cope with the malaise of teenage angst. Mother knew the sweet nothings that spoke to babies, not the tougher logic of keeping a young adult away from sex, drugs, or any other temptations found easily in an overwhelming and unforgiving city.

In 1992 Los Angeles rioted against a decade of inner-city neglect. We had been living in Reagan's fabled, Hollywoodized America for too long. Even we, the movie lovers, admitted that something was broken, even the Maria von Trapp Syndrome. It had helped, in so many ways, to inspire my mother to survive a riptide in Ensenada. It had permeated her lovable personality and made her a fun mother, and an inspiring one to other people's children, but they were growing up in Los Angeles now, in modern times, and no longer selecting Rodgers and Hammerstein tunes to sing along to. Rap and hip-hop had supplanted even hard rock. The times had moved on, and we were still living, literally, at the movies. *Boyz 'n the Hood* was now the choice of B-boys and B-girls, the language was rough, the life it portrayed violent and deadly. My mother was watching *Driving Miss Daisy* while her niece abandoned the old women's sensibility altogether. She got herself a man and was out there doing it for herself, a modern young woman living independently, but unfortunately in the streets. Something was wrong with this picture. Mother came home one day from Ensenada, shook up but unscathed, and would live another twenty-three years, but clearly a story of courage and survival would never suffice to keep the peace at home. She was up against an entirely new set of values, and they inevitably clashed. Catalina had listened to all of Mother's stories about hard work and survival, and instead of feeling the inspiration and the need to sing along to "Do-Re-Mi," she went packing, out into the streets, from which she has not emerged.

4

The Subject Was Roses—or Was It?

It started in adolescence, as it usually does. In junior high school, to be exact, in Silver Spring, Maryland, our second home in the D.C. area after landing in our own private Plymouth Rock/Ellis Island America. Mother doesn't notice at first. I wasn't about to talk about it. The embarrassment of being seen naked in front of strangers takes on an absurdly bizarre, crippling confoundedness in me. *Nausea, panic, trauma.* But, still, I'm a practical teenager and devise a quick solution: I avoid gym class altogether. I do well in school otherwise. I enjoy those moments when actual learning gets done, but why put up with the sick feeling of being seen au naturel? So why not forego that part of the day, bypass reality altogether, and avoid at all costs a place with public showers?

For the entire seventh-grade year, I spend the gym period either going to the library or walking around outside the school, hiding behind bushes when school officials come around to inspect and playing hooky for an hour until I must go back to classes looking innocent and well behaved. I get A's, but the gym teacher has never met me, so he can't complain about my absence. A grade card is given to each student to collect grades from each teacher. I fake the gym teacher's signature and assign myself an A, and then hand the card back to the homeroom teacher. This act of delinquency is not expected from me, and that works in my favor.

At the end of the school year, however, two days before the actual end of school, my homeroom teacher, a Mrs. Wilkins (her real name escapes me) approaches me and says, "The gym teacher says he can't record a final grade. He doesn't know you. How can he not know you?"

The Subject Was Roses—or Was It?

Only now has that teacher noticed? But Mrs. Wilkins thinks of me as an honest, reliable student, and she won't let herself believe the logical conclusion, that I haven't attended that class the entire year. It's unthinkable to her. I'm not afraid of getting caught as much as I fear having to explain the reasons. One could just die of embarrassment, or I felt I could at that age. I play the usual innocent, one more role I excel in.

"He never remembers my name," I say, and I play the race card. "Spanish names all sound alike to him."

Mrs. Wilkins lands squarely on my side. When she goes to a teacher's meeting, she insists that I couldn't possibly have skipped class, that I am one of her best students, that there is no truancy in her class, and the gym teacher finally relents: "Oh, I guess I confused him with that other Mexican kid who withdrew at the beginning of the year. I've got more than a hundred kids; can't keep track of all their names." He records a grade, and Mrs. Wilkins proudly returns the next day with the news that she's straightened things out for me. I am a straight-A student and, apparently, a smooth-talking delinquent. I never have to explain myself.

If nobody caught my absences in gym class, my mother noticed the trends. I stopped going to pools, vehemently turning down her offers to drive me during the summer. She could have lived with the idea of me staying away from the pool, but she also insisted on vacationing at Rehoboth Beach, and I couldn't stay behind on my own during vacation. She wouldn't let me even though I proposed it. I treated my mother to the spectacle of tears welling up in my eyes as I boarded the back of her friend's car, and she witnessed me sobbing all the way until we reached the seaside resort in Delaware. We unloaded the car, accommodated ourselves in the rented cabin, and then I insisted on staying inside instead of going to the beach. "That's not normal," Mother claimed. "We didn't drive all the way to Delaware to stay inside." I resisted, and my poor mother mollified me by promising to let me wear clothes the entire time I was there. Only then did I, surprisingly, relent and agree to go to the beach with her and her friends.

"*Pero por favor,*" she said, almost every day when we'd go through this ritual of tears, resistance, and capitulation. "I don't understand this. I don't understand you, and maybe I don't want to understand. I can't believe you're my son. We came from the sea." She reiterated her identification with Neruda. "We will return to the sea when we die. That's in our blood."

The Subject Was Roses—or Was It?

"Maybe they gave you the wrong baby at the hospital in Mulchén," I said, the smart-alecky. "I came from a family that stayed inside and doesn't want to return to the sea."

"No," she said. "You're mine all right. You're my burden to bear."

At the beach itself, I managed to strip down to my bathing suit and to stay in the water, my body covered by the water for as long as I could. On the beach, I built sand castles over my body. But this was barely a compromise on my part. Once we moved to Los Angeles, trips to the beach stopped. My resistance had grown stronger. I had grown into a temperamental young man, more insidious and impetuous than ever.

"If you force me to, I'll throw myself down the pier! I will commit suicide."

My mother refused to believe I was serious, and yet the threats made her think twice. They began to frighten her. She loaded up the car and drove away, looking back through the window up to the balcony of her apartment, wondering if I would be all right. Alone with my books, TV, homework, and a copy of *Time*, or occasionally the more sophisticated political journal *New Republic*, I was in charge of my space, as long as none of the actual matter that occupies space, my body, was exhibited to the world. Even at home, I wore long pants and long sleeve shirts. The shame of seeing myself outdistanced the fear of having others view my purported ugliness.

Despite living near world-famous beaches celebrated in songs by our surfer troubadours, the Beach Boys, I ceased all interaction with the beach or with beachgoers, or pool and Jacuzzi rats, until I was in my late thirties. My mother tried her best. She thought of the beach as a wholesome environment, a place to soak in some sun, and even bond. My excuses became more creative.

"I can't go to the beach today. I have to watch *The Subject Was Roses*!"

"The what was roses?" my mother asked, suspicious.

"A movie with Patricia Neal. She was nominated for the Oscar, and that was after she'd had a stroke, so she had to go into rehab, and she regained her ability to talk. It was very courageous of her, so I have to watch it. It's based on a play by Frank Conroy. It'll be on at two p.m. and you never know when they'll repeat it."

"Well, OK, I guess," said my mother, perplexed. "I mean if Patricia was nominated . . ."

The Subject Was Roses—or Was It?

My mother didn't know what to make of any of this. She thought it was great that a child would read up on things, particularly the movies, the news, and literature. It made me informed, something most kids my age were not. I could hold conversations with adults about these things, but I was using my knowledge to get my way and, more importantly, to hide.

The next time I offered another Oscar excuse ("I have to watch *Cool Hand Luke*, because Paul Newman was nominated"), my mother confiscated the TV set and angrily rolled the stand over to her friend Rosa's across the hallway of the apartment building for safekeeping. "You're not watching any more TV until you stop this strange behavior," she said.

"But what about *Cool Hand Luke*?" I insisted.

"*A la mierda con Cool Hand Luke!*" she retorted. "Fuck *Cool Hand Luke!*"

Without TV, however, I still had books, dozens of them. She would have needed boxes to take them away, and what type of mother deprives her son of books? You're a good parent if you take away the TV set, but the books? Still, she had taken a stand. She left me alone without TV as my companion. No *Cool Hand Luke*, but no problem really. I read Leon Uris's *Exodus*, and I told her so afterward, and that novel was made into a movie for which Sal Mineo was nominated for the supporting actor Oscar. Then the news came on one day: Sal Mineo was killed in our neighborhood, knifed down by a stranger. The once prominent actor died penniless, renting a cheap apartment in West Hollywood.

"I have to mourn his loss!" I said one day, one more reason not to go to the beach. "I will write a one-man show about him, and I will play Mineo himself because I kind of look like him in *Rebel without a Cause*, don't you think?"

My mother stood no chance. She brought back the TV. I wouldn't step onto a beach until more than twenty years later. I won that fight, but what exactly did I win?

The fear—the anxiety, the condition, the whatchamacallit disorder—began to assert itself in my imagination through a nightmare. I am twelve years old. I am dreaming that I wake up and I'm naked in bed. I open my eyes, and my body is covered by hair—coarse, thick layers of fur that make my legs feel spidery. Worse yet, I metamorphose from a child into a hairy creature, a beast in some fairy tale who would never convert into a fair prince.

When I woke up, I saw my teenage body growing body hair out of proportion to my age. I was too young to look this hairy. I borrowed my mother's Lady Razor and shaved off the hair on my legs, but it returned overnight like kudzu weeds that take over a southern landscape, stubborn growth that spreads and entangles itself in every nook of one's home. I was being transformed into a monkey, a wolf, or a half-human creature like the Sasquatch. Chilean kids teased me once for being a sissy, now American kids could do the same for being both a sissy and a hairy ape—an accident of testosterone run amok. A symbol of virility had invaded my body, making me a freak of nature. I could almost hide being a sissy, but it was much more difficult to camouflage the sprouting hair without hiding the entire body, which is what I had to do. I made the choice of wearing long sleeves and pants from then on, forever if necessary. But hair grew on my hands, too. I couldn't very well wear gloves all the time—that's one bit of freakishness I didn't indulge in—but I covered the rest of my body in all seasons. I'd become *A Man for All Seasons*—also winner for Best Picture and Best Actor. My life was a mockery of fate, and there was always an Oscar winner playing to come up with a new excuse.

"I can't go to the picnic. They're playing *The Apartment*, 1960 Oscar winner, on Channel 5."

"I can't go hiking. They're playing *Room at the Top*, starring Simone Signoret, 1959 Best Actress Oscar. It's, like, French retrospective week on the public channel."

And there was always the more standard *The Subject Was Roses*. It just sounded good when you were trying to change the subject.

At school, I feared something would betray my alarming deficiency to the world, that somebody would detect the monstrousness of my appearance, spread the rumors, and I would be finished. The shame would destroy me in the full blossoming of my youth. It made sense to hide. I rarely looked into my peers' eyes, hoping most people let me be. Don't notice me; go away. Most people were quite glad to concur. What a strange boy, they concluded, if they noticed me at all. My withdrawal from the world might have been complete if I hadn't been so loquacious and eager to raise my hand and volunteer an opinion about Chaucer, or Shakespeare, or whatever the English teacher had brought up on that day. But raising a hand was dangerous in my precarious mental state. People might notice it, my one exposure to the world, and then where would I be? I didn't know about burkas, but seriously, could one hide one's entire body, including one's face, from the world? How extreme would that have been? My mental state was beginning to deteriorate. We couldn't afford an extra bedroom, but it was perfectly possible that if we had, I would have remained in it.

"You have no friends," my mother said. "That's not normal."

"Well, we're new in Los Angeles," I said. "Give me time."

"Giving you time doesn't seem to help any."

"What would it solve, having friends?"

"Young people go out."

"And then they get into trouble, like drugs, crimes, teenage pregnancy. Is that what you want from me, Mother? In order to prove to you that I'm a normal teenager?"

"No, that's not what I mean, and you know it, and don't come up with some Oscar nominee to watch as an excuse. You need to think about dating, in a wholesome way, of course. There are girls out there dying to be asked out."

"They don't pay attention to you if you don't look like Robert Redford."

"That's not true. They just want you to make an effort."

"If I try, then what?"

"Oh, something beautiful could happen—*algo muy bonito*—like a teenage romance, something sweet, but not too graphic."

"Like *The Blue Lagoon*?"

"No, that was teenage pornography. More like *The Summer of '42*, a young man losing his virginity to a war-time widow."

"Who just happened to look like Jennifer O'Neill, a model! Come on, most widows don't look like that."

"Then what on earth will you do the rest of your life? Hide?"

"Some people do."

Becoming a recluse didn't seem out of the question then, and I said so. My mother was alarmed. She was trying to get me to rethink my teenage years, not plant a seed for a future lifestyle. She spoke about me to friends who recommended church activities, youth groups, and heavy therapy. My mother didn't know which would help.

The Subject Was Roses—or Was It?

I couldn't speak about it even to the therapist she finally sent me to, a graduate psychology student who volunteered his services at UCLA, as part of his training. I mentioned to him not feeling any urgent need to join any groups, and he encouraged me to find something to belong to. I knew that my problems were not entirely about belonging. Yet, I continued to think my problems were about my appearance, and there was nothing to do about that except avoid exposing too much of it to the world.

Later, in my late thirties, I found a book on a shelf at Borders that described my strange psychological disposition and gave it a clinical, absurd-sounding name, *The Broken Mirror: Understanding and Treating Body Dysmorphic Disorder* by Katharine A. Phillips. I discovered that BDD sufferers perceive in themselves bodily flaws unseen by others and build their entire reality around avoiding the discovery or exposure of such flaws, to the point that some people literally seclude themselves from society altogether. As a teenager, I was thinking in those terms, but I thought of it as an extreme eccentricity, not a disorder.

At the time, I settled for the simple explanation that I was unusual, and that I had to live with my flaws and do my best to mitigate its horrors. There were no words to explain the revulsion I felt toward myself. I threw away my swim suit when I was thirteen and eliminated all shorts by fourteen. Mother knew by then to buy me only long sleeve shirts. I wouldn't wear any other sort.

One summer day in 1974, when we were still in Maryland, Mother went to work and decided to make one desperate attempt to get me out of the apartment. In summer, she decided, children should be playing in the park. But most children didn't look like me, I felt. She called a woman neighbor who, with the best intentions, sent her teenage son over to invite me to the pool. I told him I didn't have a swim suit. Not to worry, he said, my mother sent an extra one for you. I looked furiously at him and didn't let him in. I told him I couldn't go. Why not? he had the temerity to ask. I slammed the door in his face. This was my mother's idea. I was furious with her. What was she trying to do to me? How could she use this boy to try to bring me out? He was an unwitting go-between. I still feel the guilt and embarrassment of slamming the door in that kid's face, and I never apologized to him. He must have hated me, but how could I stop to explain my situation to him, to anybody?

The Subject Was Roses—or Was It?

My fears were, in part, justified. Hair did eventually envelop and overpower my entire body. The kudzu weeds sprung from every pore, taking over my legs, my arms, my chest, my back, and threatening to cut me off from normal existence altogether. By sixteen I had become the monstrous creature that I feared when the sprouting had begun a few years earlier. I couldn't imagine going through life this way—hence I never walked into a room until I felt I was properly covered up. It still pains me to know how little understanding there is for what people call "self-consciousness." While I never talked about it with anyone as a kid, as an adult I have tried telling friends about this strange condition, and people still snicker. You did what? You hid your body? Still hide your body? This is followed by some pat advice—if you only let go, try hard enough, it can go away. That first year hiding from the gym class was only the start of a downward spiral of "closetedness." It took over every aspect of my youth. With every move I made, I had to consider how well I could hide my body, and what would be my level of comfort doing so. The pools and the beaches were immediately out, as my mother discovered. But a picnic would have to be weighed carefully. Long sleeve shirts made me feel uncomfortable outdoors in the summer. I turned down invitations with polite excuses, but an afternoon at an air-conditioned movie theater was certainly acceptable. In a mercifully darkened theater, the focus would not be on my ugly body but on the images projected onto a screen. A night event in fall weather, such as a night at the Greek Theater with outdoor concerts justifying more formal clothes that covered everything except one's face and hands, was acceptable. But seasons changed: winter came to my rescue, a cool season of freedom. I finally felt fully (if deceptively) normal. I wore a jacket, or long sleeves, and nobody noticed that or found it out of place. I was the counter-spirit of Persephone, visible to her loved ones only in spring and summer, kidnapped in fall and winter by Hades. I would be her winter replacement, arrayed behind layers of clothing, often fashionable clothes. People were distracted by a designer shirt or a lovely sweater or a bomber jacket and thus were less likely to notice my bodily flaws. I spent my summers thinking strategically about how best to camouflage and hide my body in ways that did not invite too much speculation, but people found me odd, uncomfortable, or nervous. I made others nervous, and I was terrified at the very idea that they might notice.

The Subject Was Roses—or Was It?

There was a brief respite from the condition. Mother moved us to Arlington, Virginia, and for some miraculous reason my fear momentarily abated. The school seemed friendlier, more middle class than working class. It made a difference. The kids didn't seem as judgmental, and the gym teacher structured his class around team spirit—even the sissy boys were welcome. How bizarre and unnatural to find that in an American junior high school. The teachers exerted greater control over their students. I couldn't have gotten away with skipping a class, and the students didn't get away with taunting and teasing during class either. From day one, I slipped into gym clothes and I would strip to take showers like everybody else. This brief sense of normalcy made me feel that one could "get over it." I would avoid kids' stares, but otherwise nobody ever made a comment, at least not to my face. Politeness and civility somehow abounded, for a short while. One day I was sitting in a ninth-grade drama class, and I must have made an unusually obnoxious comment that prompted a fellow thespian, an obnoxious overachieving Diva Actress whom most teachers honored with awards and praise, to bark back at me: "Well, I hear you're a hairy ape in the showers." People had noticed after all, and they had talked about it among themselves. I naively thought I could "overcome" my condition because the school seemed more peaceful and not lorded over by bullies. Yet, that one remark prevented me from showering in public *ever again.* When we moved to Los Angeles, I discovered, to my great relief, that for whatever reasons none of the kids in the gym class ever took showers. We changed quickly and then got back into regular clothes all sweaty and smelly. The teachers at Fairfax High had probably given up on us altogether since it was one of the first schools to install security check points, many years before Columbine. Nobody was about to enforce a shower policy when preventing weapons from entering the campus was a higher priority. This worked in my favor. Nobody paid attention to my habits. And because I was on a college prep track, I got away with not taking physical education altogether during my final year. The result also meant no exercise, but the benefit of youth was that lack of exercise had no effect on my waistline, and I somehow remained thin by eating normally.

On the surface, I was a fairly reasonable kid. My homework was done and turned in on time. I got mostly A's. I was a model student, even a model immigrant who had learned his English and adopted American culture. But deep down inside, I feared I would explode in anxiety over the very odd shell case that enclosed my hideously flawed body. I disdained it along with my looks altogether and had by then become the Creature walking the hallways afraid of the truth. This double life created a fear that went deeper than any closet. Homosexuality had begun to be discussed out loud in the 1970s, and rambunctious pride parades were staged every June a few blocks away from our Hollywood apartment. The general public had begun to at least tentatively accept gay people, so I sensed less fear in that regard than I did of my other deadlier secret, that of being a hirsute American. My poor mother, caught up in that immigrant struggle of ensuring a living, had to maintain a balance between paying too much attention, which annoyed me, and not paying enough of it, which of course isolated me further. My mother was working for Bel Air matrons, cleaning their homes and playing their faithful companion, and I spent most of my time being a decent student in class. In the afternoon, it was homework and prime-time TV. I was not on the surface a kid in trouble, but it wouldn't have taken much to get me to go overboard. I never attempted suicide, but my mother had to hear about it constantly.

"I'll get a high school degree first," I said one day, "and then throw myself out the window."

My mother and I never discussed the real issue. I never spelled it out for her. She knew something was wrong, but she had little inkling of the private anxieties about my body. I didn't speak to anybody and didn't have the language with which to speak it. Gay was mentioned prominently on national television. I could have spoken that language, but hirsuteness was ridiculed, and BDD, the anxiety disorder that had taken over my life, was not yet understood or named. I never told my mother I felt monstrous, and she never suspected I suffered from an officially diagnosed "syndrome." My isolation from other kids meant at least I wasn't hanging out with the wrong crowd. I was my only companion, and I was clearly the wrong company for myself.

Regardless of the social acceptance of homosexuality, the idea of sexuality alone had begun to take a toll on my self-esteem. In Hollywood, a young gay kid merely has to walk the streets of Santa Monica Boulevard to get picked up by some scary old queen trying to lease him for the afternoon. At least that would have meant somebody noticed you, but I clearly didn't possess that skill. I grew up in Hollywood with all the resources of cheap sex available down the street, and I never stopped to look. I was, frankly, afraid to. I didn't think I would be capable of it. Sex frightened me because it meant revealing my body to somebody. As a result, I didn't have actual sex until later in my twenties. Most people assume sex is a given with the modern teenager, but I proved that wrong. I could barely walk out of my house without feeling inadequate to the entire task of living, let alone mating. How would I even seek sex when that activity required one to act upon desire and to nail down a partner who willingly followed along? Reciprocity in both love and desire was something I would rarely find. How much of it was my own fault, or the fault of this independent parasite that ate away at my self-confidence, I can't tell. I have rarely acted upon my impulses, and as a younger man, I was paralyzed and walked around in a daze of extreme caution, fear, and trepidation. Not that anybody could tell, or care. Sexless in Hollywood—I managed to invent that possibility, a truly alternative lifestyle.

Around this time, I found friendship, not an unusual development perhaps for most kids, but for me a momentous achievement, caught up at first in repressed homoeroticism. It became more valuable to me than a teenage romance. I met Eugene some time in the eleventh grade when I sat behind him in a history class. Eugene was a Korean American teenager. His father had died in South Korea, and he now lived with his mother in Los Angeles. I felt an immediate bond to him, and more than anything else, I thought I felt something, a love deeper than any sexual crush. I felt I needed to be around him all the time, and I took the initiative to ask him out. He didn't always understand what this meant. Going to the movies with a friend was a significant break from solitude for me. It was one of the first incidents of sociability I experienced. What did I speak about? I rarely spoke about myself. I mentioned my father was dead, but I never revealed the condition of "bastardom" that seemed like just another of the many secrets I was conditioned to keep, along with my sexuality and my fixations on body image.

Eugene, nonetheless, became the first young man I tried to "pick up," and the first who rejected me.

"Can I be your friend?" I asked. This was on the patio of Fairfax High School, where we spent our break and lunch periods. This conversation had gotten off to an awkward start, but it wasn't merely a conversation.

The Subject Was Roses—or Was It?

"Sure, I can be your friend," he answered, smiling nervously.

Silence ensued. I might have followed up this request with a deeply felt definition of what I meant by friendship, something about bonding and comradeship. Instead, I invaded the comfort zone.

"By any chance," I asked him, "are you gay?"

The denial was immediate, loud, and unmistakably panicky. "No! Absolutely not! No way!"

That was clear.

"Why are you asking?"

"Because I think I'm in love with you."

I give him credit for not running away.

I was sixteen. That was my finest hour until then. It was the type of bluntness I would rarely ever bring to a gay bar in the future where picking up a man would have been a more likely possibility.

"Well, I'm sorry," he said. "I'm a Christian."

What seemed unusual about Eugene's rejection, however, was that he never hated me, nor did he turn against me for this oddly timed attempt to, well, start something, anything. Instead, Eugene took me, *not* into his arms, but straight to church. A Presbyterian one. I would tag along with him and his girlfriend, Anne, a Korean American whose father was a successful dentist. She had actual brothers and a mother and a house to go to at the end of the school day. Eugene appeared to be in awe of her, or just plainly in love. Eugene's fatherless family was, in fact, closer to mine, and we could at least compare notes. His mother was a reclusive woman still recovering from the loss of her husband. Eugene and his brother didn't always get along with her. He expressed misgivings over a certain distance she put between herself and her sons. Eugene ended up warming up to my mother a lot better than he did to me. He felt María was lively and outgoing, things I wasn't. I think he had a crush on her—a reflection of my own jealousy, perhaps, that he found her more attractive than he found me. Eugene had strong opinions about everything, and I think, at first, he believed I wasn't really gay and that my alleged attraction toward him could be explained as a form of fraternal affection. I never became a Presbyterian. I had enough problems believing in my own church. But my ability to maintain company with him proved life-altering. If one gains love through brotherhood, it's still love. As an only child, it was crucial to develop this type of bond as well, and for a teenager who spoke of suicide, it became a lifesaver.

The Subject Was Roses—or Was It?

I don't always understand this friendship. The level of comfort between us would have struck anyone as bizarre. I declared my love for him one day and suddenly became one of his best friends, riding in his car with him, and even sleeping in the same bed with him. I never understood Eugene's comfort zones. I never understood why I also put up with it. I thought I felt something for him, so I slept with him, literally, and that seemed good enough, like a sexless marriage arranged to meet a certain emotional need. It helped me cope in some ways with sexual repression, by drawing closer to a man through bonding. I thought of it as "homoerotic," and I'm sure he thought of it as spiritual. Either way, he didn't balk from it. He wasn't concerned about appearances either.

The first time I went to his apartment in Koreatown, I brought heavy-duty pajamas. I wore nightwear that covered my body no more comfortably than anything I wore to school or to the library. Eugene laughed the first time he saw the thick, flannel, long sleeve pajamas meant for some Rocky Mountain escapade. He wore his underwear to bed. I had not slept with a nearly naked man in my life, and it provoked insomnia and nervousness. Then, later that night, his mother came home. I watched everything from a half-open eyelid. She peeked into our room, and saw her nearly naked son sleeping next to a strange young man she hadn't seen before. She came into the room, slowly, as if figuring out what to do, and then covered his exposed chest with a blanket, tucking him in. Her protective reaction conveyed a strange body language, and the kiss on his forehead something more maternal, even a little desperate: who is this fag sleeping with my son? She seemed to be praying, I hope he hasn't corrupted my son. I don't know if a Korean mother would have thought that way, but I sensed her discomfort. When he woke up that morning, he asked, "Did you cover me?"

I said, "No, that was your mother. I didn't touch you one bit."

All I can say now is I marvel how Eugene, the Christian boy, had no qualms about sleeping with a gay teenager who had admitted a crush on him, and I understand all too well what his mother's misgivings must have been about. This friendship fed itself like a hurricane through warm waters. It was provocative to my senses, frustrating at first, and yet ultimately a lot more lasting than a simple case of sexual release. It was a form of love, I suppose, but companionship seemed fulfilling in and of itself.

The Subject Was Roses—or Was It?

Throughout the remaining part of high school, this sexless—yet intimate—friendship helped provide me with validation. My mother was glad to hear I had, of all things, a friend. But the most important aspect of this friendship was the openness and sincerity of the conversations. In Arlington, I concocted an elaborate tale about how my father worked as a diplomat for the Chilean Embassy and wrote propaganda for the Pinochet dictatorship. Nobody questioned it. After all, my classmates were sons and daughters of D.C.-area diplomats, and some had been stationed in Pakistan and Nepal, among other places. There was nothing unusual about a diplomat's son attending that particular school. But I had to be careful about not calling too much attention to my big lies. I kept my mother away from school to begin with and never invited her to PTA meetings or other functions. I did not introduce her to my teachers, as she was too shy and self-conscious about her English, so she never made the effort to speak to them. Her absence helped sustain my double life.

In Los Angeles, the double life began to crumble as I opened up to Eugene. He eventually learned about my past, my fatherless childhood, my sexual orientation. I felt the weight of the big lies lifting gradually around me. I felt it was possible to be myself. Eugene had a talent for a no-bullshit approach to life, a directness that was often disarming. I needed the safety of the space, the ability to speak in full confidence with somebody, and to extricate myself away from the lies that I had told back in the D.C. area. He even began to question my need to cover up.

"Why can't you wear short sleeves?" he asked once, the first time anyone other than my mother had asked such a thing.

I explained to him the entire history of how and when this habit had started.

"It doesn't seem normal. I wish I had some body hair."

True enough, Korean men as well as other Asian men seemed bereft of that one thing that had horrified me since the onset of puberty. I had never countenanced that someone might wish to have more of it.

"It's a sign of manliness," he said. I winced in pain. I didn't need so many signs of manliness all over my body.

"Well, one day, you'll grow out of it," he said. "But you do know you are a handsome man." I hadn't heard this either. "You have that Al Pacino thing going."

The Subject Was Roses—or Was It?

It didn't seem fair that he would size up my allegedly good looks. A straight boy, who wouldn't be mine anyway . . . why was he doing this? I often wonder what he said to my mother. I imagine her asking him with great concern what exactly was wrong with me, and he telling her what he knew. That's because at my next birthday my mother didn't just present me with a cake. She said the strangest thing: "You do know you're a pretty boy, don't you?" No, I didn't know, and I knew a mother's need to reassure her child. Eugene's words had become hers. It was a conspiracy of sorts, but they were trying their best to keep me from becoming another depressed, suicidal teenager. Something worked. I never thought of myself as "handsome" or a "pretty boy," but their language communicated concern. I couldn't let them down. Eugene had become part of my family.

I finished high school, and I didn't commit suicide. As for sex, it would wait for what appeared to be a decade.

There must be an entire body of literature on the psychology of repression. Sexual repression. I have not read it, but I was the expert. Repression means you have established your boundaries—or social pressure has established them for you, but you've adapted yourself to them. You are a physical being, but you are not an affectionate one. You do not touch others, nor let anyone touch you. There is an unspoken assumption that you would die if the bond were broken; there is a fear of even coming near anyone for any reason whatsoever. That's why sex seemed so frightful, no matter how desirable. I accepted Eugene's terms of friendship because he felt like a genuine friend, but I failed to explore other outlets for releasing sexual tension. This isn't to say I didn't try. I continued to ask my male friends if they were gay. I was blunt enough, and desperate enough to just get to the point. I was fishing for an answer and for a moment of reciprocity. I shocked plenty of my high school male friends—a half dozen or so, but none of them were gay or interested. I sensed rejection of my entire being, and—in spite of reassurances to the contrary from Eugene and my mother—I blamed it on my looks, my hairiness, my foreignness, and my strangeness. My mental disposition was to accept celibacy and to move on, to live as the only teenager in Hollywood without sexual experiences to tell. Yet, the simple act of establishing a friendship was a first step toward some form of socialization for me, if not something I would entirely master.

The Subject Was Roses—or Was It?

I was accepted to UCLA, and Eugene to a private Christian college in Santa Barbara.

"Why don't the two of you go to the same school?" my mother asked, imagining some sort of fraternal bond continuing beyond high school. Perhaps she hoped I had found love.

"Mother, he's a Christian. He wants to be around his people."

"Why can't you be a Christian?"

"Because I don't want to, Mother. The Catholic Church alienated me a long time ago, and I'm not going Protestant just to piss off the pope. I am not a follower."

"But when did this happen? I never realized."

"When I stopped going to church maybe?"

My mother wasn't a frequent churchgoer either. She hadn't noticed I wasn't a Christian, and that I had no aspirations to go in that direction, let alone enroll in a religious college.

"But what did it exactly?"

"I don't remember an exact moment, Mother," I said. "I must have read too many reports about the church disapproving of almost everything, including birth control, abortion, or sex of any sort."

"But you don't have sex of any sort, so what do you care?"

"It's true. But you need to have choices."

"So you abandoned the church because it disapproved of choices you don't even make?"

"That I don't make yet," I added. "I want to see what happens, and I don't want to feel guilt over everything. Maybe that's it; I want to renounce guilt."

"I'm not sure that's entirely possible. But I can't blame you. Just be careful whatever you do. I just wish you and Eugene could be together."

I don't know what she meant by this. Clearly, a woman who was still watching *Love Is a Many Splendored Thing* in retrospective movie theaters held romantic notions of some kind. She wanted to see contentedness in me and imagined that perhaps Eugene could bring that into my life in some manner. She had noticed something between us and knew that, at least around him, I was altered. I seemed more carefree and relaxed around him. I glowed. She wasn't blind. She lamented Eugene's departure more than I did. I expected UCLA to offer more than a Christian college could. I valued Eugene's friendship, but I felt ready for a secular college to bring me some extreme culture shock that might include sex and rock 'n' roll—not drugs, since I wasn't comfortable with them either. That was my problem, always trying to shirk the full experience.

The campus of UCLA turned out to be a bustling center of activity, and a world of temptation. Young men walked around in shorts and tank tops on a year-round basis regardless of weather. I walked around in long pants and long sleeve shirts, also regardless of weather. The contrast must have been remarkable to onlookers. I didn't belong among my classmates. I began to repeat the initial high school experience by walking around with my eyes down, hardly making eye contact, and staying out of trouble. Then there was the dorm. I moved into Sproul Hall and shared a small room with a student from Modesto, California, a young man from a middle-class family with a certain attitude about the Mexicans who'd "taken over" the peach-picking jobs in the town. I sensed his relief to hear I wasn't Mexican, and he felt comfortable enough then to start going off on Mexicans as if I wouldn't care. I patiently reminded him that Mexican workers wouldn't have ended up in Modesto if the peach growers hadn't employed them to begin with. Even though I wasn't Mexican, I would make him realize that the most unnerving aspects about me did not involve my ethnicity. I could not bring myself to shower in the morning and there were days when I couldn't shower at all. Anyone walking into the communal bathroom in the morning would find a dozen young men taking showers openly and visibly; there was no attempt at modesty at all. The showers were like an open window of shamelessness, and I didn't belong in them. A shower was a spectacle of debauchery for someone with my fears and repression.

I was beyond modesty by then. I was in full panic. I tried to get up every night around three a.m. when everyone was asleep and take showers quickly, with a simple need to get clean and rush back to my room. My roommate, at first, woke up and asked what I was doing.

"Just taking a shower."

"At three a.m.?"

"Yes, at three a.m.; go back to sleep."

He stopped asking after a while and got so used to it that he didn't wake up at all when I climbed down from my upper bunker. Unfortunately, I couldn't wake up every single night at three a.m., and there were days in which I walked around without a shower for nearly a week. I don't want to remember what I must have looked like or smelled like. One night I walked into the communal bathroom around 2:30 a.m., and I was shocked to find somebody else taking a shower. I made my way into the toilet, pretending I had come there to use it, and then when I was done—or faked being done—flushed the toilet, walked back to my room, without the shower. During the weekends, I visited my mother in Hollywood, and I was so relieved to be able to shower any time of day in my own enclosed space that Mother felt unusual warmth emanating from my singularly twisted disposition. I was glad to see her, but my affection was more calculating. I was obsessed with avoiding the embarrassment of exposure, and this took precedence over anything else in life. What was I hiding? My own body. Only the dead can do that more effectively.

The patterns of isolation and alienation that I encountered in high school reinforced themselves at UCLA. With Eugene gone to Santa Barbara, I didn't have many other friends. I didn't belong to any particular groups. I tried attending some peace and freedom rallies, but I didn't have the stomach for the heavy Marxist agenda that came attached with them. I tried reading up on Marx but always feared I'd become a psychotic totalitarian character. I certainly possessed the extreme psychology for it, and I also discovered Ayn Rand's books and became a free-market fanatic type for a while, but even then I had trouble joining a group to promote such ideas. Group settings were discomfiting.

I calculated my moves, yearning to do something big, yet wondering how I would take a leap forward. I wanted to be an actor, but actors were called upon to take off their shirts, or at least wear shorts, or, just as bad, short sleeves, or the new trend, nudity altogether. Being a writer—an anonymous and sentient little being hiding behind a typewriter—seemed like a better manifestation of my habits. But what type of writer? I was discouraged by the indifference of many of my American friends to my Chilean past, so I didn't write about it at all. Most Americans my age seemed oblivious of any world outside their own, and talking about the Chilean dictatorship seemed like a bit of exotica they didn't need. I was in the closet even about my Chilean identity. I stopped talking about my family—precisely the type of secretiveness I thought I had climbed out of in my friendship with Eugene, and I rarely, if ever, spoke at all about the historical circumstances that prevented us from returning to Chile. I developed a friendship with a young woman, Valerie, who actually spoke politics to me, trying to counteract the free-market ideology I was learning from Ayn Rand. Even though Valerie annoyed me with what I considered to be her "leftist bias," I was saved from complete reticence and solitude by her friendship. Her insistence, her ability to seek me out, even finding me a part-time job in the campus computer facility where she worked, seemed like a small miracle. Why was she so nice to me? At that time, I didn't ask questions. She actually seemed interested in Chile. Her boyfriend had lived in Peru for many years, and she had a curiosity about Latin America that seemed somehow un-American.

A few other people contributed a touch of companionship at this time. Robert was a young man from a Jewish family who'd lived in Israel, and I constantly stopped him in the hall of the dorm to ask him questions about that. He suffered from retinitis pigmentosa and was losing his eyesight. I became his official reader. I dictated his required reading onto a tape, and sometimes I added things I was reading for my own classes. A salacious story from Boccaccio's *The Decameron* was particularly welcome. Valerie became Robert's friend, and to this trio joined a young woman called Marlene, who lived in the dorm as well. We were good friends, chatty intelligent young people who seemed to be in school to actually learn something. While these friendships developed, I couldn't express the more dominant tyranny of self-hatred that accompanied and dominated every walking step of the day. My friends never understood this and linked my eccentricities to my Chilean background. Oh, that crazy Chilean. All of Chile was blamed for my strangeness.

A curious and fervent obsession developed around this time. His name was Santos. He was a young Cuban American who struck me as the most astonishingly beautiful man I had ever seen. I was as extreme in my longings as in my actions. I couldn't just be ugly; I had to be the ugliest. I couldn't just fall in love; I had to become overwhelmed, debilitated by the feelings that accompanied every waking hour. This obsession became a form of transcendence since it came with a hands-off policy of its own. I could feel and harbor strong feelings, yet all longings were stymied by a sense of impossibility, of limits, and of barriers. Still, the discovery that Santos was gay made the situation even more frustrating. It's one thing to fall in love with someone you can't have, but it's another to sense that you can't have what you might have gotten because you're altogether too inadequate to the task of seduction, or too ugly for it. Since I had never fallen in love with an openly gay man, which meant at least a shot at reciprocity, I became even more obsessed with simply staring at him from a distance.

I was working as a cashier at a UCLA cafeteria where I stood behind a register, wearing appropriately stiff clothes, long sleeves and slacks, and a name tag. Santos came in with a friend, paid with a check, and showed his ID, which meant I knew his name and address. What a strange sensation—to fall in love and have his driver's license in your hand. It was information that had immediately fallen into the hands of an obsessive personality. It's a scary thought, except it feels worse when the scary person in the scenario happens to be you.

He was a young man of olive skin and bright eyes, hazel if I recall correctly and—something that seemed important for my self-esteem—about my height, around 5′ 6″, with a sort of lovely, square-jawed face. I had never been struck by looks quite that way, and from that first encounter I couldn't stop thinking about him.

He came into the cafeteria every day and then into my line several times. I looked down or looked away. I couldn't let on that I had feelings for somebody I had never formally met. I let him walk away.

At college, I was convinced that I would join the Young Democrats and become some sort of activist. I went to a meeting. The student chair passed out an agenda that included a field trip to a state convention of Young Democrats in Sacramento. I was excited about taking a trip with a group, getting out of the dorm, and combating solitude. I rarely got out of the campus, let alone Los Angeles. I came back for a follow-up meeting to find that one of the new organizers was this young man called Santos.

I was taken aback by the coincidence. I couldn't contribute a word to the meeting. I listened to others talking about how to organize the trip. I was supposed to take an active role in the organization, but due to Santos's presence, I withdrew. I went home that day repelled by my feelings. I called the head of Young Democrats to let him know I wouldn't be going to Sacramento but didn't offer an explanation. I did yearn to be near Santos, with him, in him even, yet I didn't want to be exposed to the fantasy that he had become. I felt pain more than an opportunity. I sensed rejection. I didn't go back to the Young Democrats.

There was no staying away from him. He cropped up at the unlikeliest of times and places. He seemed to inhabit my world in many different ways. He started writing a column for the school newspaper, doing movie reviews, or writing on political issues, criticizing some aspect of Reagan policy. He became even more of a leftist, which was unusual for a Cuban American, I thought. I somehow resented having his presence in my school paper. He was an ongoing reminder that he lived as an example of fate's retaliation against my very life. Love was the impossible dream, and Santos was the stranger who proved love's disdain for me. That year, in a theater history class, I discovered Racine's *Phedre*, in which the title heroine would utter the words that described my own experience: "Hippolytus feels, but not for me." The idea that he was available to other men made the pain more searing, and ultimately more fateful. Phedre would die of her unrequited passion, expiring out of an internal logic as if her body imploded from within.

Even more unfortunately, I found a copy of Goethe's *The Sorrows of Young Werther* in the library. Somebody had left it out on a return shelf, and I remembered my theater history professor mentioning it as part of the Sturm und Drang movement of German literature, which promoted irrational emotions as a counter-Enlightenment stand. If there's one book one should keep away from the impressionable young man who feels unloved and unwanted, this should be it. *Don't try this at home*, should read the warning label on Goethe's book. This illustration of youthful suicide brought back the feelings I had entertained back in high school, to die young and unloved. How marvelously glorious it seemed. I discovered that Goethe's novel inspired a spate of suicides among young men whose lifeless bodies were found dressed in Werther's blue frock coat and yellow waistcoat, with copies of *Werther* in their pockets. This knowledge made me give out a nervous laugh rather than rush to imitate it. That's all my immigrant mother needed: to find her only son dead and dressed in nineteenth-century garb just to make a point about unrequited love. As a result, I had to learn to manage an obsession, not an easy thing to do when a powerful cultural marker makes self-destruction seem so highly dramatic and even beautiful. My obsessions continued, and yet I had found an absurd image with which to laugh at death. Further research showed that Goethe, in spite of his own bout of youthful regrets about love, lived to be eighty-two and felt greater remorse that his novel had inspired suicide in others when he simply had sought psychological release from his youthful pain. Old age seemed feasible if only one could learn to release pain. The writing of

The Subject Was Roses—or Was It?

Young Werther had been part of his healing, not a prescription for suicidal young men. That was a relief to discover.

One day, I took a classmate to see an Ingmar Bergman double feature—*Shame* and *Persona*—at the Nuart, a revival movie house on Santa Monica Boulevard. There was a signup sheet by the door for patrons to get on the mailing list. Santos had just signed it. He had also given out his address, all laid out right there for me to see. I already knew his address, but this was a reminder. A less stable mind would have camped out in front of his apartment building. What if I did start showing up at his door? I had elements of a stalker's psychology, but a sudden burst of sanity and caution constantly pulled me back.

I moved into an off-campus, university-owned apartment that summer to share a three-bedroom suite with five rowdy roommates who stayed up all night, and who often didn't pay the rent. When I went to the Student Housing office to pay my share, they told me that they'd no longer accept individual payments, and that we'd have to pool our resources and hand over one payment. When I tried to collect rent from my roommates, one moved his things out in the middle of the night. Since we couldn't afford to chip in for one more payment, we were evicted. One of those roommates who was kicked out along with me was a young African American man who worked at a copy shop. We kept in touch, and as I began to write more plays for a playwriting class, he saw me frequent the store more often. One day, he made a point of speaking up about a new roommate of his. "We got this gay guy as a new roommate. He brings over his male buddies all the time, and I think they spend time in there, you know—I don't really want to know what they're doing. His name is Santos."

"Santos?" I said. That name again. "He's that dark-haired, Latin guy, kinda cute?"

I failed to stop myself from letting out the word "cute." The roommate gave me a look: you're not turning that way, are you? Such strange language, "turning that way," as if one suddenly turns around one day and decides to go in that direction.

"No, I'm a sexless human being," I said, which was perfectly true, and seemed an act of conviction by then. But now I knew. Santos was not only gay, he was sexually active.

Finally, in response to one of Santos's reviews that appeared in the student papers on the Costa-Gavras film *Missing*, I decided to contact him and to actually speak to him. I'd heard that that's what you did when you were interested in somebody. *Missing* was a great film that finally brought partial attention to my native country's tragedy, the 1973 military coup. I say partial because the film wouldn't have been made if it hadn't been about a young American man who gets caught up in Chilean politics and disappears with the apparent consent of the U.S. embassy. The film had to be angled to appeal to an American audience with the added scandal of American complicity in the killing. Chileans were minor players in the story. It starred Jack Lemmon and Sissy Spacek, two reliable, even legendary, American actors. I resented the insinuation that Americans wouldn't have gone to see a film about Latin America without the American angle, but nonetheless the movie became the excuse I finally had to contact Santos.

I called him up at home and asked him out for coffee. Just like that. Obsessed people, even while shy, manage to pluck up some courage. I had found mine. "I read your article about *Missing* and thought maybe we could talk about it."

"How did you get my number?" the very befuddled Santos asked.

"Your roommate was my ex-roommate," I said, truthfully. I didn't tell him that I knew his address and had written down his license number on his check as a cashier. I didn't let on that I had dropped the Young Democrats because of his presence in it, that I had seen him at the Nuart Theater, that he'd written his address on the mailing list.

Satisfied, he was amenable—even generous—to meet me at the student coffee house in Kerckhoff Hall. Santos was polite, but it was obvious that he was popular and highly sought out, from what his roommate told me. I had my sources. I knew more about Santos than he would ever realize. He certainly didn't reveal any aspect of his private life during this brief meeting. I told him *Missing* had affected me deeply; it was a personal film that I could relate to. But his take on the film revealed his Marxist leanings, which annoyed me because of the fanatical way in which he expressed them (or so it seemed to me at the time). He said he had drifted away from the Young Democrats because he felt the need to fight for social justice from a Socialist angle. I told him I had drifted away from the Young Democrats because I read Ayn Rand and believed in the free-market system. Big mistake. The one rule of thumb of dating that I eventually learned (although it was too late for this encounter) was the need to pose, to feign, to appeal to the potential mate's interests, to lie if you will. Being yourself could be dangerous if you were a misshaped personality like me. If he's a Socialist, then identify with his struggle and throw in a name or two— Rosa Luxemburg, cool chick; Che Guevara, hot dude; how about that *Reds* movie with Warren Beatty? Instead I mentioned Ayn Rand, who was anathema even to moderate Democrats. Santos didn't have much else to say after that. He politely finished his coffee and left. That was the end of that.

UCLA had a directory of student addresses and phone numbers. Not only was the directory published, but it was kept in a file in the hallway of Kerckhoff. Anyone could walk in and get those numbers. Some students chose not to be listed, of course, but others neglected to check a box saying so, and the phone numbers could be accessed by anybody. I had originally sought Santos's name in the directory out in the hallway and found his number, but then I remembered that I had his house number already because I knew his roommate, so I didn't need it. Nonetheless, it was there. That day, immediately after our meeting, I noticed Santos walked in the direction of the file out in the hallway. I was curious about what he would do. I lounged around on the other end of the hallway, hiding. When he left the building, I walked toward the directory and discovered that Santos's card was now gone. He had removed it only seconds after our meeting. I had actually managed to scare him. *Had I become a scary person?* I was clearly not a lovable one, and I was also a lousy seducer. I had asked him out for coffee, but during coffee, I never made any overtures. No flattery, no hints that I liked him, nothing. I was essentially waiting, hoping against hope that he would come on to me. But he didn't. I had shaved and showered, had perfumed myself, and was wearing a beige (although acrylic) sweater my mother had bought me (my mother still bought most of my clothes at that time). I looked fairly presentable, maybe even "cute," but when I discovered that Santos's card was gone, I realized I had been a lousy date. It took me years to ask anyone out again for coffee, or for anything else for that matter. Santos's card was gone, I would remind myself. He had removed it himself. That spoke loud and clear. Life at zero self-esteem. And I was scary, to boot.

I had applied to go to Italy on the education abroad program. I had taken two years of Italian, warmed up to the language, found it graceful and even sexy, and felt I needed to get away from the many anxieties that were eating away at me. Brazil could have been a second choice. I still liked the idea of Brazil, a warm country of supposedly sensual people, but ultimately—face it, I told myself—they're gorgeous people who live in a tropical climate, which means wearing more revealing clothes, and I knew what that meant for my condition. I opted for a cooler climate. Northern Italy fit the bill. Padua was cold in winter and mild the rest of the year. I applied and got in, and UCLA gave me a scholarship. Again, by appearances alone, I was a good student. A high GPA made me eligible for grants, fellowships, and all other forms of government support that would make my education abroad experience practically paid for. I had been working for three years straight to get myself through college, so one year's rest from the routine of school and work would be welcome. I went to do more photocopying of my student plays at my ex-roommate's copy shop.

"How's Santos?" I asked him.

"He's leaving, finally."

"Oh, where is he going?"

"To Europe."

"Europe?!?"

Alarm bells went off.

I investigated the matter. I sought out the assistant at the education abroad program. I wasn't quite sure how to state my request, as in, "Would you find out if this guy I'm obsessed with is going to Europe on the education abroad program, and if so, where? I'd like to know because I want to stalk him."

I had to ask, out of curiosity. "A friend of mine from high school mentioned he was going abroad, that he'd been accepted, but I forgot to ask him the details. Is he going on this program?"

The assistant could have easily told me the information was confidential, but I sounded innocent enough. She looked up the name. Santos was not enrolled in the UCLA program. "But there are other programs hosted by other universities that some students enroll in," she added, listing some examples. I resisted the temptation to call him up and ask him myself. I was pessimistic. I didn't have the skills to seduce anybody, and I was reduced to admiring this young man from a distance. I decided I would never bother with Santos again. It was simpler to let him go. I would go to Europe and start a new life. The theater department, of course, tried to play a game of obstruction. "You can't be a theater major and take a year off," said the counselor. "There are technical courses—lighting and costume design, for instance—that you need to take here." I had enough credits to become an Italian major, and the Italian department welcomed my application.

A strong reaction from my mother: "A theater major was useless enough. What are you going to do as an Italian major? You should be studying accounting or something, anything, practical."

For the first time, I made it clear to my mother: "I am going to be a writer, and travel is part of the writing experience."

"I give up," said my mother, but she decided that she would find a way to benefit from the decision as well. "I'll make a visit," she added. "My boss Mr. Galanos has plenty of friends in the fashion industry in Milan. He can put us in touch with people there. *Italia, aquí venimos!* Italy, here we come!"

"How does this end up being about you?" I complained.

"Well, it does. If you're going to be impractical and full of dreams and pretensions, I am going along for the ride. I'll see you there."

My mother would make her way to Italy, and I would have to end up hosting her, at a time when I needed some distance. But the most welcome part of that trip would be a quick visit to Salzburg, Austria, where *The Sound of Music* was set, only an overnight train ride from Padua. We found a way to take Hollywood with us wherever we went.

"Going to be a writer." That was new. I had barely written a few scripts for a playwriting class. The consensus from my classmates: "You write as if you had an accent. You sound foreign on the page." Not foreign, I wanted to say, but rather eccentric or just plain unique. My first play featured desperate characters on a raft sailing out of Cuba. It turns out they're all dead. It's *No Exit* on a raft, I explained to people; it's Jean Paul Sartre, existentialism for the age in which we live. A Communist woman is stuck on the raft with the same people she persecuted. Unique, I insisted, not foreign.

Flash forward to Padua, Italy. A student from UC Riverside, English major, on a grand tour, also in the same education abroad program. We purchased an inexpensive pass sold exclusively in Italy that allowed us to take trains all over Western Europe (except England, ever the noncooperative European nonpartner) for a mere $150. In two weeks, we rode the train from Padua to Barcelona, Madrid, Paris, Amsterdam, and, for an extra fee, London, and then back down to Italy. This was Europe on the cheap, on a fast track. Impressions were formed; trains proved comfortable; the landscapes flashed by the window as a gallery of quick glimpses into a fairy-tale world of woods and lakes. Other young people traveling through the continent appeared unusually friendly and eager to share their experiences. People spoke to me, the scary guy. In Barcelona, a group of American students took us to a local pub where we drank oversized mugs of beer for fifty cents, and the only side effect was a sense of joy; no hangovers for me the next day. I made a discovery: that I felt comfortable talking about my Chilean past—not the illegitimacy part, not yet—but the culture and history. People sympathized with Chilean exiles living in Europe. They knew about Chile. They had opinions, had seen the film *Missing*, and I was back to a grand loquacious manner that had inspired me once to play Aunt Augusta (see chapter 1), this time playing the seasoned traveler holding a giant mug of beer in my hand. The gregarious role, like Aunt Augusta, suited me well for that time and place. I was theatrical even without a stage. It was a role closer to my personality, and I didn't have to put on a disguise.

On our overnight train ride from Madrid to Paris, I went out into the hallway to avoid offending riders inside the compartment with the smell of a rich mortadella and pâté sandwich bought at the Madrid train station. The odor proved a bit repugnant in that enclosed space. Another American student came to join me, and he talked about his experiences in Spain. I was listening closely. But I was surprised that I thought I saw, in the corner of my eye, a familiar face, moving forward through the hallway of the train. I stopped talking, not believing what I was seeing. Or thinking I was imagining things. Walking through the hallway directly toward me was, of course, Santos.

I stopped him with my hand firmly on his chest, the only time I ever touched him. I told myself this can't be; this is impossible, there is a look-alike in Europe. Santos, as usual around me, looked annoyed and stood there in front of me for about thirty minutes listening to me make a fool of myself. I talked about Italy and this cheap pass that was taking us everywhere. I could never get to the point. My body had long ago disintegrated into a flaccid mush of unfulfilled desire. The American student I had been talking to had already withdrawn since my attention had long stopped acknowledging him.

When it came time to speak up and contribute something to the conversation, Santos was blunt. "I love Paris. The clubs stay open late, and the men are great."

I was unable to contribute much more to this conversation. I had not been to a gay club before. I had never expressed anything resembling lust, not openly anyway. The only person who'd heard any of it had been Eugene, who had reacted by saying a prayer and by trying to convert me to Presbyterianism.

The seduction of Santos would prove equally elusive. I was grateful that he had stopped to talk to me at all. He didn't have to, but the strangeness of running into me there on that train had been enough to surprise him as it had me, and he'd come to a halt. Did he ever realize what I felt for him, how long I'd felt it, and how mind-boggling this encounter was for me? Yet again, when it came to the things that mattered, silence emanated from me. I could always blab on about superficial aspects of the trip. I could become loquacious and yet say nothing. My feelings were kept strictly in check, which meant they'd begun to erode all defenses. I will spontaneously combust, I feared while standing there, and the train kept going at its pace, and bits and pieces of my body would disperse through the windows into the mountainous landscape. The hills are alive with the carnage of a young man's devastated, mutilated heart. The young Werther in me continued to think in terms of physical disintegration.

"I was staying with my Cuban relatives in Madrid," he added. "They escaped Castro and left everything behind. We get into arguments over politics. I told them I was a Socialist, and of course, they felt betrayed and hurt, and I had to watch what I said from then on. It's not easy being Cuban and Socialist—outside of Cuba."

"Yes, we all have to watch what we say," I said, feebly. It was the best I could muster.

"But at least the men in Madrid were hot. As hot as in Paris."

"Of course," I said, trying to sound so knowing. "Really hot, I'm sure."

"And I have good luck with them."

"I'm sure, yeah."

Inappropriate bragging, I thought. I get the point; you're popular, you're beautiful, you deserve all those men.

He was headed back to his sleeper car. I told him that if he planned to come out to Italy some time, look me up. I might just do that, he said. I gave him my number and address in Italy and hoped, merely hoped, that he'd use it. He took the information and made vague, evasive promises to come visit.

I ran into Santos back at UCLA a year and a half later. He stood in front of a bulletin board, in the lobby of Melnitz Hall in the theater department. He mentioned wanting to apply for film school, but he knew UCLA was competitive. He didn't know yet what would work out. I was polite; I was nonchalant. By then, I realized Santos was not, nor ever would be, interested in me and never had been. I let it go—or, let's just say, I thought I could simply let it go by saying so.

A year later, a new acquaintance at school told me he was hanging out with a new buddy called Santos. I don't want to know, I said, although I did. Santos must remain firmly in the past. I repeated to myself the official policy but nonetheless goaded this new friend to sit down at the coffeehouse at UCLA for more details. He let it be known that Santos was single and looking.

"Well, he's not looking for me, so shut up about him!" I blurted out, rather bitchily.

"I don't know what you mean by that," he said, suddenly interested.

Equally out of character was the sudden urge for me to readily confide my feelings of obsession to another young man whom I barely knew. I told the new friend everything, the early days of obsession, the strange meeting at Kerckhoff Hall, the cosmic coincidence of running into him in Spain on a train.

"I just love it!" the new friend said with a nelly flare-up in his smile. His hands had gotten all fluttery, even queeny. "You should have walked back to his sleeping car and gone down on him. Big blow job! He was dying for it."

"I don't think so!" I said, flinching from such a possibility of being wanted.

"Those trains have tiny little bathrooms where you could have fucked the hell out of him—or let him fuck you. I mean, that's hot."

"Well, I'm glad my story of denial and repression had that effect on you."

"I don't deny nor repress," he said, "and neither should you. What were you thinking anyway? About endless love? You didn't even consider the possibility that you're young, that your feelings will wear out one day, and that you might as well make a play for his ass, and then be done with it? Did you really think you'd have a love affair, you know, that movie-style love affair that lasts a lifetime. Please, Miss Scarlett! That was old when Ashley and Rhett Butler divided Miss O'Hara's heart. What exactly were you thinking?"

The Subject Was Roses—or Was It?

It was the first time somebody had actually put my feelings in this perspective. I had spent all that time thinking precisely in those terms. My obsession had nothing to do with sexual release alone. I had thought in terms of possession, and owning a man, and settling down with him, and experiencing some form of—heaven help me—endless love. I didn't know I was supposed to think any differently. I had interpreted attraction as a form of undying loyalty that had the power to destroy. No wonder I could barely bring myself to talk to him. I had burdened myself with all that pressure to conquer a man, and then do who knows what with him—settle down in a cabin? No wonder I couldn't be casual about my attraction, and I couldn't relax around him. *Te hiciste toda una película.* I had projected a future of marital bliss onto a screen and made it play out with a happy ending.

"I should go now," I said, exhausted to realize I had talked about it, him, the Thing, the Creature, and gotten a new perspective out of doing so, something I had trouble squaring away with my illusions.

A few years later, I saw Santos once again for the last time outside a gay nightclub in West Hollywood. He was either drunk or looked unusually incoherent, but that incident supported further evidence of the Santos Way of Life that I had amassed through time. In the two years that had gone by, I managed to hear about Santos's exploits. A law student, a friend of my roommate, discussed his date with this attractive Cuban American man, who of course happened to be Santos. At that time, I did not go into my history with the impossible-to-pin-down culprit. The law student in question happened to be impossibly attractive himself. The fact that Santos had gone out on a date with a handsome—probably the most handsome, blond, august, intelligent, and available law school student I had met—did not bode well for that conversation. I wasn't in the mood to hear one more instance about Santos that might manage to provoke jealousy in me. Another school acquaintance talked about working out with this beautiful young Cuban American man, who, of course, happened to be Santos. This was Los Angeles, a city of millions of people, the nation's second largest city, but apparently neither here, nor in the entirety of Europe, could I get away from this man.

That night when I ran into him outside a West Hollywood club, I was simply walking home. I lived in the area, and it was a cooler night than anticipated. I was for once underdressed with a light jacket. A cold breeze blew through the city, provoking a light shiver uncharacteristic of the Southern California lifestyle. Outside a club on Santa Monica Boulevard, Santos stood beside a thin, recently planted tree, as if clinging to it, probably a bit drunk or high—I couldn't tell. I thought he'd break the branches of that skinny, baby tree if he leaned any harder on it. He made eye contact, and I, of course, panicked. I decided for once to, finally, walk on by.

I was too young to recognize the antisocial, melodramatic gesture I made that night. I was acting the protagonist in a couple of popular songs that set the agenda and revealed to me what to do: Dionne Warwick's "Walk On By," and the Simple Minds' "Don't You Forget about Me," which tauntingly asks, "Will you recognize me, look my way or walk on by?" Warwick, in turn, more assertively commands (courtesy of Burt Bacharach and Hal David): "If you see me walking down the street and I start to cry each time we meet, walk on by." It seemed important at that age to make decisions with a chosen soundtrack in mind. I felt the need to punish this obsession for being who he was. He was my obsession. I was not his, and all that time and energy that had gone into thinking about him and, more importantly, reacting to his presence everywhere I went, including Europe, felt wasted. He was a constant reminder I couldn't have what I wanted. My first serious obsession as an adult required me to stage the ultimate, final rejection of the object of desire. It was an impromptu dramatic moment. I had spent my youth mostly as a nonparticipant in my own affairs of the heart. I was a passive character, waiting for a twist of fate to change favorably in my direction. I took the initiative to walk on by. Unlike the hero of *Death in Venice*, an older man in love with a much younger one, I was the personification of youth rejected by itself. I didn't have to wait till old age to feel that type of humiliation. I was young and rejected by the young. What would Santos have said if I'd spoken to him that night? The same trivial things he always said to me, quick sound bytes of his fabulous life and how much fun he was having in WeHo, as he did in Paris, or at UCLA, or wherever he could be found being his magnificent self, while I could reveal very little that I actually could boast. Same old me, hiding my body—I couldn't quite say that, and so I chose to purposely deflect the opportunity to say anything at all. I walked away from him, but I also walked away from any opportunity to speak to him about my feelings. More importantly, the other role I could have played was the one of the young man who's over such hurt, the one who moves on and can proceed to befriend his obsession because maturity has brought much wisdom.

I wasn't quite there yet. I moved away from West Hollywood and never found out what became of Santos. Warwick sings some more: "Foolish pride, that's all that I have left, so let me hide."

I didn't accomplish anything by hiding. The most that can be said about surviving these years was that I can now acknowledge the bad choices. Another pop song at the period commanded zealously: "If I can't have you, I don't want nobody, baby." I apparently lived by that dictum. I had grown up with a highly sheltered frame of mind, not because my mother didn't approve of my choices, but because I had obeyed the dysmorphic disorder that caused me to hide my body and not live joyously within it. It would take decades to be rid of such behavior. It would take a lifetime to reverse a state of mind, one that called for extreme solutions. There would be other challenges ahead, but my mother wouldn't have to fear walking into a mess of self-destruction in her living room. Sanity had prevailed; enough of it needed to remain alive, a momentous, if small, achievement in the scheme of things. María had saved herself by pulling herself out of the ocean when rip tides threatened to carry her away. Similarly, I had to avoid making a bloody mess of myself. That much cruelty was mercifully avoided.

A Memory: When Grandpa Accuses You of Spying

It's spring 1980. I look emaciated in trousers too big for a slight frame, and I am not one to buy clothes, used or otherwise. My mother delivers a set of pants and shirts, I wear them, then wear them out, and so it goes. They're Galanos's cast-offs, not a bad deal if one noticed that the famous designer wore fine clothes suitable for a middle-aged man. But since my mother works comfortably inside his Bel Air home, washing and ironing his clothes, she is the recipient of his generosity, and I get to wear yesterday's fashion, which I barely notice anyway: elegant slacks, decent long sleeve shirts, but altogether stiff for a teenager. There are no hints of the California dude in me, at least in the fashion sense, but my black hair does grow long, disheveled, and it covers my eyes. I'm a mess of contrasts—the well-dressed, long-haired guy. I walk the hilly UCLA campus as a bespectacled youngster

The Subject Was Roses—or Was It?

overwhelmed by freshman terror, the sudden realization that I'm called upon to be an adult when I know what I've read in books, but nothing practical about sex, war, freedom, and, more importantly on the well-kept Bruin campus, landscape design, let alone fashion. I am still a virgin, and a novice in many other ways. I am in need of brushing up on Chilean culture and history. Perhaps a visit to the homeland might do me some good.

This year, on my second trip to visit my relatives in Chile, Tata accuses me of spying. *Whatever*, one might say today in teenage parlance, but in Chile, this is for real. My grandfather's experience as a supporter of the Pinochet dictatorship makes him aware of what to fear—the same government he supports, in other words. Intimidated by his own dictator, my grandfather finds me suspect. But really, I am only guilty of one true violation of my grandfather's trust: I have uttered disdain for General Pinochet, my one attempt to declare my independence from my grandfather's influence. The rest of the family is leftist, and few people bite their tongue in their denunciation of the dictator. They're a lively bunch, these relatives with their fists in the air and their denunciations crisp and clear, and at this time in Chilean history, that's a risky position to take. A secret police exists. It abounds in and permeates our world like foul air, but it can't jail everyone. Chileans will riot when they have to, and the dictator will eventually lose his standing even with his own military supporters. But that is still in the future, not easily foreseen in 1980. My grandfather sees himself in the general's light, as a misunderstood patriarchal figure, and the moment he hears me speak against the dictator, early on in my stay, he feels betrayed.

I will eventually lament my own absolutism, my inability or unwillingness to see Tata again. This mostly kind and generous man, my mother's stepfather, once gave my mother the gift of a home and a semblance of normalcy as he anchored a fatherless family. My mother had spent her childhood bouncing around from the relatives who took care of her when my grandmother worked as a live-in maid in Santiago to the austere German nuns who treated her as an orphan when she was interned at a girls' school. Before I knew him to be my mother's stepfather, I knew José Bravo as Tata, or Grandpa. If no one had informed me otherwise, I would have considered him my actual biological grandfather. I never had any reason to think of him as anything else.

By that summer (a Chilean winter), I had completed my first year at UCLA and been exposed to radical writings of both the Left and the Right,

The Subject Was Roses—or Was It?

from Karl Marx and Rosa Luxemburg to Milton Friedman and Ayn Rand. More importantly, Jean-François Revel had taken on the Marxist Left in *The Totalitarian Temptation* and exposed the Left's own heart of darkness. I might have been ripe for conversion to free-market economics had my exposure to General Pinochet—a major proponent of free-market reforms—not been so up close and personal. If nothing else, Revel's writings left me feeling skeptical about the totalitarian temptations of the free-market Right itself. A book written to denounce the Left had provoked the paradoxical reaction against the Right. Revel's writings would—probably for the better, I dare say—complicate my sense of belonging in any political movement at all. Revel's other book, *Without Marx or Jesus*, captured that dilemma of living in the modern world without the icons that enthuse the minds of fellow citizens who'd turned to the fervid dogma of those two gentlemen. I was barely nineteen and already living without Marx or Jesus, a dangerous place if you were going to visit relatives in Chile in 1980, when the political currents required you to belong to one camp or to the other, but not neither.

In addition to the sway of competing ideologies, my own citizenship was in flux. The Immigration and Naturalization Service (INS) managed to bungle my paperwork to become a U.S. citizen. Unlike the average American, I was eager to vote, a privilege already rescinded from the voters of my native country. The face-off between Carter and Reagan would become an epic struggle between Carter's idealism toward human rights and Reagan's firm resolve against communism. Carter's denunciation of human rights violations in Chile was admirable, even inspiring, but Reagan's anti-Communist resolve seemed to fulfill a national need for strong leadership against totalitarianism. I had become what they now call a swing voter, but only in spirit, because I wasn't yet eligible to vote. The Cold War struggle in Chile, and the tug of war between my relatives, had left me discreetly in tune with both sides of the equation, and it was only a matter of time before I took sides myself. But first I needed the ability to at least make a statement. I needed the basic right to vote, which neither country could give me.

In fall 1979 a letter arrived from the INS, announcing an appointment to finalize my papers to become a full citizen. I was required to bring witnesses who had known me four years. But I had moved to Los Angeles and enrolled at Fairfax High School in the fall of 1976. My friends there, Harris and Craig, agreed to be my witnesses, but they had known me only three and a half years. When I arrived at the INS, I was hoping for some leeway.

The Subject Was Roses—or Was It?

"I'm sorry," said the INS officer, smiling gently, but remaining firm. "They must have known you for a full four years."

It wasn't even clear to me exactly what Craig and Harris were required to have witnessed: that I wasn't a dangerous Communist, that I was entirely and sexually untouched, that I wasn't a cocaine addict? My good character was affirmed by mostly straight A's in school and by the fact that I had only tried once to test the waters of these young men's sexual identity, but had failed miserably, and yet they had remained friends because teenagers didn't seem shocked by such things, at least in the heart of the Fairfax District, where tolerance reigned. They were cool, and they were friends, and thereby good witnesses.

But no, the INS officer adamantly adhered to the rules and sent me away, saying I would receive another appointment in six months when these friends will have known me for the required time. I didn't get that appointment for another twenty-two months. In the meantime, Kate Hepburn won a record fourth Oscar for *On Golden Pond* and Henry Fonda his first for the same film and, quickly thereafter, he died. Reagan got shot, survived, and claimed he forgot to duck. Deborah Harry of Blondie sang that "the tide is high and I'm holding on." History churned along, and I didn't get my citizenship until the feds decided it was time. When I eventually got my letter for the new appointment, I was surprised there was no requirement for witnesses mentioned in the letter. There must be a mistake, I thought. I called the INS, waited an hour for a live operator to pick up, and once somebody did, the officer told me they eliminated that requirement back in 1980 about two months after I had made the trek with my friends. No more witnesses are needed, the INS operator told me; come on your own.

I missed having to decide between Reagan and Carter in the 1980 election (the independent candidacy of John Anderson would eventually prove more appealing to me anyway, but still I stood on the sidelines watching as a foreigner) over a requirement that was already on its way out when I was turned away. But history had another proposition for me that year, the last one spent as a Chilean citizen.

As I landed in Santiago, I discovered I was eligible to vote on General Pinochet's felicitous self-crowning called *el plebiscito*, the plebiscite. In a few weeks, the dictator would hold a referendum on a new constitution that a carefully appointed commission had written up with the intent of, basically, appointing Pinochet president for life, à la Fidel Castro, yet another reason I had become wary of dictators of either the Left or Right. The ego needed to rule for life requires no ideological position. I spent that summer taking my own polls in what today would be called community forums with my family members. It became clear that most of my relatives hated the general or had turned against him if they had ever held a positive view of him. Based on my family's vote alone, it was easy to conclude that he would lose the plebiscite by a wide margin. Except that I would discover my grandfather's sole vote would count many more times because that was the family in which I was staying. His vote would define our relationship and ultimately destroy it.

Nonetheless, I was excited about the election. My first lesson in citizenship would not be the Carter–Reagan match, but that one opportunity to use my first vote against an entire dictatorship. It's quite a statement for an idealistic young man. Maybe there was a reason for the bureaucratic bungling of the INS after all. I was meant to vote first in my native country, and to make a particularly crucial statement that, for once, would mark me for life—preferably in the right way—as a proponent of democracy. I was growing up among young Americans who didn't care about voting. Revel's next book would be ominously titled *How Democracies Perish*.

On a cool morning on September 11, 1980, I got up at six a.m. to follow my cousin Patricio to a local poll station. Pinochet had chosen the anniversary of his infamous coup to schedule the voting. When he had initially staged his coup, he had done so as part of a four-man military junta with the pretext of bringing stability to a country that was declared to be on the verge of civil war. The military had, in other words, acted in a "nonpartisan" manner to prevent further chaos. The junta would, the military said, rotate powers among the four men involved: representatives of the air force, the army, the navy, and the *carabineros* (the military police). Instead, Pinochet eventually bypassed his colleagues and declared himself president, and now what he sought on that day was a cleverly redefined lifetime appointment. There would be no rotation of powers. The new constitution would officially declare him president, with an eight-year term that would supposedly be renewed by the intimidated voters in 1988. But in 1980, we were not entirely naive; we had reasons to suspect fraud.

My cousin and I took a bus to the National Stadium, once the sight of detentions, executions, and torture, now the polling booth for the dictator's

The Subject Was Roses—or Was It?

goal of declaring himself a constitutional president. No registration was required. Any citizen was allowed to vote anywhere in the vicinity, show some permissible, vaguely credible ID, and then get a ballot. The informality of the arrangement made almost everyone, except perhaps diehards like my grandfather, suspect this was an electoral scam. Since when did Pinochet make it easy for anyone to cast a ballot? Especially for a complex constitution that most Chileans had not read. In the streets, peddlers sold copies of it, and admirers kept them like a souvenir. Anyone who could wade through the complex legalese and "pinochetese" with which it was written noticed that it would elevate the military as a permanent member of government. Even if Pinochet were to lose an election, he would remain head of the army and a senator for life. Senators appointed by the military would serve for life, skewering numbers were the opposition ever to win a competitive election. That night, Pinochet greeted his supporters at a televised rally in which he declared an overwhelming victory—not the 99 percent vote that most dictators usually proclaim. This was still Chile, and Chileans still liked to believe their country differed from the so-called banana republics of Latin America. We somehow expected our politics, like our weather, to be cooler and fairer. No, this dictator only claimed some 66 percent of the votes in his favor. His supporters dominated the airwaves and proclaimed his divinity as the will of the people.

I was left with a bitter memory of the scam, and yet a certain pride that I didn't fall for it. For years to come, I remained excited about my first election, and to commemorate it, I had my cousin stage a picture of me at my aunt's home in which I am casting a ballot clearly marked "No" into a box. If I couldn't get a picture of myself casting the ballot at the actual polling place, I would stage it. It was a private theater of resistance.

In the late 1970s, in Los Angeles, my mother and I met a Chilean political exile, Miguel Navarro (a pseudonym). Miguel wasn't a Marxist exile. He belonged to the centrist and moderate, some might even say conservative, Christian Democratic Party. Once General Pinochet ruthlessly swept away the Marxist Left, he turned against centrists such as the Christian Democrats, who advocated a return to democracy. Miguel had been arrested and put on a plane to nowhere. He was given a United Nations passport, which meant he was a man without a country. Thanks to sponsors in the L.A. area, Miguel settled in Southern California and worked as a watchman at a

The Subject Was Roses—or Was It?

hospital. He immersed himself in a growing community of Chilean exiles and helped organize anti-Pinochet rallies in Los Angeles. He and my mother became friends, asexual ones, like *comadres* who sit down to gossip about love affairs and husbands and other girlfriends. I thought of Miguel as a repressed gay man. I knew the signs at that age. His bizarre ability to be an ebullient noisy "girlfriend" to my mom seemed to me like a shoe that fit. I usually left the two alone to do their girl talk, and I would condescendingly pick up some serious book, a Dostoyevsky perhaps or a D. H. Lawrence. I was a teenager with an attitude and a belief that I'd grow up to be wiser, more knowing, indeed more courageous, than my elders.

That summer, as I was leaving to visit my family in Santiago, Miguel asked me to get in contact with his sister in Santiago, who wanted to send him a couple of gifts with me upon my return. Most importantly, he was writing a book, a collection of short stories that he had initially published in Chile and sought to reissue in the United States through a local, Spanish-language press. He entrusted me with the task of bringing back the original plates for the cover art that his sister had stored for him in Santiago. It was a simple request, and I agreed to do it. I didn't know this request would escalate into a disastrous confrontation with my grandfather.

Not long afterward, Miguel's sister arrived at our family's house in La Palmilla, asking for me and bearing gifts for her brother, along with the cover art. I happened to be away visiting relatives in the south, and she went ahead and left a package for me in the hands of my grandfather's younger wife, Teresa. When I got back from the trip a few days later, Teresa alerted me to the seriousness of the situation.

"Your grandfather really needs to talk to you," she warned.

I was due to fly back the following day to Los Angeles. I hoped to get out and do some last-minute shopping, but my grandfather held me up for hours in the most disturbing discussion I ever had with him.

"Who is this woman?" he asked with a tone of eerie resolve as I entered the living room. Grandfather began acting like a member of General Pinochet's secret police. He sounded grave, even threatening. I was still a teenager after all, and something of a wimp as well. I was impressionable and soft-spoken, easily intimidated. His wife came in carrying the package and placed it on the table.

"The neighbor saw her come in here, and afterward came to talk to me. This woman is a terrorist!"

The Subject Was Roses—or Was It?

"A what?" A smile crossed my face, incredulity breaking through the tension he had provoked on it. It was a misunderstanding, I was about to explain, but his face wasn't budging. He was not amused.

"Yes, she is involved with Marxist terrorists who seek to overthrow the general, our general."

Teresa opened up the package containing the evidence. I looked into it and saw some old records, small 45 rpm recordings of old boleros, hardly the subversive stuff that spies might carry around. "We listened to them, and we believe there are hidden messages in them," my grandfather said.

"Hidden messages?" I asked, stopping myself from breaking into laughter.

"That's how the terrorists communicate," he said.

"Grandpa, I think they're just love songs," I argued. "Really."

"Don't talk to me that way!" Grandpa raised his voice. My smile only angered him more. I wasn't taking this seriously. "This is what those people do! They smuggle messages to their contacts abroad, and those messages could be anywhere! They've found documents hidden behind frames in art work. They could arrest you at the airport. It's very important for you to tell me the truth. How do you know these people?"

I told him I knew Miguel in Los Angeles, that he was a Christian Democrat and not a Marxist as far as I knew, and that the package was just made up of gifts from his sister.

"Then what's this?"

Finally, Grandpa pulled out the incriminating evidence. It was the plate for the front cover of the book. It was a landscape of snowy Andean mountains with the title of the book and Miguel's name on it.

"We tried to open it," he said.

"What do you mean, 'open it'?"

"But we couldn't. There's hidden film in there. If they find it at the airport, you could be held prisoner, you could be tortured!"

At that point, I began to entertain some doubts. What if Miguel had set me up and conspired to use me, a teenager, to smuggle important documents that could be used in the underground struggle against Pinochet? Aside from the pleasant, even romantic memory of the film *Julia*, in which Jane Fonda smuggles papers for her lesbo-buddy for whom the movie's named, played by Vanessa Redgrave, I could barely see myself as a teenage smuggler and underground spy.

The Subject Was Roses—or Was It?

"So if you know this man," said my grandfather, his voice becoming more severe, "then that means you're a part of it."

"A part of what?"

"That you're agreeing to spy against your own country."

"What? Tata, please."

"I'm serious."

I was getting nervous. "Well, I don't know anything."

"No, don't say a word!" he said. "I'm taking you to meet my neighbor. He'll tell you the whole story."

I followed my grandfather, a tall man, through the neighborhood looking like a tiny, compliant vassal to the king. I kept my head down and felt humiliation, even fear. As soon as we entered his home, the neighbor, an older gentleman in his late fifties, short, stocky, graying, and looking ill and vulnerable, appeared defensive and astounded to see my grandfather arrive with this intimidated kid by his side.

"Tell him what you told me," my grandfather practically ordered him.

The man clammed up. He was suddenly watching his words. "Well, I just heard that . . . that woman's a Communist, that's all."

My grandfather looked bothered, even outraged. "Tell him the rest of the story, what you told me!" He raised his voice at the man. "He needs to know everything before he gets in trouble."

But the man didn't want trouble of his own. He looked frightened himself. "That's all I have to say," he said. "Please leave now."

My grandfather looked outraged. He turned, signaling to me to follow him. Outside, he cursed the man, "*Pero qué cobarde el viejo!* Now they're all scared!" he said. "After everything he told me about this woman! It's important for you to know who you're associating with. She's dangerous! You're being used."

We arrived home and then he made himself clear. "I won't let you take this package to the airport. It's for your own good. I don't want you in any danger. You must call this woman and ask her to pick it up in twenty-four hours or I'll burn it all up."

I found myself hesitating, then picking up the phone slowly, stalling, but finally calling Miguel's sister and leaving her a message to come pick up her package. I was leaving for the airport the next day, and the package sat there on the bed opposite the one I'd be sleeping in that night. My grandfather looked at it as if we would all be in danger that night, until that thing, like a piece of radioactive material, was removed from his house.

Before going to bed that night, Teresa brought a cup of tea to console me. "I listened to all the records, and they were just songs that remind me of the old days," she said wistfully, then hummed a few bars from "Sabor a Mí." I smiled at the incongruity of the moment. Ten years had passed since she married my grandfather in a rush, three months after my grandmother's death, provoking a scandal in our righteous, Catholic family. She had given birth to two children, Pablo and Paola, and they were, legally speaking, uncle and aunt to me, tiny things who were barely running around the backyard, making noise, jumping all over me with the type of unconditional love children can give. But they were growing up in Pinochet's world, a country steeped in fear.

"Things are better now thanks to Pinochet," said Teresa, as if wanting to convince me that my grandfather was right. "There are no food shortages, and I don't have to worry so much about feeding my family. Pinochet saved us from all that." She reached forward to tap me lightly on the shoulder. "I'm sure you didn't mean any harm."

"Of course I didn't!"

"I don't really think there are any hidden messages in those records, but then I have no idea how to play the records backward."

"Backward?"

"Yeah, to listen for the hidden messages."

"Where did you get that idea?"

"Well, that's what they do. You should have seen your grandfather trying to make that record player go backward to see what it could reveal. I had to slap his hand. 'You're going to break the record player!' I had to shout at him."

My grandfather's paranoia had marked us all. We were all imagining some strange Communist conspiracy landing on our doorstep hidden in 45 rpm records. More frightful was the actual reality that the secret police did exist, that it was active, that people had been arrested for a lot less than a suspicious package.

My body felt tense, racked with anxiety. I feared I wouldn't get any sleep that last night. When I finally began to nod off, I dreamed of an assault on our house, secret policemen surrounding it with machine guns, then taking me in as prisoner. I woke up and noticed I had left the light on. This wasn't a far-fetched scenario. My uncle—who still lived with my grandfather at the time—had been accused a few years before of buying stolen goods for a flea market stand where he sold all sorts of used items. The police didn't just arrest him. They used the neighbor's house in the middle of the night to slip in through the walls and climb up onto the roof. The first thing my grandfather, his wife, and children heard was the hard stomping of boots on the roof, breaking tiles, as they invaded from on high like jaguars assaulting from trees. My uncle and his children were woken up as the assault began, and they felt under attack. A squad of men jumped onto the patio, lined up the entire pajama-clad family against the wall to frisk them, even though the only one they were looking for was my uncle. The point was made—they were the people in power, and they must show off their authority. My uncle was taken into custody, where electric rods were applied to his genitals. They wanted him to talk about his contacts. He wouldn't so they continued to torture him for days. That was for a common alleged theft.

With all that in mind, I knew my grandfather was not acting entirely out of paranoia in his dealings with my alleged terrorist plot. He considered himself a Pinochet supporter, but he wasn't naive about what the general's ruthless police could do. Even a simple accusation of theft could be accompanied by dramatic displays of authority, ending in arrest and interrogation techniques that included torture. My uncle was released and not tried for anything. He was innocent, but there was no doubting the police's resolve to get their way.

I feared arrest, which wasn't as preposterous as I first must have thought. My grandfather's suspicions were not at all out of sync with the reality of their lives under Pinochet. Still, even though I understood my grandfather's fear, I resented him for creating this scene to begin with, and for supporting the dictatorship in spite of what he knew about it. I was determined not to have anything more to do with him, the Pinochet regime, or the entire country of Chile. I was determined more than ever to become a U.S. citizen and, better yet, a white American, whiter in fact than most Americans, seeking an identity I would wear snugly for years. It didn't fit, but I was determined to stifle and overcome memory. I suffered from the youthful hubris of believing one could possibly do that.

The next day, I packed quickly, and in spite of my fears, in an act of defiance, I threw the suspicious package into my suitcase and left it there. I stared at it. I was going to be strong like Lillian Hellman in *Julia*. I was going to defy my grandfather and to condemn Pinochet and his pack of wolves who invaded homes and took in prisoners. And even if I had been taking secret papers to the Underground, I would have done so gladly. I was going to be the courageous, teenage, sissy spy. Except maybe not. I thought twice. Then I split my decision in what can now only be called a Clintonian compromise such as don't ask, don't tell, the type of thing that doesn't please anyone. I kept the records in my suitcase but threw out the artwork. I figured the plate was the more suspicious item since it would be used on a book that was likely to be anti-Pinochet. I rationalized my cowardice, and I reasoned I was at least halfway heroic. I hid the records in my suitcase. How much courage did it take to smuggle old records out of the country? I ask myself that today, but at the time, it seemed it was the best I could do.

I even announced it to Teresa. "I'm taking the records, but I'm leaving the artwork."

She looked befuddled. "Then maybe I just won't tell your grandpa what you did until after your plane takes off," she said.

So that's where it stood. My grandfather was already upset at me anyway for the alleged company I kept. He refused to go to the airport to bid me farewell, and he would later tell people I had given in to the Marxist temptation. Of course, back in Los Angeles, Miguel wouldn't speak to me again because I failed to bring him the artwork—I'd given in to the Pinochet temptation. I called Miguel up repeatedly to apologize, but he only took my call once to tell me I was a coward. Don't ask, don't tell. My policy preceded Clinton's, and I could have warned the future president that everyone would be upset and unforgiving.

I didn't return to Chile until it was time to bring my mother's ashes for a ceremony with my family in 2003. My grandfather had died by then. He never saw me again, nor I him. I see pictures of him in which he aged gradually, surrounded by this new family of children that Teresa created around him. She renovated his life and gave him a renewed purpose in life, but I am a link to the past, to that life we led in the late 1960s when we were still a family: my grandmother, the expert cook; my mother, the businesswoman who set up our magazine stand; and my uncle, the lively teenager and loyal son, playing his electric guitar and insisting on buying mod clothes. That family was gone, that way of life shattered by politics on the one hand and by the march of time and death. My so-called betrayal was, in fact, political. I hadn't embraced the Marxist underground after all, just the "bourgeois" temptation of wanting democracy to mean something—fair elections and civil liberties, at the very least. I associated Grandfather with the frightful era of torture that had managed to turn him into a truly frightened and frightening man. I rejected Pinochet, but in the same breadth I cut off my grandfather as if they'd been one and the same. In later years, through letters and phone calls, Teresa would tell me my grandfather still thought of me. Yet, I never acknowledged it. He's the only person I ever systematically turned against, to the point of successfully avoiding him for nearly twenty years before his death. I don't like the feeling still. If I'd been stronger, I would have learned to say no, to confront yet manage to understand. That's a lot to ask of a teenager, but I continue to think I should have known better still. That's regret for you. It somehow makes you think that the wisdom of an older age could have been transferred to that time and place when partisan passions ran high. If my grandfather still thought of me, as his widow now says, then that's one small comfort. I managed to remain in his memory, and he in mine. Today Chileans have seemingly moved on. They haven't forgotten the past, but the maturity of their current political leadership suggests there's more forgiveness in the air than rancor. I'd like to believe I have learned some wisdom since then as well, and that I learned to forgive myself, the second person I was hardest on, the first being my grandfather, who, I hope, died with a sense of forgiveness toward me. I never heard from Teresa or his children whether his political passions lessened, or whether he would have been ready to lay down the partisanship he carried with him like a security blanket. It's easier to imagine him forgiving me now, but the dictator left behind a dark legacy of sins himself and often inspired more defiance than regret among his followers.

María sneaks into Charles Jaffee's house to hold the Oscar for *Annie Hall* in 1978

Above: The author at UCLA, spring 1984 (photo by Eugene)

Left: The author as ASU professor, 1997

Above: The immigrants land in Washington, D.C., on a windy day, 1971. *From left*: Aunt Nelly, María, the author, and Rosa

Right: The author as high school student with rock 'n' roll hairdo, 1977 (photo by Eugene)

The marriage of Teresa and Tata (seen here with their children, Paola and Pablo, in 1980) provokes a scandal

The author wearing fake Versace outside Il Duomo, Milan, Italy, 1982

The author in gondolier shirt in Venice, 1982

Mother and son in Vienna, 1983

María poses with her citizenship certificate outside Dorothy Chandler Pavilion in Los Angeles, 1983

María as a nanny in North Hollywood, 1997

5

Italian Holiday

My mother may have embodied Maria von Trapp, the caretaker
nanny, as a role model, but she eventually also evolved into one
of Tennessee Williams's lovable neurotics—Alma Winemiller would do,
the undefiled woman in the first half of *Summer and Smoke.* Yet, my
mother never became the town's libidinously inclined wallflower of the
second half of the play/film, as played by Geraldine Page. That honor
would have to pass down to me. From a silent, repressed sexual entity, uncomfortable in my body, clothed to cover up every bit of skin except hands
and face, I became sexually active—for a while anyway. Desire overpow-
ered my body in specific periods of time, then retreated into hibernation.
The pattern persists today. Periods of isolation followed by outbursts of in-
discretion. It's the Winemiller syndrome.

But *Summer and Smoke* won't do as an analogy any longer. My actual
fall from grace as the male spinster boy virgin in Italy resembles more
closely *Summer Time,* starring Katharine Hepburn as a middle-aged
woman who finds romance and physical intimacy in the arms of Rosanno
Brazzi. I watched the film in our dorm-sized apartment off Sunset Boulevard early in the late 1970s as a late show one lonesome Saturday night. I
was fourteen, and Mother had seen it in Santiago in the late 1950s and
watched it again several times on TV. Italy as the place one goes to get laid
is, of course, flattering to Italians, assuming they care about so many tourists defiling their streets and expecting sexual favors and romance and all
other demanding expectations of affection-deprived Americans. Italians

may be romantic, but they're not to be used for our purposes, unless they wish to be, and some of them do, so God bless the willing.

Mother went to Italy first in 1980 on a Europass tour but never spoke of getting laid. She missed a deadly terrorist bomb in Bologna by a couple of days, and that was the most excitement she got out of the trip as far as I knew. When I announced that I was going to Padua, Italy, through the education abroad program, she was overjoyed for me, and for herself. Mother followed me there in 1983 to visit me, and we managed to bicker like cantankerous old ladies. Who got laid first and who overcame some powerful hang-ups is not for me to say here. I don't know everything about Mother's private life. She was never one to tell. All I know is that the same syndrome of Catholic virgin that Mother struggled with in her youth was inherited by her son, a virginal, feminized, puny, and asexual young man who arrived in Italy sensing he needed to let go of the past.

I did let go, not for the obvious reasons of quick conquest, but because, in the lesson of Hollywood romances, I learned something about myself that went beyond sex. Yes, there was sex, and there was also romance. The soundtrack played out in the background; the gondolas sailed. Italy, the wine, the pasta, the men—it worked as it was meant to. It also brought me into life and initiated me to the spontaneity of love and sex, which is what I remember best about this period of life. The poet Pablo Neruda titled his memoirs *I Confess That I Have Lived.* The confession also assumes there's a way to exist without living. I have gone through periods of great danger doing precisely that, of repressing my feelings and my instincts and therefore shying away from living. This period is not one of them.

I discovered creative writing at UCLA, and even though my only experiences in life up until that point seemed to be about hiding from reality, at least I had something perversely real to write about: sexual repression. All my early efforts, however, were disconnected from that reality. I was too self-conscious to delve into my specific fears about sex and other aberrations. I wrote fantasy scenarios, melodrama, detective stories, sci-fi, things that I eventually kept away from people but retained in my files as reminders, the way parents keep baby shoes. After writing on my own for so long, I finally sought to enroll in a fiction class, but all the classes were full. There was an opening in a playwriting class, however, and the theater professor, Carol Sorgenfrei, welcomed me into it. I was theatrical at least. Scratch the surface of the quiet boy virgin, and you'd find the makings of a neurasthenic Tennessee Williams heroine struggling to break free. I do sense a female quality about me, a sense of polite reticence worthy of Alma Winemiller. Williams wrote successfully about boozy, sexually repressed, middle-aged women falling apart, but as a teenager, I felt he was writing about me. I was a perfect fit for a playwriting class. I had aspired to be an actor, and while I had given up on the idea, the thought of writing for the live theater seemed to fulfill a theatrical yearning.

I started writing about Latino immigrants. Nobody else seemed to be doing it at the time. One of my first efforts, as an exercise, was about an INS officer who gets seduced by an illegal alien/femme fatale who then takes off with his money. Then, my first full-length play, *Flute of the Andes*, depicted a Peruvian family in Los Angeles with lots of kids, too many for modern staging capacity. Nonetheless that play allowed me an opportunity to write about a warm, loving family the likes of which I'd never really experienced in the United States. Some vague memories of my grandmother donning an apron and cooking French cuisine like an expert rubbed off on this play, but as an idyll, it blurred like an imperfectly captured memory.

I was floundering as a student, a creative writer, and a human being. It seemed perfectly reasonable to attend an education abroad program far away from home. I imagined myself as one of those writers, scribbling away on a journal in a café in Italy, which is exactly what I would do for almost a year. My life became literary even before I could accomplish anything as a writer. I believed at least in the posturing of writing. It sustained a fantasy life I needed. I was turning twenty; I was an unattractive, hairy virgin. My mother and my high school best friend, Eugene, were suggesting my self-image was to blame for how I felt, that I actually wasn't that ugly, or some such condolences. Sex was a remote possibility, and if I had failed to get laid on Santa Monica Boulevard, or Hollywood and Vine, I had probably missed the boat altogether. I believed I was headed for a life of celibacy. Reading Dante in the original didn't help. His chaste love for Beatrice, the ideal woman he never touched, struck me as an act of masochism. At least he was married to somebody else. I was more afraid of Mann's *Death in Venice*, a fateful tale of obsession and death. My Santos obsession had been an early warning that I was developing an extreme psychology. A major getaway trip seemed like the answer, and the need to write was another. I started short stories, novels, a couple of plays, and, most importantly, a journal that I've kept to this day.

"It's a wonderful thing that you have all these opportunities," said my mother. "At your age, I had dropped out of school and began working at a vitamin factory in Santiago. Americans invest in young people, in education in particular. I hope you're grateful for all these things."

I was grateful, but I was also surrounded by young people who were learning that the United States was "imperialist" and racist. When my mother spoke of the great advantages of living in this country, I felt myself being pulled in various directions. I trusted my mother's instinct to be grateful toward our adopted country, but anti-Americanism was the cool disposition at a public university like UCLA, especially after the voters elected Ronald Reagan, who labeled the Soviet Union "the evil empire." In my first talk with an American student at an orientation meeting, he said that he was looking forward to meeting the Italian people who were being occupied by American forces.

"I'm glad to have immigrated to the United States," I said, but he looked at me with suspicion. He'd been brought up in an American suburb. He had never been abroad before, but he had taken a political science course with a Marxist professor at UCLA. He was quick to label me conservative. He would do so the rest of my stay in Italy. I would continue to project an uncool disposition because I was considered too much of a grateful immigrant.

The overnight train from Paris stopped in Padua on its way to nearby Venice. It unloaded a group of us that had flown to the French capital with other students bound for different cities in France. We had separated from them and taken a train to Italy. We congregated in our American dorm located in a quiet cul de sac close to the train station and met the other students who had arrived earlier.

I discovered I was not the only Guillermo in the program. In the United States, even in Los Angeles, I had been used to the fact that my name—William in translation—still proved to be unusual, even "exotic" wherever I went. I was living closer to West than East L.A., so I wasn't living in a "Hispanic" area. My classmates and my professors knew me as William; my mother knew me as "Willy," which I had tried to ban to no avail. The Other Guillermo, as I began to refer to him, was a Mexican

American young man. He was handsome, outgoing, popular, and, of course, excessive. He considered himself bisexual and found himself partying on down in the daytime anywhere with a couple of beers, and sometimes drugs, with boys and girls, sometimes at the same time. He was a chick magnet. He was the opposite of whatever it is that I was. I could have blamed my solitude on being too Hispanic, or too queer, or too shy, or too unattractive, or everything else that suited my need to blame anything other than my choices. In Italy, the Other Guillermo emerged on the first day to shake my hand and confront me with some other self I might have been in some other life. The Other Guillermo was the living refutation that attitude mattered more than ethnicity, hang-ups, or teenage depression, for that matter. I had no valid excuses. White people, Italians, Americans, Latinos and non-Latinos, men and women—he seemed to draw them all as I watched in amused silence from a distance. But not for long. The Other Guillermo felt compassion, maybe even attraction, toward me. He would never admit it. There was no cachet in admitting any attraction for the uncool. I wore clothes that were too unfashionable for an older man to wear, which is why Mr. Galanos had discarded them. I clearly struck the Other Guillermo as pathetic, or at least worthy of pity. On the second night in Italy, I heard of a gathering up in his room, and I went up, uninvited, to check things out. The Other Guillermo was drinking with his buddies, both male and female, all laid out on the bed. He drew me to him and locked lips with me and everybody there laughed. It was essentially my first male-to-male kiss. But later, when I mentioned it, he didn't remember it. He was probably drunk or high. The next night he went out running in the streets of Padua after consuming drugs, and he broke his ankle while jumping from a bridge over a river bed. He was in the hospital for a couple of days. I went to visit him. I was alone with him for once, not counting Italian patients in other beds. Alone in this case meant that the other American and Italian friends had left, and I had him to myself. He looked vulnerable for once, laid out on the bed, broken. The hospital struck me as sparse, a large room with a dozen beds in it, as if in a military camp.

"How do you say 'ankle' in Spanish?" he asked.

I had to think. I had been learning Italian. When I started to think in Spanish, the two languages would cancel each other out, and I would draw a blank. He was writing a letter to his Mexican mother. "Ah, *tobillo*," I finally said.

"With a long *b* or a short one?"

"Long, I'm pretty sure."

"Would you look over my letter and see if I made any mistakes? Sometimes, my Spanish, you know . . ."

"Oh, I know how it is," I said.

"My mother only speaks Spanish. She's an immigrant and works as a maid."

"Oh, well, good," I said. I hadn't expected him to reveal his background either. That was something I never talked about. In college I didn't make up the type of stories I had told in the D.C. area, but I didn't speak about my family at all. My family was probably a bigger secret than my sexuality. I looked over his letter and didn't find any particularly gross mistakes. He disguised his own activities, telling his mother he had been running and fallen, nothing about running in the middle of the night after a bacchanalian episode.

"If you can look over my Spanish grammar now and then, I'd appreciate it," he added.

"Oh, of course."

"Good, then we'll help each other out."

The Other Guillermo took me under his wing and tried to change everything about me. "You dress like an old man," he told me one day, and I hadn't even told him that I wore hand-me-downs from Galanos. He started taking me to fashionable thrift shops, which in Italy often featured designer clothes at discounted rates. Italy was the capital of fashion. Even in a small city like Padua, the various Italian designers had their outlets, Armani and Versace particularly, among many others. Walking to school, the Other Guillermo would stop and announce, "Fashion break!" The big names in fashion were priced beyond my ability, but nonetheless, they gave us ideas on how to combine colors and accessories, and we could then find them at cheaper stores minus the labels.

He picked out various shirts and pants for me to try on. The dollar exchange rate was reasonably favorable, and I broke down under the Other Guillermo's pressure. I bought myself new shirts, shoes, jackets, and pants. The weather was mildly cool and pleasant. The Other Guillermo didn't notice my preference for long sleeve shirts because there was no need to buy summer weather clothing in September. We were preparing for a cold winter, and I got away with the typically perverse choice of hiding beneath layers of garments. But nonetheless, these clothes were fashionable and elegant. The Other Guillermo moussed up my hair, stashed my old man's slacks away in the closet, and, as his foot healed, took me to Milan for our first taste of a gay nightclub in Europe.

The Other Guillermo, for all his excess, his booze and drugs, and womanizing (and man-izing, too, for that matter), seemed to me a thoroughly compassionate being. He had a sense of inclusiveness, even mercy and empathy. He didn't know much about me, but he saw in me something bothersome, the very face of solitude and pain. I didn't have to say much. He knew what to do, and he accomplished it quickly within a few weeks of my arrival in Italy. Like Eugene in high school, and Valerie back in UCLA, the Other Guillermo realized that he was saving a life somehow. Like Blanche Du Bois, I've depended on the kindness of these "strangers" who became my friends, and who seemed to guide me in a direction that was the opposite of the quagmire I constantly built for myself. I inspired something in these people to come to my rescue.

In Milan, I accomplished my first pickup of a man and my first heartbreak in the span of twenty-four hours. The Other Guillermo had approved my outfit, a nightclub shirt with a solid color, pearly white; he bid me to polish my shoes into a sparkling dark black. Walking in new shoes, hiding behind designer clothes, I was ready to enter a nightclub for the first time in Italy's main fashion city. The Other Guillermo enjoyed his thick sunglasses and strutted through the streets across from Milan's gothic cathedral, Il Duomo, as if he were a model. Tall, lean, and statuesque, he prided himself on his style. I was his dim, diminutive copycat, but I preferred to think of myself as his apprentice. I clearly did not feel like his equal, but I was learning.

The first half of the nightclub proved to be merely quaint, disappointingly so. Older men danced to slow boleros (or the Italian equivalent). One led; the other followed. It was a scene from the 1940s. My grandfather would have felt comfortable with this scene, had it not been for the same-sex dancing. We didn't fit in.

The Other Guillermo looked around and noticed something happening through an opening in the building, looking like a small tunnel.

"There's another dance floor!" he announced excitedly.

We discovered there was a second half to the nightclub. Loud, rambunctious, with a dizzying array of disco lights flickering, this more happening section of the club lured us in, and that's where our night really began. We danced to "Gloria" in the original Italian version (Americans would dance to the song in Laura Brannigan's English-language version). We danced to synthetic Euro pop hits, and the imported American ones, and whatever else worked. Italian men surrounded us, the two Guillermos on the dance floor in a sea of handsome people.

The Other Guillermo and I took a breather. He bought me a beer. Not my first one, but nonetheless my first nightclub drink. It went to my head, this one single beer. Before I knew it, I was making out with an Italian policeman. At least he claimed to be a cop. He was short with a dark moustache, a bit stocky, but attractive, and was dressed in civilian clothes, basic dark slacks and white shirt. He took me outside the nightclub toward an unlit area and manhandled me beneath a tree. He kissed my neck, then my lips, and I for the first time felt a sensation, a weird exhilaration. It was a make-out session, a first ever for me. Back in high school, I had missed out on this, no necking in the Hollywood Hills inside a car overlooking the city. I made up for that fast. I was suffocating under this much delight, stirring my body and soul. I stopped the policeman. I tried to make conversation. The policeman had to think about what he said carefully. He insisted that he couldn't say much about his work, that Italy had suffered a couple of years of terrorist attacks, and that he worked in an anti-terrorist unit, and that's all he could say. I agreed.

Enough talking. We made out some more. I gave him my number and address in Padua, and all my basic statistics, before we said goodbye.

I walked on air on our way back to the hotel. The Other Guillermo kept telling me to calm down. I was acting like a giddy little girl, he told me. First lesson to learn is . . . not to fall in love after one make-out session. I was simply enamored of the feeling of touch, intimacy, heat generated by closeness, and the sensation of feeling wanted. The Other Guillermo had been sexually active since his teens. Early teens. He didn't think my behavior was amusing. It harked back to earlier times for him. He was cool and detached about such things as love. He took me to the hotel, and we slept soundly next to one another, but each to his own side of the bed. By then, I didn't care if he ignored me. I had found affection—even if through a temporary flirtation—all on my own.

The next day, after walking through the streets of Milan and trying on expensive clothes we couldn't afford, we went back to the same nightclub.

In retrospect, this was a bad idea. Another nightclub would have been more appropriate, if only to explore the nightlife in different ways. We didn't know another club, and that was our choice, to repeat ourselves. The policeman was back, and I enthusiastically went up to him and kissed him on the lips, and then told him how much I'd enjoyed the previous night. But this time, he pulled back. He seemed scared or intimidated by this teenage-looking virginal creature in his arms expressing an overflowing sense of joy. He took a sip of his drink, looked pensive for a second, and then, finally, let it out:

"I have a job where I have to be discreet," he said. "I can't be involved with anyone."

He walked away, lost in the crowd. I was so devastated I found myself walking out of the nightclub and into the streets of Milan. I walked slowly back to the hotel without even noticing the people or my surroundings. Whoever populates and threatens the streets of Milan past midnight blurred as a forgettable entity around me—I didn't notice it at all. I was stunned by this rejection and thought it was because of me. I had done something wrong. I wasn't good enough. The feeling returned; I'm a fool thinking I can suddenly attract anyone just because I have a new haircut and a change of clothes. When I got to the hotel, I threw myself on the bed and cried. An hour or so later, the Other Guillermo walked in, throwing down his jacket on me and wanting to punish me.

"Where the hell have you been? I was worried to death about you! I couldn't find you. Why did you do that? Explain yourself, mister."

I did explain to him in details with tears in my eyes and a childish pout at that.

"Well, you should have found me and told me you were leaving. I would have come with you. You shouldn't be walking the streets of Milan by yourself! You idiot, don't ever do that to me again!"

I promised I wouldn't. The Other Guillermo lay down next to me and bid me to sleep, which I did. His presence was of great comfort, but I felt awkward. I had shown a surprisingly childish side to him. From then on, the Other Guillermo kept an eye on me. I resented the feeling of vulnerability, something I had rarely shown anyone, caught up in my own thoughts and too guarded to show any emotions. It was an arduous step for me, to exhibit something other than caution and impenetrability. A few weeks later, I accompanied the Other Guillermo again to Milan. At the back of my mind, I entertained the thought that I would use this venture and new friendship to forget Santos. On that night with the Italian policeman, I felt justified and freed of youthful obsessions altogether. On the second night, with the policeman's rejection, I found myself right back in a childish state of mind, that I had failed, that I wasn't good enough. The Other G. got a chance to see all this, but I didn't explain to him why this happened. I never revealed to him my Santos obsession.

I took my studies seriously and integrated the weekend forays into nightclubs, momentous though they might have seemed at first, into a more balanced life. I had never made much room for socializing, and I looked forward to the weekends without becoming entirely devoted to them. I became an avid reader of Boccaccio's *The Decameron*, a series of bawdy tales that eventually inspired Chaucer's *Canterbury Tales*. Pasolini's film based on the *Tales* portrays Chaucer pillaging ideas, or even whole passages, from the manuscript of *The Decameron*. The story about the nuns who collectively screw the gardener and start a convent of their bastard children struck me as especially invigorating and funny. It was the right mood for what I was experiencing that year. I had left Kate Hepburn behind. I wasn't a middle-aged spinster. I was a twenty-year-old man. I had to constantly remind myself of that. The Other Guillermo even told me I looked good in my new clothes, that I even looked "handsome." It was the closest thing to a genuine compliment he gave me since he always seemed cool, and indifference was supposed to be part of his persona. He didn't have to compliment me. Being allowed into his company was already a compliment. Except that I awakened in him a fraternal instinct. He felt the need to flatter me, to make me feel wanted. There was no reason why he and I couldn't have been lovers, except that the Other Guillermo preferred to keep his feelings toward me at a familial level, intimate but chaste. Any contact between us would have been incestuous. Besides, he had other people to pursue. He had gotten himself an Italian girlfriend, a hairdresser in her early thirties, and I was the kid brother who followed him around. I knew that on weekends he would go out to gay bars and make out with men. It was our little secret. His Italian girlfriend was simply in love and seemed clueless to his nature. I was jealous of his, shall we say, versatility and flexibility with genders, but I felt lucky enough to have a friend and would never have called him on it.

Italian Holiday

I struck out on my own. I took the train to Bologna with another student who claimed that city offered the liveliest gay scene in Italy. We went dancing in one of the city's intimate, cavernous, little nightclubs. Young Italian men in designer clothes with white boy rhythms made up the scene, as they tried to jerk themselves up into a dance. Bologna was also the main hub of the Italian Communist Party. The Cold War raged on, with our NATO allies often having to weather the blunt criticism of local leftist or pacifist parties. Reagan was called a warmonger. It's never been easy to be an American abroad, but with this president sounding particularly hawkish, one had to be careful not to enrage some European sensibilities by speaking with a pro-American slant. A detached indifference seemed to work here as well, and we were young. One could get away with sounding un-opinionated, but I tended to listen, make notes, and formulate ideas in my mind. I came from a country torn by the Cold War, in which a dictator promised to make Chileans safe from communism. I was anti-fascist, but clearly not a Marxist either. I didn't care for the pacifist stand in Europe. If we didn't arm ourselves, perhaps they would disarm—that was the delusional belief among some of the pacifists. Still, most Italians proved to be surprisingly friendly to Americans, even when they considered themselves Leftists. Italian students sought us out. We received guests at the dorm, and while some of them were men trying to pick up on the young women, others genuinely wanted to talk about everything, including politics. They may have disliked Reagan, but that was the cool, official thing to do. Peer pressure dictated it. Politically, they didn't want to join the Warsaw Pact nations. At election time, in the privacy of a booth, peer pressure dissipated. Italians chose again and again to be part of the West, much to the chagrin of the Left. I believe our group of students also embodied accessibility and open-mindedness they didn't find in other foreign students. Across from our dorm, Chinese students congregated among themselves in their own buildings. The Italians told us they couldn't get any ideas or opinions out of them. They were afraid to speak about anything. They were in Italy to study safe, nonpolitical subject matter such as engineering. They had to speak enough Italian to use it in class, but if they ever used their conversational skills to utter a full sentence, the Italians didn't hear it. In contrast, the hospitality room in our dorm was hopping with American kids drinking and smoking on a Saturday night and often arguing. Our opinions were not monolithic. We had Christian boys and rowdy frat types and girls without inhibitions and others who were shyer and demure, and the Other Guillermo and I also represented an immigrant component among the students that impressed Italians altogether. They loved our dorm, and one of them ended up meeting a future wife there. It took me a while to contribute my own share of pairing up, but I did.

Which all goes to say that, in Bologna that night, I picked up an Italian Communist man who had strong, firm beliefs about the end of American hegemony in Italy and who believed that Italians could make communism work without the Soviet Union in a softer, more open version of that doctrine. He was deluded, I believe, but nonetheless, he was a relatively handsome man. And so was his lover. He was fair-skinned, his lover dark. A complex relationship of threesomes would begin that night. Their names were Francesco, light-skinned, and Stefano, a darker, swarthier, Mediterranean type.

At the club, they confused me for Asian because my friend was half-Filipino, half-Japanese, so the first thing Francesco asked me was "Where are you boys from? China?"

"Not China," I said. "Chile originally. But we're both now from California, USA."

"Ah, so you're American!" His face lit up in wonderment, but then again, Francesco's face would always light up in the same manner, helping Stefano's face spark in turn as a chain effect of amazement. There was something naturally gregarious about them, and they fed off each other's gaiety. "Well, you're exotic looking, whatever you are," Francesco added. *Exotic* was always the code word when you looked different, and I had no problem playing the exotic card. My friend from California left us alone. He had his own flirtations to contend with that night.

"I'm Francesco; this is Stefano, my lover. We've been together for almost ten years," he added.

"Oh, wonderful," I said, not quite sure how to react. Stefano left to get us drinks, and Francesco kissed me on the cheek. "*Che bello!* How beautiful you are!"

I didn't ask the obvious. Would Stefano be jealous? Why was he doing this in public? Stefano returned with beer bottles, and Francesco quickly moved in to corner me up against the wall to kiss me. Stefano looked on in amusement. It was one of those relationships, I gathered. No explanations were needed. The rules were understood. They were casual about themselves, about issues, about their lives. "Oh, yes," Francesco revealed after a couple of kisses. "Stefano and I belong to the Italian Communist Party. We're both very active in it."

I wasn't scared or intimidated. Italian politics mirrored the political landscape of Chile. I had family members who'd once been Socialists, as well as Communists, right-wing Nationalists, and Christian Democrats. The same range of parties functioned in both countries, and Pinochet was the new Mussolini, as far as Italians were concerned. Italians were much more aware of Chilean politics, having received a good share of exiles after the military coup of 1973. I didn't have to explain a thing, as I usually did to my American friends, if they cared at all about Chile. Being a Communist in Italy clearly had a different connotation in Italy than it did in the United States. One could not afford to play the American naïveté. When in Bologna, you do the bolognesi.

The first night, only Francesco made out with me at the club, but when I went back the following weekend to spend more time with him, his lover climbed into bed with us. I was, therefore, initiated into sexuality by not one but two Italian Communists. I kept the politics to myself, especially the pro-market, pro-individualist politics I had learned from Ayn Rand's essays and novels. I betrayed the rugged individualism of capitalist doctrine to pure lust. I had to. I was barely into my twenties, but late in life by American standards to be losing one's virginity. I wasn't entirely doctrinaire anyway. I was registered as a Democrat, but I read Ayn Rand as if to annoy my leftist friends. Somebody had to. My mother's pro-American attitude was also part of my thinking. There was no point in belonging to one group anyway. I had no qualms about sleeping with two Italians at the same time.

What were these two? What could one call them? They weren't my "boyfriends," and they were lovers only to one another. They had lived together in a small apartment in downtown Bologna for a decade now. Stefano had a teenage son from a former marriage who came to visit in the afternoons after his father completed his share of ravaging me, and then we would all go to the movies to watch some dubbed American film such as *An Officer and a Gentleman.* His teenage son was quite well aware of his father's relationship to Francesco, but I am not clear if he understood my relationship to both of his daddies.

I visited these two men throughout the winter of 1982. And each time, a slight variation of coupling took place. The two of them would serve me a lavish, homemade meal in their tiny apartment where the bedroom and the kitchen were practically attached and divided only by a thin wall. The meal would threaten to make me sleepy, but with two eager lovers, there was no time to rest. Francesco would start on me first; then Stefano would climb into bed and take turns.

"*Sei bello!*" was the only thing Stefano would repeatedly say in bed. "You are beautiful." That's clearly not something I'd heard anyone say to me, let alone in bed. I had to believe it. I felt these men made love to me in spite of what I looked like, or what I thought I looked like. If they were blind, that was their problem. I thought myself lucky that they saw only what they wanted to see. I continued to close my eyes during copulation because I didn't want to see any aspect of my body naked. It was the one way someone with my disorder could cope with a situation I hadn't been in before, the recipient of sex, anybody's sex, and enjoy it in spite of the aversion I felt toward my body.

Needless to say, I managed to shock some of my colleagues back in the American dorm in Padua. Even the Other Guillermo expressed surprise, even delight.

"I didn't think you had it in you," he said when I told him the entire story of how these two Italian men took turns in bed with me. "Go for it" was the Other Guillermo's refrain toward just about everything.

I went for it. I went back to Bologna for more. During the next school year—and yes, there was school, there was studying to be done, and exams to take—I would take time out to take a train down to Bologna and spend the weekend with my two friends. I couldn't call them lovers. I had to think of them as the men who initiated me into sexuality, and who thought of me as their willing sex slave.

Gradually, I learned about their beliefs, and their lifestyle, and I seemed to embrace an aspect of their lives I would otherwise have never understood. They were so-called Communists, but they were primarily Italian, and their working-class background made them seem like my Chilean relatives. They lived in modest circumstances. Time has passed, and memory eludes me as to their profession. Stefano complained about the repetitive nature of his work, which made me surmise he worked at an assembly line, and Francesco mentioned his own work at another factory. The most joyous part of their nature was their addiction to television and films, and here I was totally at home with them. Their politics were completely Italian—that is, not addicted to absolutes and thoroughly pragmatic. *The Fountainhead*, based on the Ayn Rand novel, played on television, and they were overjoyed. They loved the hero Howard Roark's rebellious nature, and they likened it to the struggle against capitalism. I didn't break their hearts by telling them Ayn Rand was a rabid pro-capitalist, anti-communist stalwart, the most fanatical advocate of laissez-faire economics on the American scene. I had to remain a quiet presence, slowly absorbing the lessons of their mutual affection for me, even enjoying the irony of my presence in their lives. I needed their affection, and their sex, and I kept our odd weekend friendship going until I left for the United States. I never got a sense that I was disturbing their relationship or threatening it. Stefano once stopped in the middle of our lovemaking and seemed preoccupied. Francesco had left to go pay a visit to a friend, leaving us alone. I asked if everything was going well between them. I feared I was becoming the cause of their problems, if any.

"Oh, Francesco is just a romantic," he said.

"What do you mean?"

"He falls in love all the time, and he may be falling in love with you."

"Oh, so is that a problem? Should I go?"

"No, no, *non si preoccupare.* I told him you're a young man in transit. You'll leave soon and go back to the United States or maybe even back to Chile. It'll be sad to see you go. You've brought so much love to our home, but we have to enjoy the moment, and let that be it. We take the blessings of life, and then let them go."

"That's sad," I said. "I hope I didn't . . ."

"You didn't do anything. We chose this. We chose to make love to you, and we are responsible for our actions. So no guilt; we're not Catholics."

But there were other things going on to make Francesco melancholy that day.

A woman acquaintance was courting Stefano. That is, she wanted a child and had offered him the opportunity to impregnate her. Francesco had expressed at least some envy or unease about Stefano's ability to attract women, and also about the fact that Stefano was already a father. Now that another woman had approached him to father one more child, Francesco had begun to feel possessive.

"I haven't made up my mind about whether I want another child," Stefano said, "but Francesco should approve, or at least be supportive. We live in a dangerous world, and there's no point holding back. Only three years have gone by since *la strage* . . ."

"*La strage?*" I asked. "What do you . . . ?"

He meant the worst act of terrorism in recent Italian history. A bomb exploded inside the central train station in Bologna on August 2, 1980, killing eighty-five people, wounding hundreds of others. My mother was riding on a train bound for Florence that same summer and had mentioned her closeness to Bologna on that day. Right-wing, neo-fascist extremists claimed credit for the attack, in retribution for Bologna being a main hub of the Italian Communist Party. The entire city, Stefano and Francesco included, had gathered in Piazza Maggiore to mourn the loss of life. Since then, August 2 was preserved as a memorial to all victims of terrorism.

At the train station that night, I noticed for once the monument to the victims that had been incorporated in the waiting room of the rebuilt new structure. At first I thought the architect had designed a symbolic ray of lightning parting the wall of the station, but later I discovered it wasn't meant as symbolism. That was an actual crack left from the incident that was maintained as a reminder. The clock was permanently stopped at 10:25 a.m., the time that the incident occurred.

"We're always subject to fascist attack," he said that day. "We need to live for today."

I never stuck around long enough to find out if he chose to have a second child. He had been correct about me—I was in transit.

Back in Padua, the Other Guillermo kept me busy with "fashion breaks," which came to absorb time and expendable income. Every day, I brought home new attire. Boots one day, to go with a new sweater, and a bar shirt to be worn to Cosmopolitan, the only gay nightclub on the outskirts of the city, between Venice and Padua.

"We're impressed already," said my roommate at the time, an Italian American young man from California, who thought I was becoming superficial, having arrived in Italy as well read but clueless about frivolous things such as fashion. He made it clear he didn't like the new me. "You lost your virginity to two Italian Communists; congratulations. Now you need to study."

I did study. I did my homework and kept up with everyday chores, but the winter felt long, and the need to find moments of pure diversion continued to claim time. The Other Guillermo was never satisfied with only studying. The need to improvise a party claimed his life at times, and there was no stopping him as he dragged me along.

He and I took a bus that left us in a small town where the only gay nightclub had been allowed to open up at the time. At least it allowed for men from various parts of the Veneto province to gather in this one hot-spot of nightlife in the middle of nowhere. The buses stopped at midnight, and we were forced to hitch a ride from a willing Italian gentleman with a car, most likely someone the Other Guillermo skillfully flirted with.

I seemed unable to "pick up" strangers in that club until I met a middle-aged man who owned a furniture company. He gave me his number, and a few days later I was receiving a gentleman caller up at the dorm. He'd take me out to dinner and talk about his wife—his soon-to-be ex-wife. He had come out recently at forty and had made arrangements with her to keep living together until the children grew up. I had no qualms about seeing him, although I considered him too old for me. But there was something inherently interesting about a man who could speak about culture, art, politics, and books. Moreover, he looked like Rosanno Brazzi, the middle-aged suitor Kate Hepburn picks up in *Summer Time*. I was supposed to have made a break with the spinster drama. I had to start thinking of myself as a young man. But still I kept seeing him for the Rosanno Brazzi resemblance alone. I enjoyed his attention, and his kisses seemed needy and appreciative of me, for someone who'd been denied same-sex affection his entire life. He decided, finally, that he wanted to fly off to Rio with me, all expenses paid. I'd come as his younger companion. Before I could gesticulate like a grateful boy toy, my sense of geography spelled out the obvious: Rio meant beaches.

"I just don't go to the beach," I told him rather bluntly without explaining the reasons why. The speed with which I rejected the offer came across, of course, as a slap in the face. It spoiled dinner at a small family restaurant in Padua.

"I don't understand," he said, looking befuddled. "Why on earth not? *Ma perchè, Guglielmo, dimmi perchè?*"

"I just can't!" I even raised my voice. I was adamant.

He didn't insist. He went off on his own and found boys quite easily in Brazil a lot more eager to don a Speedo and sun themselves at a beach. It was impossible or imprudent to explain to him or to anyone else that I'd stopped going to the beach as a teenager because I couldn't take my clothes off in public, and that I held to that policy because my mind was twisted by a form of social anxiety disorder I could not name or understand. I made do with excuses, school being an acceptable reason for skipping Brazil, all expenses paid. I had taken my dysfunctions to Europe with me.

The Other Guillermo was spending more time with his Italian girlfriend and decided he didn't want to go out to Cosmopolitan with me one weekend. He encouraged me to strike out on my own. He'd also grown impatient with my irascible moods and habits. He had once wanted to go to the gym to work out. I told him I would gladly go except that I didn't have any gym clothes. He told me he could lend me some shorts and a T-shirt. Finally, I told him the truth, in part, that I'd find them too revealing, and that I didn't want to show any skin at the gym.

"OK, that's enough," he said. "I've had it. Your shit's gotten too weird for me."

I couldn't argue. I understood people's impatience with my strange condition, and I didn't think my eccentricities were particularly bearable. Yet, I bore the brunt of them and found myself alone that weekend. One more instance of solitude wouldn't hurt.

I took the bus to the nowhere town by myself, wearing my white ruffled shirt with a bowtie and black pants. To avoid resembling a caterer at some debutante ball, I piled on a wool black sweater that glimmered in newness and elegance. I wasn't afraid to go out by myself, but I also knew that meeting anyone while alone would prove difficult, if not impossible as well. I needed the Other Guillermo to make the rounds, speak to men, and introduce me to some of them. I needed that extra push from an emphatic, relentless person that the Other Guillermo proved to be around strangers. On my own, I rarely opened up to anyone, and since I didn't initiate conversations, by the end of the evening, I was incapable of asking anyone for a ride, which you were supposed to do if you wanted to get back home. The buses had stopped after midnight. The nightclub was closing at three a.m., and the men had started to drift away. I went out into the night not knowing how I'd get home. I tried hitchhiking, but nobody stopped. A light drizzle had started, and I was a rare sight out in the middle of nowhere. I was a sad sight, a young man dressed in an elegant white ruffled shirt with black pants and an elegant sweater waiting at the curbside while the rain picked up in intensity and cars passed him by.

Italian Holiday

I decided to try walking the thirty kilometers or so toward Padua. Or rather, I knew it would be impossible to walk the entire way, but walking kept me warm, and I figured sooner or later, something would happen. For better or for worse. Somebody would have to stop, the police at least. The road began to feel dark and foreboding. Only a car or two drove by, and nobody stopped for me, but by then, I'd stopped trying to hitchhike. I kept on walking in the dark, guiding myself by the small glint of light emanating from a partly clouded moon, and continued to do so for nearly an hour before I could see any lights in the horizon. Deep inside, I felt this walk was what I deserved. I'd failed to initiate the conversation and ask for a ride. It wasn't in my character to initiate conversations with strangers, even when crucial. They usually spoke to me, if they chose to. I had no choices—or so I felt. I even silenced a cry for help that night. Would I be this silent even while dying out on the road by myself? What would it take for me to speak up? I continued to walk as if to find out.

I arrived in a small town called Dolo after four a.m. A few street lights guided me toward a couple of brick buildings that could have been factories in the middle of nowhere. I opted to walk around and see if a late-night diner would be open. Instead, I found a bus depot and an office where bus drivers went to rest before and after their shifts. Three bus drivers, older men in uniforms, were watching a late-night show on television, and I walked in looking like a lost boy, already drenched in drizzle, my shoes dipped in mud. I disturbed their rather noisy conversation in front of the TV. But I must have awakened some fatherly instinct in them. They took immediate pity on me and asked me to sit down. One of them brought me coffee and asked me what the hell I was doing out there in the middle of the night walking by the highway like that.

"*Ma cosa faceva Lei nel pieno della notte nell'autostrada?*"

They seemed genuinely concerned, but in all honesty, other than darkness and solitude, I had failed to find any real danger, not even a stray dog. Perhaps I'd been lucky, and the rain had scared away creatures, thieves, terrorists, who knows what. The bus drivers' concern did reveal that danger was to be found out there, but I had arrived a little wet, yet unscathed.

"*Volevo camminare a Padova,*" I said, managing to break some sort of record in naïveté, judging by the resulting laughter. "I wanted to walk all the way to Padua."

They made it clear that might have taken me some twenty hours, nearly an entire day, but I told them I walk fast. They still laughed at my strangely unrealistic demeanor. I finally asked about a bus. They told me the next bus to Padua would be leaving at 5:30 am, and I was welcome to wait for it in their office.

"*Il conducente sono io,*" said the bus driver, proudly, an older man with gray hair and a pot belly, slipping into a jacket, as the night had turned colder. "I'll be your driver tonight."

An American TV movie starring Candice Bergen played for the next hour and a half, and we all watched together. A young woman moves to New York City and gets a job in a slick new corporate building.

"Is that how it is in America?" one of the men asked me. "You work in a big building?"

"*Sono uno studente,*" I said.

I was a student, I revealed; I wasn't working right now, I didn't know much about the working world—well, other than maintenance, I should have added, but didn't. A would-be lover was off to Rio de Janeiro without me, my best friend had dissed me because of my inscrutable behavior, and I couldn't speak up in social situations; I was lost and wet in some small town waiting for a bus. I did not explain all that, just smiled, and enjoyed the warmth of the waiting room. Candice Bergen spoke in Italian, and I nodded off until one of them woke me up.

"*Parte,*" one of the bus drivers said, shaking my shoulder. "*Signore, l'autobus parte adesso. Venga subito, venga.*"

The bus was leaving. I yawned and shook off my sleep to get up and walk out into the street where the bus waited for me along with a couple of old ladies in some sort of gray, factory uniform. I looked out the window as we pulled away from Dolo, that small refuge from a drizzling night when I'd been too shy to ask for a ride. I got home safely, and I have been grateful to the polite bus drivers of Dolo ever since.

My other relationship with a young man in Italy ended up a sexless encounter. It certainly created a contrast with the double pack of Communist lover men. But it showed this double-sided nature in my character. I could allow myself to be sodomized in Bologna, but I could be the perfect gentleman in Pisa. I'd met Ricardo almost as soon as I arrived in Italy. I took a train to Venice from Padua and found myself in the midst of a lively regatta festival. Gondolas paraded themselves through the waters of the city as people applauded them from the galleries above. On a ferry from the train station to St. Mark's Cathedral, a young man struck up a conversation with me. He was also a reticent, soft-spoken, and shy person, and I suspect that I at least didn't intimidate him. It was safe to talk to me. I also suspected he was gay, but I couldn't determine so at that point. What was important was how close we drew quickly, and how we later failed to draw closer.

He and I spent the day walking around Venice, comparing notes on living in Italy versus America. I told him I wanted to be a writer, and that I'd started a series of plays for a class at UCLA. He told me he lived with his parents in Livorno, but studied in Pisa, and that I should come visit him so that I'd get to tour another part of Italy. I could have taken the train back to Padua that night, but instead he and I went to the local Youth Hostel in Venice, where we spent the night on separate bunk beds. This rather chaste flirtation seemed perfectly abnormal for me at that age. I was not one to make friends this easily, and besides, every conversation I struck with men my age jumpstarted a guessing game for me—guessing what was up, whether I was picking up on homoerotic longings, or whether, as usual, I was imagining them. I liked Ricardo and was drawn to his pleasant quiet nature. When it was time to go our separate ways, we exchanged information. We kept in touch.

That Christmas, I took the train down to Pisa, where he was waiting for me at the station. He took my picture in front of the infamous Leaning Tower, which would eventually need major restoration to prevent it from leaning any further and falling. Ricardo lived with his parents and an aunt. They were equally reticent people. His aunt had suffered the loss of her husband, had come to live with her sister, and while they seemed like an average family, I couldn't help but feel a certain discomfort—if not with me, with the idea of them sharing their mourning with a stranger.

The mother told me she had imagined a blond American. "You're darker than the average American," she said. "*Sei moro*," she added, the Italian word for dark, but it also meant "moor," the invaders from the south who'd once conquered Spain.

"Well, I'm Latin American then," I had to say, and that seemed to quell their suspicions.

"No problem," she said. "Just wondering."

Italian Holiday

This befuddled but attentive host cooked the best Christmas meal I could possibly remember eating—turkey, ham, lasagna—and I can remember trying everything and having to stop eating. I ached, burdened by food and gastric maelstrom.

That same evening, after dinner, Ricardo took me to a radio station where he worked as a volunteer. Co-op radio stations made it possible for young people to conduct their own programming, and he was part of one of them. He introduced me as his American friend over the airwaves.

"*Ecco qui un'amico americano*," he said, bidding me to get closer to the microphone. He wanted me to introduce his radio listeners to Blondie. I told the listeners in my imperfect Italian that the lead singer Deborah Harry represented a new wave of female vocalists with a tough, rock 'n' roll sound such as Pat Benatar and Chrissie Hynde of the Pretenders, that Janis Joplin was an early precursor, and women were no longer expected to sing the "suono dolce," the sweet sounds of love ballads, and that they could also be expected to get down and dirty. It seemed like a fair analysis, rendered in an American-Chilean-accented Italian.

"*Ecco qui la bellissima Deborah Harry di Blondie.*"

He played "Dreaming" and "The Tide Is High," and while the music played, he smiled at me, reaching out to congratulate me.

"You know so much about American music," he said. "Why can't you come back during the summer and help me put together programming? You can be my co-host. In our spare time, we'll go to the beach."

He said the cursed word, the *beach*. Livorno is a port city, which means, of course, a beach, and nakedness, and all that. I saw it all crumbling down fast.

But Ricardo continued to insist, thinking he could entice me with summers at the beach. "Come back and we'll go swimming."

Finally, a few days went by, and I had to come up with some explanation. "I've already made arrangements to go spend the summer in Paris learning French at the Académie Française." It wasn't true when I said it, but when I got back to Padua, I got my *Let's Go: France* book out and made contact with the Académie Française. I enrolled myself in a French class in Paris because I'd be far away from a beach. It was something I couldn't explain to Ricardo. It was one more offer I turned down because of the Condition.

On the final night of my stay, I was in the guest room lying down, ready to fall asleep, when Ricardo came into the room to get something.

He opened up drawers in a chest and pulled out a shirt or two. But ultimately, he wanted to talk and sat by the edge of my bed. This was the closest thing to intimacy I could get out of him. Ricardo was no more forward or outgoing than I was, and ultimately, he proved himself equally frightened. If he meant to initiate something other than a conversation, if he meant to make a pass, or touch me in any way, he failed to do so. I failed to do the same. I clearly wanted something. I'm not clear on what he wanted, or what he could bring himself to want.

"Why won't you come back in the summer?" he insisted. "Why couldn't you spend only part of the summer in Paris? You could do both."

"I don't know—I've always wanted to spend time in Paris," I said, in an awkward tone. I had to look away because I didn't have a better excuse. I would have liked to come back. I would have liked to have embraced him, and at least shown some form of affection for him that very night—whatever he'd allow, whatever his own inhibitions would permit. I would have liked, in fact, to have spent the entire summer in his arms. But he had brought up the beach, a forbidden zone for me. I had managed to disappoint him. He got up from the bed and then left the room carrying two white shirts. The next day, he would shake my hand goodbye at the train station. I failed to hug him as well. Although we wrote to each other a couple of times, I never saw him again.

My relationship with the Other Guillermo became more distant during the rest of my stay in Italy. We were still friends, but ultimately, he had found his own companionship. The Italian girlfriend got serious. She started to spend more time at his dorm, which was one of the few that came with its own kitchen. She began cooking for him, inviting other people over. Every afternoon, a small party would gather in this liveliest of dorms, in which the girlfriend would preside over what appeared to be a quickly improvised marriage. He sat down, she served him a meal. He played Mexican husband, she Italian wife. Then, the Other Guillermo's roommate would bring his own girlfriend, a German exchange student. They'd pull out bottles of *il vino* and then some recreational drugs, and the party would intensify. I wasn't exactly invited. I would just show up and mostly observe. The couples would start making out, and I would still observe. In front of me, and in front of his other friends, the Other Guillermo seemed eager to emphasize his heterosexual side. A wild, rambunctious side, and yet my presence invited resentment. He didn't want to be pigeon-holed. He went out of his way to remind me that he and I never had sex, as if I needed the reminder. He even chided me for telling people we'd slept together in Milan. People would get the wrong idea. If he wasn't ashamed of being bisexual, then the only reason he was behaving this way was because he didn't want people to think he'd had the bad taste of once technically sleeping with me—again, this is how I took things at the time, with a posture of extreme defensiveness. His possessive girlfriend was a woman in love and—in my rude opinion at the time—without a life. She didn't seem to aspire to anything much. She threw herself into a torrid love affair with the Other Guillermo because her work as a hair stylist had become routine. She was in her early thirties, if I can gauge age, but clearly, she was older than him by some ten years. She must have known he was going back to the United States, but he needed company, and he had to have it at any cost. He wasn't going to be caught without it. He wanted to prove he was the one Guillermo with a life, and I was the other one who had trouble getting one. Nonetheless, I had thrown him for a loop as well, acquiring two scandalous lovers at a time in Bologna. The Other Guillermo sought to prove his competitiveness, making it clear and obvious to everyone he didn't do "dry spells" in relationships. He had sex, and he could get it on his schedule.

More seriously, for all his fashion breaks, his illicit drugs, and wild times with the boys and the girls, the Other Guillermo held one dirty secret: he wanted to become a lawyer. He entertained a conventional future for himself, in contrast to the free spirit he sought to exhibit in his youth. He held a not-so-secret love of fashion. He sketched vivid, colorful portraits of himself donning ambitious outfits of his own creation. When I first saw them plastered all over the wall of his dormitory, I stopped to stare and then observe their great detail.

"These are amazing!" I told him, sincere in my praise. "You should study fashion."

"Oh, I'd love to chuck everything and go to Milan to make my mark on the world."

"You should."

"I'd love to dress up beautiful models in Milan, make them stunning."

"Well, what's stopping you?"

"My parents want me to be a lawyer."

"Why is it up to them?"

"Because they're poor people. They want certainty."

"I hate that. Certainty."

"Well, it's what they want."

"But—"

"There's no point in arguing. There's work and money in the law."

I looked disappointed. He clearly possessed the talent, if not the will, to pursue fashion. Years later, when I graduated with a master's degree in playwriting from UC San Diego, I looked back upon this conversation and thought how odd that the one man who sought to give me a makeover and transform me into a more fabulous version of myself ended up opting for a profession he felt no real love for, and I—the square, repressed, Catholic virgin—ended up in a career that's all about risk and multiple rejection. He became practical. I became the "risk-taker." I often wonder if, without his constant, persistent goading of me, I would have broken through my inhibitions. Yet, he chose conformity, having done a wonderful job of inspiring more from me.

That spring as the Other Guillermo prepared to return to the United States in June, I opted to stay longer in Europe. The boyfriend of one the UCLA students was subletting a tiny hole of an apartment in Paris at Rue de Cherche Midi during the summer, and I took it. I would spend the summer of 1983 without discretionary income trying to write another set of novels and short stories. The Other Guillermo was already thinking of going back to UC Santa Barbara and worrying about his LSAT.

The time had come to say goodbye. But I couldn't let go of the Other Guillermo with a solemn hug and a kiss. In fact, I got nowhere near him that afternoon at the train station. His girlfriend stood by his side. She and I both went to bid him farewell, but she took center stage. In the most dramatic fashion possible, and emblematic of many scenes one might imagine in a neo-realist, Italian film, in which a Sicilian momma (played by Anna Magnani) grieves the loss of a loved one, the Italian girlfriend began to cry, throwing herself at the Other Guillermo's arms, circumventing any chance for me to show emotion. She outshined me, stole what would have been my scene (more subtle and without the tearjerker), crying in a loud, panting manner. The best I could do was pat her on the back, and go "there, there, there." The Other Guillermo pulled himself away and made a quick ascension to the train, as if scared. He barely waved at me, looking worried for the mental state of this woman. What had he done to her? The sadness I felt at seeing him leave was compounded by a simple realization: nobody had ever cried for *me* with this type of energy and conviction. I doubted that anyone would ever want me in this manner. The girlfriend's genuine grief was proof of the dynamic personality the Other Guillermo represented, in contrast to my own relative insignificance in the scheme of things. The Other Guillermo inspired passion; I didn't. This contrast between me and my more charismatic friend would always haunt me, from the moment I consoled his intense, anguished girlfriend as the train pulled away. The Other Guillermo was gone, leaving behind a devastated woman. Immobilized and outflanked by the Italian girlfriend, I had trouble expressing my own grief.

The Other Guillermo had also left behind a fairly presentable young man, expertly clad in Italian fashion, with a good sense of color and coordination. He had helped my transformation from that sickly frail creature into a more fully realized version of myself. His artistry was expended, somehow, in the creation of the new me, and often I felt I was wearing his clothes, his fashion, and emulating his walk. Still, even borrowed style was better than none. I would develop my own one day. The Other Guillermo eventually applied and entered a law school, as planned. I was his only (if flawed) masterwork. I was no longer the repressed neurasthenic maiden of a Tennessee Williams play. Something had changed, and the Other Guillermo had left me more firmly planted in reality with new powers of transformation and, even, sexuality. That was his gift to me. I often wonder what I did for him. It hadn't occurred to me at that age that I could contribute something to his life. I was too busy absorbing the lessons of his teaching. I would have to go on to finish my novel or my play, or whatever I was meant to write, I thought. I had no idea how to repay people with something other than the fondness of memory.

6

Éxito, or the Language of Success

I flew alone into the United States at ten years of age, and the first word that caught my attention upon my arrival at JFK International Airport glowed in the various signs that pointed toward the world outside: *Exit*. The Spanish word for "success" is *éxito*. My translation was, of course, wide of the mark, but my child's eye saw something else: what a great country, I thought; it wishes you success as you leave the building. Today, I would advocate changing all the exit signs to *success*. Give your best wishes to people. Let them feel confident as they go out of the building into those streets where they might well be devoured by people who lack success or, conversely, zealously cling to their own. Be an optimist, and let your best wishes prevail. I would eventually learn the flat, unadorned meaning of "exit," but I haven't forgotten the translation that amused me at that age and that I thought was so original, an optimistic one for a child who constantly sought to bend the world to his imagination.

The United States felt welcoming to a child of ten, impressions colored by my mother's rosy disposition, her Maria von Trapp aura of seeing the world through a wide angle and Cinemascope lens with a bouncy soundtrack playing in our heads. The music and the rhythm of the streets invited one to think in terms of music and dance. The juke box in the diner across from the Manhattan hotel featured the hits of the times, and I could choose Diana Ross's "Surrender," the Jacksons' "Going Back to Indiana," or Joan Baez's "The Night They Drove all Dixie Down" with haunting lyrics by Robbie Robertson that I wouldn't understand until I learned English. My mother didn't hesitate to give me enough quarters to play all three selections and then poured raspberry syrup on my pancakes. That's how she welcomed me into the country, through a glimpse of the Big Apple, both my taste and aural buds appeased. We took the bus to D.C., where we settled down in the nation's capital—for a short while anyway. Settling down did not suit us well. We turned out to be restless immigrants on the go. We started in D.C. and then bounced around the country until we reached L.A., the last station for fidgety people before the ocean put a stop to us.

My mother had arrived a year ahead of me like a scouting agent looking at the schools and the way of life. She had been working for a family in Bethesda, Maryland, as their house- and life-keeper. Mother claimed she ran the house, the lives, and the everyday rhythm and traffic of her chosen home. Housekeepers try to believe this, but I suspect my mother was right. She had yet to learn English fluently, but an irrepressible smile conveyed plenty of meaning, and she could communicate loudly with her broken new language. She was well loved by the American family for whom she worked, but she couldn't surrender her need for independence and self-sufficiency. Within a year, she had saved enough money and moved out. She continued to work for several families in the Bethesda–Chevy Chase area as a live-out domestic, but only for families she'd select. She shared a diminutive apartment with a Mexican woman on Bradley Boulevard within walking distance of a bus stop that took her to the various homes she cleaned. Her roommate was Flora, a hairdresser, who let her stay in a foldout bed in the living room. No problem. While Americans see overcrowding and poverty, an immigrant sees an opportunity. Americans who bothered to notice may have wanted to define us as underprivileged. But poverty is a way station on our road into the American way of life. María appreciated the United States and considered herself lucky to be sleeping on a foldout bed in a cramped Maryland apartment. She bought herself a modest camera with a flashcube. On weekends she and her cousin Nelly hopped on the bus to Washington, D.C., where they posed for pictures in front of national monuments and mailed them to Chile. A picture of my mother standing next to anti–Vietnam War protestors shows her smiling in sweet innocence. The hippie protestors struck her as exotic creatures, part of the free-love lifestyle that she had once seen in the movies, and that she could now join in as a shy young Catholic woman who had no trouble getting male admirers, yet kept her distance. Another picture is a glamour shot. My mother poses in a miniskirt in front of an average home in the Maryland suburbs, showing plenty of legs and a sensual pout with painted lips. On the back, a dedication to her son. All the homes look like this, she writes, in front of a cobblestone entrance to a gorgeous house.

What is remarkable in all the pictures she leaves behind is the adventurous spirit of an immigrant woman chronicling her eagerness to see it all for herself. The Lincoln Monument: we must stand in front of it. The Washington Monument: make sure it appears in the background. The Jefferson Memorial: let me move to the side for you to catch the cupola. It was a long way from the girls' school in Santiago in which food shortages had forced her to eat spicy ants off a stick.

A year's worth of paperwork, and I became entitled to join her in the adventure. I've always been grateful for this, even today when immigrants get attacked, and conservative politicians write that we're unwilling to learn English, that we refuse to assimilate. My mother and I arrived in a confident country that still welcomed immigrants. We sensed it. We felt right at home. We had trouble believing that there were Americans who resented us, who felt threatened by us. That's not the people we met in this suburb of D.C. Americans seemed sane. Anti-war protests revealed a democratic process, not chaos or hatred. Learning the language would take time, but there'd be no deep alienation for us (maybe mild befuddlement at times), no obligatory inner-city malaise that required us to, say, denounce our oppression as Third World people. That type of thing wouldn't come up until I went to UCLA, a shocking new political reality that tried to tear down my American childhood, deconstruct it for me, and spit it back as an imperialist, oppressive reality. My childhood had been the mirage. The luminous world into which I thought I had immigrated, in which my "poverty" seemed brighter, cleaner, more comfortable than any middle-class status I had experienced in Chile, would eventually be ridiculed—by more than one professor and several of my classmates. A Marxist history professor asked me about my background, and when he heard Chile, he was overjoyed. U.S. intervention, the CIA, the martyr Salvador Allende. When I told him we immigrated before the military coup, he was unfazed. He said I needed to pick up the struggle. When I told him I liked moving to the United States, that's when he replied, "That's all bourgeois illusion."

"You need to struggle anyway. You must find out the truth about Chile."

I agreed. "But I don't want to seem ungrateful to the U.S."

"The CIA destroys your country, and you're supposed to be grateful?"

"I'm getting an education because of the U.S."

"Milk it for all it's worth," he followed. "The Republicans are going to cut down on student aid, and then don't come tell me you feel grateful."

I couldn't argue. I didn't want to come across as naive, as I continued to cling to memories of my initial days as an immigrant as days of liberation. I also came from a school in Chile where bullying was practically required as a social norm. I have learned plenty about bullying in the United States, especially in the aftermath of the Columbine tragedy, but I thought that any meanness I encountered in U.S. schools did not compare to my childhood perceptions of cruelty in Chile. I wanted to listen to everybody and learn from all my teachers, but I often felt that they wanted me to fulfill their image of the victimized minority. I was poor. I was supposed to be angry. But my mother and I experienced exhilaration instead, a honeymoon with the much-denounced Empire. Even my Socialist aunt in Chile had warned me: the moment you get there you'll turn into a *gringo.* This was her specific lament. Still, my Socialist aunt was practical. She talked of a Cuban Revolution but understood with some fatalism the lures of the capitalist empire. She sent me to the United States to experience it for myself. She claimed one day the Socialist countries would also be ready to welcome immigrants, but for now, people tried to flee Cuba and the Soviet Bloc countries and risked their lives doing so. She recognized it as a temporary historical phenomenon: people wanted to live in the United States, but one day they would actually choose socialism. Until that happened, off I went into the United States, and she found that perfectly acceptable, for the historical moment.

The Chilean relatives who put me on the plane wished me luck. Success, they whispered among themselves, *éxito. Hacerse la América,* they said, yet another expression that connotes success. It literally means "to make yourself an America," your own America, your own creation of the Big Time. The expression started with the European newcomers, for whom all the Americas meant finding gold. That's how you made your own America, by migrating to it, but now the term had turned north. Latin Americans used it to imply the United States, where you went to make yourself an America. To leave for the United States was considered a lucky break, leading inevitably to making it. My relatives, dozens of them, came to bid me farewell at the then-called Pudahuel International Airport of Santiago. Most had never seen a plane up close. There were still literal gates, the type that swing open, not simply the holes in the wall in which a moveable unit (a jetway) connects travelers to the plane. They could stand behind those gates, and I—a little person traveling alone—went with my ticket and my legal residence papers into a bus that transported me and the other passengers to the plane. I got out of the bus and gave a final farewell to this throng of supporters cheering me on. The stewardesses gave me a suspicious look: a child traveling alone, something for us to take care of. But I gave them no problem. I was too busy inspecting the plane, playing with the buttons, and then admiring the clouds and the moon outside the window. I was an astronaut. I was Neil Armstrong. There had been a time when our teacher had made us memorize the names of American astronauts.

A friend of my grandmother, the indomitable Mother Lolita, who lives on into her nineties and looks as spirited and lovely as ever, slipped a bottle of her homemade liqueur into my backpack, a sweet concoction she called *dulce Lolita*. This was her farewell gift—meant for my mother. I chose to sip *dulce Lolita* on the plane ever so slowly, to calm my nerves. The stewardesses kept looking at it. At a distance, it might have looked like a sugary drink, yet they didn't realize I was a ten-year-old enjoying a happy hour. Once I landed in New York City, the customs officials smelled it and gave me a strange look. Half the bottle was gone. Then, when they looked into my suitcase, they found herbs. Yet another aunt had slipped in bags of herbal remedies, which were packaged in loose, plastic bags. The customs inspector smelled them just to be certain but determined that those suspicious-looking products were what they were, rural medicine. They're good for your mother's digestion, the aunt had said. To top it off, an uncle had crowned me with a *huaso* (Chilean cowboy) hat at the airport, and I had boarded the plane wearing it. As I slept on the plane, it slipped somewhere into the crevices. I forgot about it altogether, and it disappeared into the night. At JFK customs, I suddenly remembered. I told an official who spoke Spanish that my *huaso*, my hat, was missing. She let another officer know. The officer made a phone call. "Go find some wa-zoo hat," he ordered somebody. Nothing turned up. I had moved on to notice the impressive exit signs with their wishes of success.

I was in New York City. My mother stood above, waving from a viewing station overlooking the customs desks. I recognized her face immediately, a glowing, welcoming smile. We hadn't seen each other in over a year. My mother's first action was to walk me into the city, to 32nd Street, where we'd hitch a ride to the top of the Empire State Building, something I'd seen in the movies, with Deborah Kerr and Cary Grant kissing.

"How was your plane ride?" Mother asked.

"I barely slept," I said. "I kept playing with all the buttons, then I read all my magazines, Archie comics, Batman, Lone Ranger, and Barrabás (the Chilean cartoon about an indefatigable soccer team). Then the mean stewardess came by and turned off my light and told me to sleep, but I couldn't. I looked out the window and stared at the moon and the clouds the entire night."

It was the longest trip of my life, in child's time, which slows down to the minute and split seconds. Awake and aloft while cruising through clouds, I was an introspective child, ascertaining the meaning of this new life, imagining who knows what—excitement, glory, glamour? I felt no sense of loss. I didn't miss my native country. I didn't think I had left Chile forever. People talk about their exile, their need to abandon their homelands, perhaps for political reasons, perhaps risking their lives on rafts or, worse, walking by foot through a desert. I had left Chile on a joy ride, with a full set of papers because my mother had planned it that way. Luck had allowed it to happen precisely as she planned it. Boring immigrants, that's what we were, ones who came without the drama of danger, risk, potential oppression, or alienation as "illegals." We felt the welcome and the transformation of a new life. Our optimism was probably justified—although today I have learned enough skepticism to ridicule it myself before others do. We were trained by Julie Andrews to think of our favorite things, and even our local church in Santiago had adopted the song in a Spanish translation. The American nuns who presided over the church kept up the Maria von Trapp allure of thinking good things. "Raindrops on roses, whiskers on kittens." Not much of a believer nowadays, I'm still grateful for the songs and the music the nuns gave us, like gifts wrapped in good wishes. There was something unhip about us, immigrants who actually enjoyed their immigration. I've learned today, through my academic friends, that a rosy disposition is considered square, even reactionary. In intellectual circles, I've learned to turn on the heavy sarcasm and irony, if only to hide a Catholic childhood in which we could sing songs such as "My Favorite Things" without being ridiculed.

Éxito, or the Language of Success

In Maryland, we were newcomers, and yet we felt, of all things, at home. Mother and I shared a sense of excitement and adaptability. The first lesson: other immigrants complain about everything; we annoyed them by liking everything. What better lesson than to find the *West Side Story* soundtrack in the mobile library that parked in front of our building every week. A mobile library was exciting enough—did we also make people sick by being excited by that, too? There were no public libraries in my neighborhood in Santiago at the time. The only library was the used book and used magazine store we ran ourselves. We were the facilitators of culture in the La Palmilla neighborhood at a time when television hadn't yet established itself in Chile. We didn't sell books. We rented them along with magazines. That was the essence of the economy. People were too poor to buy them, and the content was populist—cartoons, serial illustrated romances, movie gossip. But in Bethesda, the library came to us with books, for free.

"There are some books in Spanish in the back," I remember the librarian saying. Was she a librarian or just a driver? I didn't know the difference. There were indeed children's books in Spanish, which I checked out. But I plunged into English-language books at the same time. I didn't have to know the language. I wanted to stare at the words and the illustrations and try to match them. My first "Cat in the Hat" books were a surreal experience, drawings of a funky cat with language that expressed who knows what. The early playwright in me was writing his own script.

But much more important for the long-term imprint upon my imagination was another finding: the soundtrack of the Sondheim/Bernstein/Robbins musical *West Side Story*.

"I like to be in America," said the lyrics. One group of immigrants yearned to go back to San Juan, and the other wanted to give them "a boat to get on." I have spent the rest of my life acting out those lyrics. My mother was Anita, the lively Puerto Rican woman in love with Manhattan, singing about how much she likes to be in America. The rest would be the other people—the morose, the pessimists, the realists, the academics—who tried to point out all the problems with life in the United States.

"But there is a reason why we came," Mother said. Gatherings included friends from Peru, Mexico, Guatemala, and other Latin American countries. "Let's not forget that we left behind countries that had no future for us" (in Sondheim's words: "Always the hurricanes blowing, always the population growing").

This basic lesson was never lost on me. Our native countries would fall into the hands of dictators throughout the 1970s, one by one, with the help of the CIA. The economies could not catch up with the basic human yearning for some breathing space, even a small touch of magic, of hope for oneself and family. Out of frustration, people rioted or joined revolutionary movements, in which case the ruling class cracked down, imposing curfews, then dictatorship. The pattern repeated itself over and over again throughout this period. Relatives from Chile wrote short narratives, a paragraph here and there, revealing food shortages, riots, police brutality, and eventually the tragic military coup.

My mother had no time to look back. For her the United States was the place to dream first and then to work to pursue those dreams. That night at the Empire State Building, she laid it on the line: "*Ay, pero mira esta gran ciudad,* how the lights shine upon into the night. People who worked hard put up those buildings, not some *flojos* who do nothing all day. You build it day by day, brick by brick; it's about the choices you make every single day, from the moment you wake up."

It dawned on me that she always introduced a new task in the context of play. A free afternoon? Why not go over the abc's? Or the multiplication tables? Or use that new movie with Liz Taylor to talk about the history of Rome and Anthony and Cleopatra? A certain dutifulness came attached to the everyday life, but she always made it seem as fun as riding the elevator to the top of the Empire State Building.

In looking back, I questioned her tone, her tendency to dismiss people as *flojos* the way some Republicans dismissed "welfare queens." I understood eventually why she didn't consider herself a Republican and still voted for Reagan. She resented the people who she thought dismissed hard work and who supposedly glorified dependency. I never met a "welfare queen" personally. But my mother recognized that I couldn't get an education without government aid, and that free lunches helped us make it through the day without experiencing hunger. She was a hard-working woman, but she could certainly use the subsidy. It became simply a matter of style—it was optimism that got you through the day, and the mantra was obligatory. Make fun of that optimism, and María made the unsuspecting victim get back that dismissive attitude Anita perfected so well: "I know a boat you can get on."

I still didn't know exactly what success entailed, but I knew early on in my first days in the United States that all the exit signs wished it for me. It was time to exit the building and start living out there in the new country, and to start getting the translations right.

Ten years go by. I am in the Café Figaro of West Hollywood, a fixture that has since disappeared. In my neighborhood in the 1980s, it was the precursor to Starbucks. Devoted to espresso, yet with a larger lunch and dinner menu than the current ubiquitous chain, not to mention an actual bar, Café Figaro fulfilled my fantasy of a literary life—books, notebooks, espresso, and a pen in hand to capture the moment, but also booze as well, if necessary. To others, it may have been a restaurant, but in the late afternoon, as the lunch crowd thinned, idle writers moved in to camp out for a couple of hours. I was one of them, and it behooved me to look debonair and witty when I was actually trying to write into a notebook. Conversations with the servers soaked up time, but it helped me stay for hours, and it broke up the monotony of actually getting some writing done. A Saturday afternoon around three p.m. was perfect for the cappuccino and the slice of chocolate cake. Death by Chocolate, they called it, a thick concoction, more dark chocolate cream than actual cake. I had picked up the habit of carrying both a notebook and a journal in Italy. The notebook was for dialogue and scenes for plays, sometimes short stories. The journal was to record experiences, ideas, sensations. An actress/waitress approached me one day. "UCLA, right?" she asked. "I saw you in that scene in drama class."

Yes, I'd done a scene from Sartre's *No Exit*, playing the bedeviled hero. For the first time since Charo in Chile, I'd kissed a young woman. The director made me get on top of her as the psychotic lesbian character bid me to penetrate the younger woman—at least that was our interpretation. I gave it my all. I crushed the poor young actress writhing beneath me, and she looked like she enjoyed the endless humping the director made me do as the aggressive female character bid me to take her. One of the young men in the class analyzed our scene afterward, saying that her breasts threatened to pop out of a tight outfit giving "new meaning to the term

dramatic tension." But the professor gave me a B anyway. I didn't get sufficient credit for the tension: people were too focused on the breasts.

"You were great," says the waitress. I didn't believe her. I still remembered that class as a nightmare, and a death knell for any acting ambitions.
Another director cast me in a scene as the aggressive black soldier in David
Rabe's *Streamers*, yet another case of miscasting. "It's a stretch," the director told me, "but it's a class. You might learn something." I failed to play a
homicidal deranged black soldier even though part of me wished I could
have pulled it off. I got another B. My heart was somewhere else. I was not
an actor, just a theatrical person, perhaps a literary one. I told the waitress
I was writing—well, taking notes about writing—a play about Sal Mineo.

She didn't seem to know the actor from *Rebel without a Cause*, but she
still smiled and tried to look interested.

"You see," I told her with great earnestness because I believed a play
could actually result, "since I was a teenager, I've been told I look like Sal
Mineo, and I figured I might as well write a one-man show about him and
star in it. He was killed in my neighborhood."

"Oh, no! Recently?"

"No, not recently, but in 1976 only a few months before my mother
and I moved to Los Angeles. We were originally from Chile, but we lived
in Arlington, Virginia, and suddenly I'm living in L.A. and every day I
walk by the apartment building where he was stabbed to death by a perfect
stranger, and I just think, there's something to that story."

There was definitely a one-man show in Mineo's biography, but I could
not bring myself to write it, let alone star in it. Still, I was proud that I was
talking about my ideas and getting to a point where I could one day start
and finish something. We were in Hollywood after all, albeit West Hollywood, another city altogether. But it still helped, when the waitress recognized you—you felt you belonged there. Singer Belinda Carlisle sat on the
table beside me one afternoon, as she shared coffee with a friend. She was
someone recognizable, and I even avoided staring at her. When you belonged, you didn't need to play the role of the fan, but of the disinterested
insider. It made sense somehow, my life in West Hollywood, even though
I was only accomplishing the successful writing of notes, and lots of them.

"When will it happen?" my mother asked. She sat me down shortly
after I returned from Italy. I had colorful Italian clothes hanging in the

closet, but I had no job, and I was sleeping in her living room on a foldout bed. We were still using one after all these years, and my mother was understandably concerned. "When will you get a job and start doing something with your life?"

I wasn't done with school yet. I didn't know what the hurry was. It's true that I'd stretched out my requirements into a fifth year. But the fifth year had ended, and I was enrolling for one more quarter, my sixth year at UCLA. I was making a career of being an undergrad. But I was also genuinely trying to write. How could I prove it to her?

"We didn't come to the U.S. to live like this," she said. She was blaming it, her life, on me. It was clear I was meant to be a success at twenty-three, and I was meant to be her redemption for the life that she was failing to lead. Carmen's parents had left their Florida retirement home, and they were staying with us in the one-bedroom apartment. This meant that for a couple of months, the old folks slept in the one bedroom, and Carmen, María, and myself camped out in the living room. Third World conditions. Carmen couldn't stand it for long and made her parents move into their own apartment in the same building, now owned by a Korean man, who also didn't like all the crowding of forlorn immigrants around him.

The problem was that we were still living *like this.* We had moved to Los Angeles to avoid a static, crowded life in Arlington, Virginia. We felt restless again. The nomadic instinct took hold of us one more time in the summer of 1976. Mother could not stand the repetitive task of filing for GEICO. She had previously left behind maintenance because that was not good enough for the enterprising immigrant. A government-sponsored course to teach immigrants English and basic office skills lifted her out of that one socioeconomic tier only to make her a clerk, which Mother immediately found constrained her instinct to move, to see America, to make it in America (*hacerse la América*). Rosa, her Peruvian friend, had already moved to Los Angeles, which gave us an excuse to invite ourselves along. That summer we had also had a slight problem with the landlord in Virginia. He came knocking on the door one day when I was alone and asked me questions.

"How many people are living here?"

There was my mother and I, my aunt Nelly had moved in, as had a friend of my mother's, Carmen. Four people in a two-bedroom apartment. This was shocking to the American landlord. By the standards of his privileged First World view, this was overcrowding. He came in when I was alone, and I kept my eyes down, ashamed, berated by his bullying tactics. He inspected our place as if we'd been transients camping out illegally, trespassers in his private property. My mother had ceded one of the bedrooms to me. I had a room to myself for the first time in my life. She and Carmen slept on a foldout bed in the living room. Aunt Nelly enjoyed the other room by herself. This was a standard arrangement—for immigrants. "It's unacceptable," he said. "What time does your mother come home?"

The landlord called at night to speak to the women of the house. Somebody had to leave. Three people were the most he could accept. Mother said fine, we will all move. All the way to California. Aunt Nelly, ever the cautious one, was shocked at Mother's impulsive decision and stayed behind. Carmen, who enjoyed a similarly adventurous spirit, joined my mother and me. She owned the one car in the household, an old Pontiac that survived the wear and tear of the cross-country trip, but only just. We rented a U-Haul trailer that followed us to California like a faithful pet, attached to the Pontiac. My mother hadn't yet learned to drive, so Carmen drove the whole way. I had the back of the car to myself, where I read Jacqueline Susann's neo-pornographic *The Love Machine.* It's educational, I told my mother, who wasn't buying it, but I was a teenager by then. Better that I read about it than actually perform it was her rationalization for my newly adult tastes in reading. Off we went, driving through Lee Highway until I saw my favorite school—Stratford Junior High—disappear in the rearview mirror. We were leaving behind the good, steady but boring life of settled immigrants. I welcomed the drastic move. I didn't think of its effect on me, my psyche, my strangeness. I knew we weren't sedate, average people. I knew we could pick up any time and go. It was part of the freedom of living in the United States. Until then, we had refused to stand still, so why stop now?

I must admit to one cruel trick that I played on my various schoolmates throughout the D.C. area. The first time I played this trick was on boys in the locker room at my Silver Spring junior high school. Instead of telling them I was simply moving, I told them I had testicular cancer and that they wouldn't see me again. They laughed and dismissed my folly, but they never saw me again because we moved. I wanted them to come to school and begin to ask. Not that they would be worried about me—the boys I targeted were the type most likely to bully me around—but I wanted at the very least for them to consider the possibility that I didn't lie.

Éxito, or the Language of *Success*

The second time I played this same trick was during the summer of 1976 when we were about to leave Arlington for Los Angeles. I ran into some schoolmates, two teenage girls, at a local drugstore. With a straight face, I announced again with great serenity, even acceptance, "I have cancer, so you won't be seeing me much longer."

They looked altered somehow, not quite believing it but almost, as if not wanting to dismiss the truth. Yet, these were friendly girls. They'd never done me any harm. There was no reason for me to get even with them as I wanted to against the boys in Silver Spring, and yet I thought I would test it out one more time. The girls walked away, not knowing what to think.

A few days later, I got a phone call from my history teacher. "Kids are telling me you have cancer; is this true?" I couldn't lie to dear Ms. K——, but I did anyway.

"We're moving back to Chile," I told her, "so that I may die among my relatives."

"I want to speak to your mother," she said.

"She's not here, I'm sorry," I answered, and this time I managed to cough, confusing cancer for tuberculosis. I was clearly acting out the Camille role. Few people knew of my role-playing upon meeting my father in the summer of 1975, when I created Aunt Augusta. But this time, I was looking for a grand, dramatic excuse for us moving as opposed to admitting we were being evicted for overcrowding. That would have been so Third World. I was all about avoiding embarrassments at that age. What was one more lie anyway? My schoolmates believed my father toiled as a well-paid diplomat for Generalíssimo Augusto Pinochet in the Chilean Embassy in Washington. There was no reason why I shouldn't be going back to Santiago. Most diplomatic appointments ended, and now I was struggling with terminal cancer. My teenage life had become fiction, and it saved me from the flat reality of our immigrant lives. I had found an odd, cruel way to skip town.

Out of this nomadic life, Mother felt the need to build a home in Los Angeles. Years later, she was complaining. How come we're living like this? But this was our purpose, I wanted to say. We never put that much emphasis on settling down, furnishing a place and staying put. In the D.C. area, we moved from Bethesda to Silver Spring, Maryland, and then to Arlington, Virginia. Mostly because we felt like it, because we thought we'd find a better life crisscrossing the Potomac River until we finally quit. In L.A. we'd moved from our apartment off Sunset/Hayworth to Sunset/Formosa, with only a subtle difference in size and quality. We moved several times again through the years until Mother ended up in Portland, Oregon, and I in Arizona. So I felt the blame that morning.

"When will we stop living like this?" She was accusing me of not being the breadwinner, of not buying her a home, or not providing a better way of life. "You should be out there doing something in Hollywood."

"Hollywood?" I asked. The word had become threatening, something to be used against me.

"We drove all the way out here from Virginia."

"So that's why we drove out here?" I asked. "I thought it was because we wanted to be free, and see the country, and get away from our boring lives in Virginia."

"Yeah, but we've been in Hollywood for seven years now, and what have you done?"

"I'm not an actor."

"You were going to be an actor once!"

"Well, I'm sorry! I can't be that type of son."

Unfortunately for my immigrant mother, I was a humanities student. Therefore, I wasn't going anywhere. All those books—drama, poetry, criticism—and the occasional polemical book—by George Orwell, Ayn Rand, Bill Buckley—pointed in one direction only: debt. School loans needed to be repaid. What would I do about that? We didn't come to the U.S. to . . . It's an immigrant mother's eternal lament to realize success was not guaranteed. Her son had grown up, and he now read books. That's what he did with his spare time. Could there be a greater punishment? Yes, her son could be queer, but my mother couldn't admit to that yet, and therefore she was in for a long period of adjustment. Her dilemma was clear: how to accept the overall disappointment a struggling writer represented. I, her only son, her insurance against bad times, was burdened with the responsibility of lifting us out of poverty. Why were we living like this? I had once followed Fred Silverman's career in the magazines and newspapers. He had graduated from Ohio State, gone into programming, and become the head guru of all three major networks. He'd re-created television by solidifying hits such as *All in the Family,* then creating the spinoffs that moved memorable characters into our living rooms and our imaginations: Maude,

and the Jeffersons, Mary Richards, and Rhoda, all of them our virtual relatives. At ABC, he'd do the same with *Happy Days*—Ritchie Cunningham
became a cousin, the Fonz our best friend, and Laverne and Shirley and
Mork and Mindy also emerged to play parts in our lives. Silverman had
been my hero of sorts because pop culture fulfilled my own need to popu-
late American culture with characters and situations. Yet I had fallen in
love with serious literature instead. I was clearly not following in the steps
of the successful network boss, no matter how fascinated I was by programming and counter-programming. My mother had been thinking in
terms of Ritchie Valens, the son of a Mexican American, farm-working
mother. A couple of hit songs like "La Bamba," and he's buying his mother
a home. Luis Valdez's film of Valens's tragic life didn't help any.

"What was all that education about?" asked María when she seemed to
be giving up on me. My talents, whatever they were, didn't flourish in the
teen years. Writers needed time, sometimes decades. The talent I was aiming for required the patient nurturing of language, words, and the ability
to discover a voice. A young man rarely possessed an immediate, accessible
voice. Of course, I wasn't about to tell her that my contemporary, Bret
Easton Ellis, had already published his first novel, *Less Than Zero*, chronicling the lives of spoiled Beverly Hills brats. Youthful writers could establish themselves and make some sort of impression on the culture. I wasn't
headed in that direction. I was lucky my mother had not read about Ellis,
a best-selling author in his twenties.

I heard my mother's thought process, the wheels turning. If her son
wasn't about to make a bold move, she would. This led my mother to make
a crucial decision. She would marry my soon-to-be stepfather, Osvaldo
Campos, as an odd business arrangement, but it was clearly one way to get
her closer to one of her dreams, her own house. Her son was no Ritchie
Valens. I'll show that writer, was her attitude. Of course, that still left the
matter of what I would do with my life. If anything.

Whether my mother considered writing to be real work or not, I insisted I was doing plenty with my life. I found a coffeehouse, a different one
every day, one in Westwood near the university, another one in Kerckoff
Hall inside the university itself, and there was still the Figaro. I moved into
West Hollywood—you might say—to be near it, and to streets that were
walkable and reminiscent of a European lifestyle that I still missed. I shared
an apartment with Montgomery, a friend I'd met in Italy, now a law student

at UCLA, and Jonathan, an MBA grad from UC Davis, who had secured a position with Cedars-Sinai in management. Jonathan's parents were wealthy Beverly Hills socialites. Their cast-off furniture remade our living room, turning it into something plush and sociably agreeable. I shared a room with Montgomery, so there was no private space, but I was no longer sleeping on a foldout bed. I had lucked out. I worked part-time for the UCLA Latin American Center, filling out book orders in their publications department, and the rest of the time I was somewhere in the city writing stories or reading.

Mother had reason to worry. I was clearly not enterprising. My personality was dim. I failed to do the networking necessary to meet people and get ahead. I was not involved publicly with any one organization. I was on my own out on the streets, walking, since I didn't have a car, or a driver's license, and I would stop somewhere for a cappuccino, which I could always somehow afford, and write.

"Why are *you* living like this?" Mother asked. It was no longer us, it was me. She had married Osvaldo, the Chilean immigrant who'd help her buy her house in the Valley. She was making progress, of sorts. But she still lived ten minutes away from me in Hollywood, and her phone calls were always about what I intended to do to get my house in order.

"I am a writer," I said with great confidence. "That's what I'm doing, not just intending to do."

She wasn't buying it. Mother was always, partly, right about these things, which exacerbated my moods. Why indeed was I living like this? I questioned my own goals and ambitions but never found the way to betray them. I stuck it out because there was no other way of life for me. It was not possible that I would surrender my books, my notebooks, and the countless ideas for plays, novels, short stories, and screenplays that populated my mind in a chaotic world of riches. All I had to do was extract narratives from my imagination, learn to put them on paper, and sell them to somebody, and to whom exactly? I didn't know anyone.

After the Italian adventures, I settled into a life of relative solitude. I wasn't dating. My roommate Jonathan picked up strangers at the local bars at a feverish, almost daily pace. The befuddled men he brought home found me reading a book, preferably of some literary worth, a Eudora Welty perhaps, or later, Barbara Pym, the British spinster who seemed to peer into my bizarre twenty-something-year-old's soul. I knew what it was like to be surrounded by sexually and romantically active people while staring in the background as the average Pym heroine might do. I was a most unusual West Hollywood gay man. I was capable of going out and having drinks with friends and my roommates, but I avoided becoming romantically and much less sexually involved with anyone.

My mother's worst fears about me were true. I was calling myself a writer without writing for anyone or any one goal. I was getting by on part-time work while living fairly well thanks to the relative prosperity and success of my roommates. That they put up with me was their contribution to the arts. No, we hadn't come to the United States to live like this. Writers like Hemingway had left the country to live like this elsewhere, but Paris had become too expensive to maintain a bohemian lifestyle, and I wasn't about to be down and out like Orwell. The irony was that I was *living well* in an expensive American city, but I still walked in the streets without a clear direction in the world, as a drifter would. Unlike Kerouac, I didn't set out to live on the road. In L.A., without a car or a license, my aimlessness was marked by the path of my feet walking, riding the bus, peering from its windows at the landmarks of Hollywood success.

I began to write laconically, with a sense of loss perhaps. My characters were Barbara Pym light. An early novel, *Miss Lilly's Last Stand*, features a bumbling heroine, a lively spinster involved with a religious fanatic who wants to bomb an abortion clinic. I never developed it beyond a first draft, but I still remember the enthusiasm I felt for this dark comedic tale. I wrote it in record speed over a couple of weeks, and then I inexplicably abandoned it, out of an inner fear that it wouldn't survive a rewrite, that I would find a way to ruin it. It haunts my imagination and has become a permanent fixture of my files, but I have resisted the temptation to look at it again. The style was clumsy and youthful, but the story itself had its charm. Miss Lilly is an affable, awkward woman who wears hand-knit sweaters that smell of fresh wool. Her teacups are more important to her than whether a man finds her attractive, and when one eventually does, she falls in love madly enough to ignore that he's a terrorist until it's too late.

It was another bumbling, charming, middle-aged woman who led to one of my first publications. "Miss Consuelo" was a short story about a Mexican immigrant woman trying to write a romance novel that reflected that particular anxiety expressed by my mother: "We didn't come to the U.S. to live like this."

My mother had by then enrolled at Los Angeles City College, and my short story portrays a middle-aged woman who becomes a romance novelist while attending the same college. My mother never entertained writing ambitions, but amid our many conversations, she mentioned reading Mexican illustrated romances. The heroine was often an innocent country bumpkin who arrives in the city, gets defiled by some handsome but deceitful ruffian, and then gets even by becoming a big success by opening up a successful restaurant à la *Mildred Pierce,* for example. "I could write one much better than that," she said with a condescending tone.

"Then maybe you should," I said. I made her tell me her ideas. A beautiful heroine arrives to lord over an avocado plantation in California in the days of the Spanish colony. But then she couldn't expand upon it.

"Look, I'm not the writer," she said. "You use it."

I didn't know how to write about an avocado plantation without cracking up. To me, it just seemed funny to associate romance with avocadoes. My earnest mother may have regarded plantations as the right setting for that type of steamy tale. But I imagined a heroine running through a forest of trees with ripe avocadoes falling on her head, ruining her hair, and staining her many outfits. The images were clearly comedic, and that was the spirit in which I eventually wrote the story. Consuelo pens a tale, "Romance of the Guacamoles," for her creative writing class, and the teacher, who prefers somber, Updike-like scenarios of middle-class marital disasters, ridicules it. He advises her to get in touch with her immigrant angst. But Consuelo feels she has to remain true to her instinct for passion. By the time I finished the story, I was acquainted with *The Writer's Market,* and its companion volume, *The Fiction Writer's Market.* On Saturday mornings, I walked toward the local post office on San Vicente and Santa Monica and sent off my submissions to the various literary journals that populated the land. I was determined to have them publish me whether they knew it or not. Dozens of rejections began to arrive, sometimes with hand-written comments and words of encouragement. I rarely spoke of rejections. Even acknowledging them would curse the roll I was on in writing short stories. I was enjoying myself altogether and continued to write at a furious pace. My roommate Jonathan, after saying goodbye to a trick, would sit down and help me through the grammar.

Éxito, or the Language of Success

"We have to tame the Chilean accent," he said, the one he detected on the page. He was a bright, educated young man with an MBA, whose addiction to porn, sex, and pot seemed like the perfect contrast to the more ascetic lifestyle I led down the hallway in the other room. The keys of my old typewriter made a racket that penetrated walls. Jonathan and his tricks banged into the wall with heavy sodomy. But Jonathan seemed as devoted to editing my short stories as I was to writing them. Yet, instead of being grateful, I was also judgmental. I was annoyed by his tendency to bring strangers into the house. I liked him. He was warm and personable, but I didn't like the men he picked up on the streets. When our new roommate, Sean, came to live with us in fall 1986, he immediately noticed Jonathan's habits when he heard a disturbing argument between Jonathan and a young trick who wanted money after their encounter. The argument escalated, and Sean feared they would start a fight. Finally, the young trick settled for some undetermined amount and walked out in a fury. But it came close, Sean reported. My need to remain alert became acute after that. Jonathan was picking up dangerous hustlers instead of just average Joes. I also didn't appreciate Jonathan showing me his collection of pictures of all the men he'd picked up in the past couple of years. He had stashed in a shoebox Polaroids of men posing naked, sometimes frontally, other times with their buttocks to the camera. He kept them the way others might keep baseball cards, and he often felt the need to show them off to me. As much as I appreciated Jonathan's help with my writing, I felt threatened by someone who was sexually active. It was either my own hang-up or just a gut feeling that Jonathan was playing with fire. Who was I to judge? I was the asexual artist next door. I continued to bang away at my typewriter, he banged away at strangers, both noises for neighbors to complain about.

Sean brought much-needed sanity, the right mix of someone who was involved in the gay community, and who dated often but without the excess I saw in Jonathan, and without the recourse to illicit drugs. Some time in late 1986, Sean gave me a message from an editor at *Puerto del Sol*, a literary magazine from New Mexico State University. I called the editor back, and he wanted to make sure my story "A Spring Color" wasn't being considered by anyone else. I could barely contain my excitement and sound professional.

"Yes, you may have the rights to publish my story," I must have said, sounding mechanical, and emotionless, figuring you're not supposed to scream, "Oh my God!" at an editor when your first acceptance arrives in the form of a phone call. I sounded sober, smooth, and in control. The story was a rare Joycean tale of a child roaming around a house in Santiago, a barely fictionalized glimpse into our home at La Palmilla. After reading the first couple of pages of *Portrait of the Artist as a Young Man*, I figured I could write that. This was my first acceptance outside the university, where *Westside*, a UCLA journal, had published a short story in 1985 as I was graduating, after years of rejecting me. Another tale of growing up, the surreal "Uncle Memo," was accepted shortly afterward by the *New Mexico Humanities Review*.

Then, the editor of the Arte Público Press decided one day to publish "Miss Consuelo," along with two more stories, "Pinochet in Hollywood" and "Patroklos," in the now defunct quarterly *Americas Review*. Written more or less at the time I was preparing to apply for graduate school, all three stories would be published after my graduation. It took that long to get them to print. I managed to prove to my mother I wasn't simply sitting out in coffeehouses pretending to be writing. I had acceptance letters to prove it. Much to my chagrin, my mother couldn't read any of my stories. The English was too advanced for her, but in my attempt to share "Miss Consuelo" with her, I later adapted it to a play, something Mother could experience through the visual aid of actors playing out the dialogue. Later, "Miss Consuelo" was also published in the twenty-year retrospective by *Americas Review* and was picked up by National Public Radio's short story series, where it aired on New Year's Day in 1993.

The stage continued to lure. I admired the actors. They seemed audacious and brave enough to face up to rejection. One audition in high school and another at UCLA's theater department exhausted my ability to withstand public ridicule. I could not bring myself to audition again. Literary rejections, at least, occurred in the mail. Yet, actors attracted me, and I found myself thinking I could somehow cling to them, that their beauty and appeal reflected upon me, that I could seduce them with words. The stage, rather than the screen, also proved safer to someone easily intimidated. I couldn't walk into an agent's office and convince him of my worth, my bankability, the inevitability of my success that would help him collect his 20 percent cut. Selling oneself went against my personality, hampered as it was by diffidence that was blatantly pathological. My inability to speak to strangers, let alone promote my talents, derailed any Hollywood ambitions, so it made sense to try to write for the theater. It seemed to be populated by something other than egotistical, hysterical, angry people. I was wrong about that assessment, but I believed it enough in the 1980s to think I had some sort of future in the more genteel and less threatening world of the live theater.

In time, I met a man, Michael Kohl, who worked with the Celebration Theater, the only gay-themed company in Los Angeles, which continues to thrive today, and which later proved crucial to my ambitions. Kohl had become involved in the company in the early 1980s and in time became its interim artistic director. I met him, however, when he was the only non-Latino in a mountain retreat of gay Latino men. On my return from Italy, I visited the Gay Community Center in Hollywood, which announced a retreat for Latino gays and lesbians. I had never attended a retreat, nor had I identified specifically with the Latino community nor, for that matter, was I active in gay circles, seeing myself as a loner. Solitude and curiosity made me enroll; I figured I might even learn something about myself. I discovered that I was, in fact, a Latin American of some sort, that I had no business feeling I was detached from this particular community, but that I had returned from Europe as either a true loner or a snob. Ironically enough, I befriended Michael Kohl, the only Anglo who showed up. He was more supportive of Latino identity than I was.

He wrote musicals, directed them, and stated that the Celebration Theater was open to new plays. He gave me his number. Once we returned to the city, I called him, and he put me to work. He was involved in a reading of a play for another local theater company. He needed help and solicited mine. In a few days, I was substituting for his lead actor at a rehearsal. Professional actors were crammed in his living room reading a play by a local playwright. I didn't think of myself as an actor, but I was a warm body—I could substitute and read out loud. In a few days, a public reading would help the playwright hear his work in front of a public. At the reading I passed out the program and made myself useful. I don't recall the content of the play or whether it was well received. I was thrilled to be involved. Michael was an energetic, tall man who had pictures of himself smiling next to Tennessee Williams. The great late playwright had come over to his apartment one night with a group of friends for some late-night partying. The picture, along with the ambience around the theater, made sense to me. Michael had been touched by Tennessee, who was nicknamed the magic bird.

Éxito, or the Language of *Success*

I asked Michael if he would read my plays. We met at a local diner where he lectured me for three hours on the strengths and weaknesses of my efforts. He also urged me to write gay-themed plays so that Celebration Theater could consider them. I thought such a thing would prove embarrassing to me, and to my mother, and to my entire father's family in Santiago, which was busy pretending I didn't exist. I held on to the hope that I would one day exist in their eyes, denying myself the right to exist in the here and now. Michael could see how these issues and the diffidence that plagued my personality affected my writing, and he urged me to start from a place of truth. I knew no such place. I was writing to come across as clever, witty, brilliant, debonair, European, and many things that I wasn't. I didn't identify with gay issues, and while I could write a part for a gay character, I didn't think of my work as being about gay identity. I had problems with both Latino and gay identities. I was writing for an abstract general public that could identify with the overall human experience without ever getting too specific about mine. My identities embarrassed me. I ran from them.

Michael proved to be invaluable in encouraging my work, and the privilege of watching actors and directors work in various productions at the Celebration, housed in a tiny space in Silver Lake, kept me engaged and stimulated. Yet, it would take a long decade before I returned to the Celebration and watched one of my plays debut.

Another small theater on Wilton and Sunset Boulevard, the Nosotros Theater, was founded by the legendary actor Ricardo Montalban to promote Latino talent in Hollywood. It featured a playwrights' unit in addition to an actors' lab. I joined both. I began to write scenes for the actors' lab and enjoyed watching actors memorize my lines and interpret them. More importantly, I wrote my second full-length play for them.

The ongoing turf wars of Nosotros Theater kept us all guessing about the organization's viability. Would it be there the next day? A meeting of the board and its members led to shouting matches and death threats. The board members hired security guards, fired the artistic director, and brought in a new one. He taught at the local Los Angeles City College and had great ambitions to turn Nosotros into a regularly producing theater company, as opposed to a support network for actors. He was looking for a play to do. The director of the writers' unit pointed to my play, *Exiled from L.A.,* about an errant Mexican family that moves around, in this case from L.A. to D.C., the exact opposite of our family's journey. One phone call, I hoped, would transform my life. I called my mother. "They're going to do my play!"

"That's wonderful, but are you sure it's ready? Are you sure you're ready?"

"Of course, I'm ready!" I said. A young playwright will always say this, but I was terrified.

I hadn't been offered a production. I had been asked instead for rewrites for a possible production. I had interpreted the phone call as a tentative acceptance, a mere formality that would become the real thing. The artistic director needed some rewrites, which was natural. I would provide them, and the production would happen. I started to alert my friends that the Nosotros Theater would be producing my play. In a few weeks, a flyer would be forthcoming, I announced. For an entire week, I skipped work. I made serious cuts, reshuffled scenes, took out characters, added one or two. I was convinced I'd transformed this simple family comedy into a precious, promising play that would alter my life for good. Things were looking up at the Nosotros. The infighting that had threatened to dissolve the theater went into temporary hiatus. Ricardo Montalban blazed into a meeting one night like a knight, descending from his limousine, and accompanied by his own set of security men. With all the members of the organization present, I among them, he made the feuding board of directors embrace and publicly apologize to one another. Wearing one of his dapper suits, this overpowering gentleman, superstar of Latino actors, with his suave, sophisticated voice and charming accent, spoke of the importance of unity. The organization he'd founded threatened to evolve into trench warfare, but Mr. Montalban's charisma allowed for a truce in the constant backstabbing that went on behind the scenes. I introduced myself to Mr. Montalban as a playwright. He shook my hand and said, "I hope there's a part for me in one of your plays."

"Always," I said.

In truth, there wasn't a part for him, but that was all speculation anyway. Next time the playwright's group met, the head of it informed me the artistic director had found another play, a trial drama that better suited his needs.

"So you're saying you're not going to do my play?" I asked.

"Well, who knows? Maybe in the future, but not now," he said. "You're young, though."

Young and devastated. I went into a depression that only a kid high on his horse of invincibility could plunge into. It was difficult to eat for an entire week. It was difficult to go to work and smile through my pain. Telling my mother meant further humiliation. I made a quick phone call and simply let her know the facts and tried not to show any emotion.

"They're not going to do the play," I said, and then cut it short.

"I'm sure other things will turn up," was all she could say.

I left it at that. At work, it was back to the book orders for the Latin American Center. I asked myself if I'd spend the rest of my life there. It wouldn't be a bad prospect if I became a full-time clerk, with health benefits, and a possible retirement fund. I found some level of satisfaction taking care of my books, as I saw them, as if they'd been pets and I worked at the zoo feeding them. Johannes Wilbert, the head of the center, had written an entire series of *lore* books, among them the *Folk Literature of the Selknam Indians*, and the Chamacoco Indians, and the Toba Indians, and other such titles that published the mostly forgotten literature of Indian tribes in South America. I never read them entirely because I tired of creation tales, wise-talking animal spirits, and other such spiritual niceties. I needed more modern psychological perversities in my reading (Dostoyevsky and Camus, for instance). But Professor Wilbert gave me a copy of Carl Jung's *Man and His Symbols*, and I was mesmerized by the discussion on archetypes, which enlightened me at last about the purpose of characters in a story. The professor didn't realize that I took reading seriously—enough to threaten my clerk duties. I read more books on the Latin American Center's dime than I should have, but I hope today that they'd appreciate that the ambience—along with the professor's gifts—helped me develop as a writer.

Only a few weeks later, in early 1986, the *Los Angeles Times* featured an article that changed my life: a report on the state of Latino theater in Southern California, of which there was a dearth in contrast to the huge burgeoning population of both immigrants and native-born Latinos that was transforming L.A. into a virtual Latin American city. I learned that the South Coast Repertory Theater, an important regional theater in Orange

County, was sponsoring the Hispanic Playwrights' Project, a unique project that aimed to develop Latino playwrights and Latino-themed plays, coordinated by a young director recently graduated from UC Irvine, José Cruz González. The article listed an address for sending submissions. I had nothing to lose, so I sent them *Exiled from L.A.*, the play that the Nosotros had briefly considered, then dropped.

A couple of months later, I got a phone call from José Cruz himself. Three playwrights had been chosen to present their plays as part of the project. I wasn't one of them, but three more playwrights were invited to participate during a week of conference talks and readings. The artistic committee at the South Coast Rep was improvising; and how grateful I was that they were. They wanted to be inclusive without necessarily opening the doors wide to all playwrights who had submitted material. They decided that this project would benefit from other voices, particularly from the participation of younger playwrights. They would *pay me* to attend this conference and house me. Since my own mother had trouble housing me, a hotel room felt like a luxury, a prize won on some TV show that came with exotic travel to Orange County.

My mother drove me to Orange County as if to see this for herself. She dropped me off at a local hotel, a modern lavish one across the street from the South Coast Repertory, where the Orange County Arts Building was being built. "Your cousin Catalina should see this," she said. Catalina had begun to fail in school, and my mother was looking for some inspiration, but I didn't think a young writer's accomplishments were of interest to my cousin.

"Mother, what does she care about any of this?"

"Because she needs to see it for herself. If you work hard, you get invited to participate in things like this. What is this exactly? What will you be doing with them?"

"Oh, talking about my play, I guess," I said, rather uncertain, but I felt the need to strengthen the argument. "And interacting with important people in the American theater."

She left me at the hotel, satisfied. Yet another point for me, I figured, something to remind her when she brought up the fact that we were still living like immigrants.

Three playwrights—Eduardo Machado, Lisa Loomer, and Arthur Giron—presented their plays, and I watched them work with professional directors and actors. Actor Danny de la Paz had recently starred in the film *Boulevard Nights*, and I spoke to him between rehearsals of a play by Giron. Seeing a film actor live still seemed to have its own cache. I was pleased at Danny's approachability. He eventually read my play, *Exiled from L.A.*, and tore it to pieces with an irate tone of voice. But a movie star was good enough for me, and when he decided he didn't want to drive back into L.A., he went up to my hotel room and slept on a foldout. I wanted to volunteer my bed, but he was humble enough not to displace me. I had a film star in my room, and it seemed, well, cool for once.

I observed the rehearsals for Giron's play for another reason. The director was Jorge Huerta, who'd written a book—at the time, the only book—on Chicano theater. He encouraged me to continue writing. Like Michael Kohl before him, such encouragement made a difference to a self-esteem-deprived young man like myself. Jorge exuded so much warmth that I couldn't help but feel a magnetic pull toward him that would last for several decades. He was a middle-aged Chicano who came across as sophisticated and dynamic, yet blunt, plain-spoken, and humorous. I was clearly in awe of him and of the affection he showed me. I readily accepted any affection, particularly when it seemed real and not a product of lust, which I secretly hoped was present as well. But just as I let an actor sleep innocently in my room during this conference, I harbored an aversion to even the idea to seduce. I lacked the skill, let alone the confidence, to seduce a scholar/director such as Jorge, a professor at UC San Diego. Over dinner he told me plainly, "We have a playwriting program at UC San Diego. Why don't you apply?"

The next morning, from the hotel, I called the office at UC San Diego and requested an admission form, nine months before it was due.

At the conference we read the plays by the other participants. This also meant reading *Exiled from L.A.* out loud. Jorge praised its dialogue but said I didn't have a plot. Everybody agreed. I had no sense of dramatic structure. Situations arose and then went in different directions all at once. No sense of unity. I would hear this complaint long into the future. I was much too carefree and improvisational up until then, not putting in the serious framework for developing a story with a beginning, middle, and end.

I returned to Los Angeles, ready to start a new play, *The Seductions of Johnny Diego*, which highlighted the seduce-able and seductive nature of a mysterious Vietnam War vet who returns home to Los Angeles to break hearts and take over the appliance sales company of his in-laws. As I saw it, the mix of grand ambitions and the banality of selling appliances to middle-class people created a world of tragicomic possibilities. This play proved problematic in its many versions. The main character's Chicano identity was inspired by Jorge's book and personality. It was as if I'd imagined the younger seductive Jorge Huerta and placed him in Los Angeles where Jorge had grown up. This became a trend: I would use my writing to initiate affairs on the page, my own way of capturing attractions and chaste love without the fear and the implications of touch.

At work, the mail carrier came in every day and initiated small talk. I took care of the Latin American Center's mail, distributed it, and kept the ones related to publication orders, which I filled. The carrier, a vivacious young man, Mark, wanted to know more about my private life. I didn't have much of one, but I volunteered that I was same-sex inclined, if not active. I told him I wasn't dating anyone.

"We'll see what we can do about that," he said.

A few days later, Mark called me at home and asked me if I minded Vietnamese men.

"I don't care," I said. I had no aversion to any race. I also just needed a warm body at that point. "Whatever works!"

Mark asked me to designate a meeting place. I didn't hesitate: Café Figaro. He said he'd send over a young man called Tyler. I showed up a few evenings later on a Wednesday night when nothing else was happening. I expected a brief encounter, an awkward routine of strangers meeting blindly, and then walking back to my apartment alone. When Tyler appeared, I sat up. Way up. Mark had described him as young, fit, and handsome, but I knew he had to say that to get me to show up. I was surprised that not only had Mark not lied, but Tyler looked like a Vietnamese prince. He had a lean swimmer's build, a smooth, medium dark skin, and a striking way with fashions, simple yet elegant, wearing black leather pants that highlighted his thin, shapely figure and a white shirt that was unbuttoned and showed a tight yet lean chest, muscular without being bulky.

I was speechless. He was a friend of Mark's lover, also a Vietnamese young man. Apparently it was his duty to introduce all Vietnamese gay men to available young bachelors like myself.

Tyler spoke English well enough for simple conversation, with a rather charming accent. He sold cars in Anaheim, Orange County. He wasn't happy with the job but thought he'd eventually get something else.

"What would you like to do?" I asked.

I don't recall the answer. Tyler didn't have the ambitions that would alter the world. I suggested he should become a model. He smiled nervously at the suggestion. He had made some head shots like everyone else in Hollywood, he admitted, but he had no agent. He didn't think of himself as an actor. He had been an extra in a film, but whatever worked, he'd do. You never knew when the industry would put out a call for a handsome Vietnamese stud to stand somewhere with his shirt off. Tyler had escaped Vietnam on a fisherman's boat with hundreds of other people, mostly men, perilously crowded and in unsanitary conditions. He had worried throughout the voyage that the boat might sink. The men were found after a couple of scary days at sea by a Thai vessel and taken to a refugee camp. He was accepted into the United States as an exile and headed for Orange County, where a substantial Vietnamese community had settled and prospered in the late 1970s and early 1980s.

I didn't know what to make of him. He was impressed that I was a writer, but he had no questions about my work. I said I was originally from Chile. He didn't know where that was on the map.

It didn't matter. For the next few months, I spent time with him in my bed, enjoying his presence and the geography of his body. For the first time in my life, I touched a man with a firm swimmer's build. When he went into the bathroom, I watched him move, admiring the perfect structure of his body.

Jonathan was impressed. He had not seen me bring anyone home before.

"I guess you were holding out for somebody special," he said.

Special indeed. There was so much lust expended in that short period of time that I knew it couldn't last. Tyler wanted it to last. He called me every day and mentioned the need to have a lover, to be with someone for life. I decided I needed somebody with whom I could speak about topics that went beyond our simple backgrounds. I wanted him to read a book. I didn't know Asian literature aside from the Japanese epic *The Tale of Genji* and some of Mishima's novels. I knew nothing of Vietnamese literature. I wanted to find something accessible in English. I settled for *The Good Earth* by Pearl S. Buck, a novel that had inspired me as a sixth grader; more importantly, I had watched my grandfather cry at the movie version when I visited Chile in 1975. The Louise Rainer character reminded him of his peasant mother. The tale had legs, as the executives said in Hollywood. Tyler was delighted about the idea of reading the novel. He hugged me when I presented him with the gift and seemed genuinely moved. We made love that night. The next day, he went home and completely ignored the book. Next time I talked to him, he said he had read the first couple of paragraphs and then fallen asleep.

"How can I be involved with someone who doesn't read?" I asked Jonathan.

My roommate stared at me, perplexed.

"He's hot," he said. "Don't give him a reading list; fuck his brains out."

I was a purist. Instead of being grateful that Tyler liked me and was willing to sleep with me in spite of what I considered to be my bodily flaws and deficiencies, I found ways to distance myself from him. I couldn't possibly build a life with him. I couldn't keep him around for long. Our conversation had become stultifying and repetitive. I wanted him to come back with a full review and appreciation of *The Good Earth.*

I was invited to the South Coast Repertory, only a short drive away from Tyler's apartment in Anaheim. When Tyler heard I was staying at a hotel in his vicinity, he wanted to come over for the night. Instead, I went with him to a Vietnamese restaurant and then spent the night at his place. I sensed that it was over. He didn't. He was talking about moving to the L.A. area, to be closer to me.

The following night, I attended one of the readings at the South Coast Rep. I allowed Danny de la Paz to come to my room, as if expecting something to happen. I was already breaking up with Tyler. I had spent a week enjoying stimulating theater talk with directors, playwrights, and actors; what I wanted more than anything was to be in the thick of things, in the midst of theatrical chatter. I failed to return Tyler's phone calls; at last he began to get the hint.

I did not appreciate what Tyler had brought into my life, including the physical beauty he possessed. I was bored with it, not because I was really wiser and brighter, but because I didn't know how to speak to him at a less pretentious level. I wanted someone to match my literary pretenses. Sex with beauty didn't seem as important as my need to do literary chatter. Now I read the *New York Times Book Review* by myself, but I don't expect all my friends to do the same. My inability to be loose and free, and relaxed, made me calibrate the value of a relationship in terms of how it catered to me. I wanted my potential lover not only to reflect my interests but to adhere to them as well.

That night, over dinner in Anaheim, Tyler revealed to me the details of a previous relationship. He had dated an older American man—in his early forties—who had become so obsessed with him that he learned Vietnamese. He wanted Tyler to come over and help him practice. That was his tactic for bringing him into his life. An ingenious ploy. Tyler said he appreciated it; even though he wasn't terribly attracted to this man, he saw him for over a year. He could at least practice his native language and share it with somebody. Later, I realized that I hadn't made an effort to find a common ground. For somebody who was otherwise curious about languages and international cultures, I saw nothing but failure in our other cultural divide—the one based on literacy, or literary pretensions. Perhaps Tyler, too, should have made an effort, but I could have used my educated instincts to find some other solution. I still regret my avoidance of him, and the complete solitude that followed this affair, which lasted some three whole years aside from a one-night stand. Gay friends seemed surprised to hear me say, "It's been three years since . . ."

A young man is not supposed to do without sex for three years in West Hollywood, or in modern America, for that matter.

When I returned from Orange County, there were several messages from Tyler. Jonathan was giving me that look of suspicion.

"What did you do?" he asked as if assuming something was wrong because of Tyler's insistent phone calls, and that I was to blame for anything that went wrong. "Did you pull out your reading list again?"

"No, no reading list this time," I said. "I just didn't call him back when I was too busy meeting important figures in the American theater."

"What a jerk!" he said. "You should have brought him along, paraded him in front of everybody, and people would have turned around and envied you. That boy's a catch."

"I should have thought of that, but I only thought about how limited our conversations are."

"So you get the worst of both worlds—you end up without the sex and without the ability to brag and promote yourself. You're hopeless."

"Well, maybe there's more to this world than just bragging and promoting yourself."

"At least keep him for the sex."

"I'll be the judge of that."

I phoned Tyler back and told him I couldn't see him any longer. I didn't explain why. Jonathan's assessment of my problems made me more defiant. I couldn't readily admit that he was mostly right.

Tyler attended a party I hosted a year later and he looked as stunningly beautiful as ever. He had a new American boyfriend, a gorgeous blond boy from Alabama with an aw-shucks smile that confirmed he was enjoying his sensual encounters with my lost Vietnamese prince. I was, and remained for a long time, alone.

I was too much in love with my pretenses and my claim to a literary lifestyle, enamored of being at Café Figaro reading Anaïs Nin, drinking cappuccinos. I don't know if this was the worst of times or the best of them. I was young, enthusiastic about learning, and collecting books from the Bodhi Tree Bookstore on Melrose across from my apartment building, augmenting a bibliophilic lust for more words, my own and those of others. My records show I was reading *Does God Exist?* by Hans Kung and *Démocratie et Totalitarisme* by Raymond Aron in French, along with Dickens's *Little Dorrit,* Márquez's *Chronicle of a Death Foretold,* and *The Rise and Fall of Athens* by Plutarch. Yet, I couldn't communicate with strangers, or keep beauty in my life, and I didn't feel confident that I was appealing to most men.

"Tyler found you attractive."

Jonathan continued to offer his unsolicited assessments of me. He urged me to go into the streets of West Hollywood with him at two a.m. as the bars were closing. He said that's when the men were most available.

"If Tyler was calling you, and you agreed he was hot, you should have taken that as a compliment. You're not that ugly, see?"

"I just don't see the world as you do," I told him.

"No, that's why you don't get laid, and you blow your own chances. You should go out with me."

"I've got the new Barbara Pym to finish."

"That's for old ladies."

"No, it's not. She's a major witticist."

"Oh, great, try fucking that."

"And then I want to finish a new short story."

"That typewriter is going to drive the neighbor crazy. You need to get a PC and join a new age."

"I'm slowly getting there. I just need time."

"It's nearly two, and I'm outta here."

Jonathan lived in West Hollywood. I was paying a visit.

One day, Jonathan succeeded in pulling me out of the house to attend a performance of a couple of artists I had never heard of.

"Oh, you'll see, they're fabulous, they're provocateurs. They're boyfriends, and one of them at least gets naked."

"On stage? Live? Do I want to see that?"

Apparently, I did. I followed Jonathan out that day, and he drove us to the little Cast Theater, where Tim Miller was performing a revealing monologue show with his then boyfriend, Doug Sadownick. I didn't think it was possible for an artist to reveal aspects of his private life in public, end up naked on stage, and provoke the audience into thunderous applause. I felt more self-conscious than the artist.

"That's what you should be doing," Jonathan told me at the end of the show, just to rub it in.

"I don't know about that," I said. "It works for him, not me."

Afterward, Jonathan insisted I should meet the two artists/writers, and he enjoyed my embarrassment in front of them. Both Tim and Doug were not simply performance artists. They also were sociable people who stuck around to speak to the audience.

"My friend here wants to be a writer," he told them. Both Tim and Doug looked delighted. Doug pulled out a card.

"You should both join us for one of our parties," Doug said. "Give us a call. Perhaps you'll perform for us one day."

I didn't call, and I never performed for them. But through the years, I managed to run into the couple and they continued to encourage me. Doug stopped me at the gym to give me the address to their home, where they were holding one of their parties, another one I skipped because I felt so intimidated by the dynamic queer duo. I feared their audacity and, particularly, Tim's nudity as if, through some trick, they would find a way to get me to reveal myself in public. Even twenty years later, Tim Miller showed up at Arizona State University and wanted to do brunch. I gladly took him to a local eatery. He was wearing shorts, exposing well-exercised dancer's calves. It was a warm day in March, and I was still relishing what passes for winter in Arizona with a fashionable winter jacket. Two decades had passed, and I couldn't help but notice his fitness and how comfortable he continues to be in his own body. Tim must have gotten the hint by then that I expressed myself in my own peculiar ways, and that I was a reticent person in contrast to his wonderfully rambunctious one. I hid it well, my personality, like my body itself. I displayed an agreeable nature but never quite my true self to him. It was something Jonathan complained about.

"You live under a strange shadow," my roommate finally told me one day before one of his forays into the night. "What I don't get is how calm and normal you appear to be. I know there's more to you than all that, because I can read it into your short stories. There's a big Chilean soul waiting to escape from the boundaries of Pinochet's repression."

He actually blamed Pinochet for my psychological repressions, and it was as good as any dissection of me at the time. I give him credit still for introducing me to a great performance artist, for helping correct my English, and then for psychoanalyzing me with some degree of accuracy. I wasn't quite as grateful as I should have been. I made fun of his insatiable need for men to my other friends and moved out complaining about him, missing out on his charm and his ability to get me out into the city. I got a call a few years later from his mother, asking me how she could publish her son's poems.

"He wrote wonderful poetry," she said, "and I know that he valued your friendship. He said he enjoyed editing your work. It inspired him to write his own."

I didn't even know he had passed away.

"He had a fatal reaction to the medicine," she explained. He had been diagnosed as HIV positive when I was in graduate school, but he never bothered to reveal it to me. He sensed that I held back, and he did, too.

After my invitation to Orange County, my mother saw glimpses of *éxito* in me. I had proved that I was not a dilettante walking the streets of L.A. and wasting time in cafés. Some good had come of my efforts, no matter how desolate I felt. I was much too used to being alone—and often, I simply chose this as a form of alternate lifestyle. It wasn't a done deal that

I would go to graduate school. UCLA had rejected me twice by then, and Nosotros had clearly put my playwriting on hold. It would be a decade before Celebration became seriously interested in any of my plays. It would be a long wait for anything to happen in my writing life, and my private life had turned into another empty promise as well, and I was to blame for it, too.

I remember a strange night in West Hollywood when I couldn't withstand the solitude that stifled my life like hot air. I needed to get out. Sean was proving himself the best of the roommates by then, a responsible prelaw student who'd eventually attend UC Berkeley and make a mark as a Bay Area lawyer. He was also generous about reading my scripts and providing valuable feedback. Jonathan continued to edit as well, so I had managed to put two roommates to work on my writing. But with Jonathan I had to cope with his unpredictable personality and the sometimes frightful strangers he brought home.

I needed to be on my own that night. I walked to the Melrose district, to a local bar. I had a couple of beers and met a young man from what was then called Yugoslavia. He didn't want to talk, which was just as well given my bad luck with intellectual chatter, and took me to his apartment around the block. I had sex with a perfect stranger; what might have seemed an average night out for some men in West Hollywood was for me completely and absurdly unknown. I did not enjoy the sex or the small talk afterward. The young man wanted to call a cab for me; I said I didn't need it. I wanted to get away. Once I walked outside, I realized it was close to three a.m. The streets of this normally noisy, crowded city looked desolate and threatening. A few cars drove by, but otherwise there was no one else around. I started to walk along Melrose Avenue, feeling the dread of being alone in the middle of the city. It was becoming colder and more ominous. A mugging or worse would not have been difficult to execute. I felt threatened, defeated by the city, endangered by the slow, dreaded pace of night.

I found a few coins in the bottom of my pants' front pocket, and called home. Both Jonathan and Sean were asleep, and the answering machine picked up. I only had two more quarters, good for two more calls. The second time, my roommates again failed to pick up. With great fear, I tried my last quarter, and to my relief, Sean answered. He'd heard the phone ring twice and thought it was a crank call, but this time he had surmised that somebody was calling for serious reasons.

"I need a ride," I said, trying not to sound too desperate. "It's kind of scary out here."

I stood on the corner of Melrose and Fairfax. In front of me was my former high school, from which I had graduated less than a decade before. I was not proud to be on my own, waiting for a ride in the virtual dark of night. If my mother had seen me, I knew her likely refrain: "We didn't come to the U.S. to so-forth-and-so-forth." The few minutes between my phone call and Sean's arrival crept along in excruciating slowness, reminding me that I was alone in front of my alma mater, that I hadn't done enough to be proud of my life, that I had broken up with the only beautiful young man who had expressed an interest in me because he didn't read the same books. I had sabotaged our relationship and didn't have much of anything to show for myself. That was not quite the message I once read on the exit signs of JFK.

7

María's Wedding

I returned from Italy a transformed man, arrayed in a fake Armani sweater and a pair of pseudo-Versace slacks. Streaks of deep auburn highlighted my normally dark brown hair, a "step" zigzagged around the right temple, and thick gel stiffened the rest of it into stringy clumps. UCLA students refused to let go of their cotton T-shirts, sandals, and shorts. I stood out: polished, tanned, rested, and ready. Slickness did me good. A young man I met at the weekly gay student group meeting asked me if I was independently wealthy. I answered that I was independently poor. He thought I was hilarious, believed my line to be wit rather than truth telling. Wit could be enticing, erotic, appealing. I made him smile, and then he agreed to sleep with me, one of the first instances in which I found myself projecting an alluring image of some kind, at least in the United States. Solitude asserted itself quickly, as did the reality that I was still the help's son. My socioeconomic status hadn't changed, just the wardrobe. Still, in this period, illusion reigned: I managed to feign a life that Americans confuse for success. Perhaps that's all success ever was: illusion. I just never knew how to project such a thing until Italians urged me to shine my shoes, and to buy new ones to begin with.

It was 1984, the year of Orwell's nightmare. Yet I lived more closely connected to the Orwell of *Down and Out in Paris and London.* I was not literally homeless. My mother would not have allowed that. She was still a force in my life. I slept on her couch and let that be my shelter. I earned minimum wage as a cashier, but I would never go hungry if she could help it. She preferred Italian slickness to grunge. She wanted me to be myself, but my Self was also a work in progress. The Olympics were coming to Los Angeles. Reagan had lulled us into complacency with his "Morning in America" commercials. Even my liberal mother would end up voting for him. I threw my vote away on a Libertarian candidate. It was a year of prosperity, not necessarily for me, but I was young, thin, and stylishly poor. Confidence made me dream of success, of love affairs, of something that might break the restlessness and eager anticipation of great things to come. My mother beat me to it. The big changes came from her, but so did the steps backward. I witnessed. I participated. I tried my best to learn.

The immigrant life continued as it was before my trip, its limitations unaltered. It was back to basics. My mother woke me up before school and asked me about my plans. My plans? I was wearing the same pajamas I wore at fourteen. I was still in school. She worried that education had become a way of life, subverting and delaying the future. I was an ass about it.

"What about your life?" I asked.

"This isn't about me," she said, but I was making her feel the heat. I was a true *atrevido*, a disrespectful brat who'd been to Italy and thought he was the shit. One good slap across that Chilean low-class face of a *roto* (the Chilean word for "the poor" but also for someone without manners), and she could have taken care of it. But she was more respectful of me than I was of her. I was supposed to be an adult, and she was trying to talk to me like one.

"You're in your forties," I went on. "Soon you'll be fifty, and you're still living like this. Carmen's still your roommate and the two of you don't do much except work at the same old thing. You're Hollywood maids for life."

"I'm not a maid; I'm a household supervisor."

"Whatever you call it."

"I came to the U.S. to work, not to study," she said. "You've had all the opportunities; I haven't. It isn't fair for you to say these things about me."

I tried to rein in my offense and attempted to answer her questions without lashing out.

"And I do have plans . . ."

"Such as?"

"I plan to write," I told her. She turned away with a look of disappointment, even grief. She knew what that meant. She saw the evidence, a grown-up man sleeping on his mother's couch. She walked away, despondent. It was not the life she had envisioned for me, or for herself. She worked for a world-class fashion designer as the "household supervisor." She saw first-hand what true success meant. It didn't look like this, the life I was leading.

I remained optimistic. I thought of writing as something that would free me of my immigrant past, but I had trouble regarding my immigrant reality as the stimulus for the writing. I thought philosophically and read Aristotle. I spent time at the UCLA coffeehouse in Kerckhoff Hall writing notes, profound statements about illusion and reality. My imagination took me far from the Los Angeles of the maintenance people who are my closest kin. I wanted to write treatises on totalitarianism and libertarianism, freedom and the arts, the politics of self-expression, and other topics suitable to someone who sought to perfect the masturbatory art of profundity. Mother had reasons to be worried. But she didn't know how bad it really was. I was not turning out anything of consequence yet. The collected Orwell sat on the lamp table, dog-eared and stained. I was rereading it for clues on the type of work I sought to do. Of what use would those things be to us? If I was sleeping on the couch, it was because I didn't have a bedroom of my own. How would Orwell get me a bedroom to myself? Not even Virginia Woolf would help provide this, a room where I could write and isolate myself. I chose a coffeehouse of my own. There I found the time, and the crowdedness, needed to isolate myself in a corner surrounded by a noisy, stimulating ambience.

One day it dawned on me that I could prove my cleverness on television and earn some much-needed cash. I filled out the questionnaire for a game show in a sparkling, shiny office inside a skyscraper in Century City: it was *Joker's Wild*, a poor man's *Jeopardy*. The pace was slower—you didn't have to accelerate and beat your opponent to press a button. The contestants took turns answering questions. I could do that. Speed intimidated me, and during *Jeopardy* I blurted out answers that often ended up as comedic relief for people in the room. But *Joker's Wild* accommodated my slower, more thoughtful approach. I knew I could do it. The young assistant welcomed me into a room along other aspirants and wished me good luck. I answered trivia questions within the allotted time, and I was happy to discover I scored in the 90+ percentile range. I was asked to stay for an interview with the producer. My luck had struck, or so I thought. A question about the late Chilean president Salvador Allende clinched the interview as if it had been tailored just for me. The producer walked in with the

intention of weeding out the highest scorers. Some twenty other participants had been asked to stay, people of different ages and backgrounds. I
looked young, confident, cocky, the one with the black, polished shoes.

He asked me what I did and what I planned to do in the future.

"I'm a student at UCLA, and I'd like to go to film school," I said, trying to sound cheerful like a game show contestant who's already in front of
the cameras.

"Oh? Why do you need to go to film school?" he asked. I didn't realize
it was a trick question. "I mean, you could learn to do it independently."

"I like the learning environment," I answered, still not realizing what I
was stepping into. "And financial aid helps pay for my education."

That stopped everyone in their tracks. The producer's assistant looked
tense, as if they knew what that meant to their boss. The producer was a
relatively young man in his thirties but acted nowhere near cool or hip
around me. He responded like a cantankerous teacher in a Dickens tale.

"Oh, you're a welfare case," he said.

I smiled. I didn't know what to say to that.

He added, "You expect the taxpayers to foot the bill."

"Ah, if you put it that way," I answered. The rest of the scorers laughed
nervously. I tried to laugh as well, managing a strange gurgle of a sound at
best.

"OK, next," he said, and then briefly interviewed everyone else in the
room without ever sounding nearly as punishing, as if he exhausted his
condescension and spite on me. I waited for him to weed through nineteen
more postulants. Then he went into a room, and his various assistants followed him with a servile posture, carrying their clipboards. We waited a
few more minutes, staring around nervously at one another. One of his assistants emerged from the conference room and then called my name
along with three others. We were the first ones to be eliminated. I was es-
corted out by a security guard and left out on the street.

What the fuck . . . ?

I asked myself the question a hundred times while waiting for the bus
to shuttle me out of Century City. I continued to ask the same thing riding
home and the rest of the night as I tried, to no avail, to sleep. I played out
the situation over and over again. I didn't get it. I wouldn't get it until a few
years later when President Reagan announced another round of cuts in
student financial aid. People who remember the gentle, kindly grandfather

figure forget that this president cut student aid to the bone (even while students voted for him). Living in the Democratic bubble of Los Angeles, it's easy to forget people still believe student aid constitutes a waste of taxpayers' money. I hadn't realized that some people in so-called liberal Hollywood would think the same. Or perhaps the savvy producer who's read his demographic studies must have sensed my attitude would turn off viewers who wanted to see reliable, enterprising, Republican-leaning racial minorities on the screen, not welfare queens. I knew I'd blown it with my words. His answer revealed a deep contempt that I eventually blamed on the Republicans. I felt redeemed when, in a frank interview, Benjamin Aaron, the doctor who saved Reagan's life after his assassination attempt, revealed that he couldn't have made it through medical school without the financial aid the president was trying to cut. The president had gone into the hospital bleeding, and he'd told the doctors, "I hope you're all Republicans." The Democratic-leaning doctor reassured him, "Today, we're all Republicans, Mr. President." You'd think the president would have been grateful to us welfare queens after that. I can't blame the president for my elimination from *Joker's Wild*, but I learned to connect the dots. The producer saw a Latino-looking kid who was getting educated at the taxpayers' expense, and he chose not to put such an offensive entity on national television. I could have used the opportunity to reassure my mother I wouldn't end up on the streets like Orwell. Anything would have helped at that point to remind her that a liberal arts education was not a ticket to poverty in America. But I was proving that argument wrong.

My mother softened up. She offered to ride the bus if I went ahead and borrowed her new Nissan Stanza to drive to school. I reminded her that if she took the bus, she would have to get off on Sunset and walk up a hill. Women walking up that hill wearing uniforms were invariably maids. She chose to be identified as such for me. That was her first new car, bought as a cooperative venture with her roommate Carmen. She had saved enough to buy off Carmen's half and then decided to hand it off to me. This is what parents did, apparently, when they prospered. She expected me to jump for joy.

"That's not necessary," I said. I didn't know what was worse, being a brat because you take your mother's means of transportation or an ingrate because you don't. But this was about her pride, not mine.

"University students must have a car," she said.

"We can't afford a second car," I reminded her. "We're not that type of family."

"You can borrow it every other day."

"It's all right; I've got a bus pass. It takes me everywhere."

I insisted and stuck to my principle. My mother was weighing the evidence: in L.A. the bus system transported the elderly, the student, or the help. I qualified as two out of three, and my mother hated that. I didn't have a license, and I couldn't afford a car. I took up part-time work as a cashier in a UCLA dining facility. I'm a good cashier, I figured, with an ability to close the register and balance it to the penny, but the young man who slept with me because of an Armani sweater walked in one day and saw me working there. He stopped returning my phone calls. I had not lied to him or anybody else about my financial status, but my clothes, my talk of art and theater, my Italian holiday, and the various indications that I was writing a novel or two and a play and a philosophical notebook had endowed me with a cosmopolitan flair that was illusory. Another piece of wardrobe—the dining facility's apron, clearly non-Armani—spoiled the effect for him. I wasn't just the help's son any longer. I had become the help.

I'm getting married!"

One evening that spring, my mother surprised me during supper with an announcement of rushed and sudden nuptials. Nothing really surprised me, I thought. I remained cool and calm. Secretly, I was stunned. How did this happen? It was a marriage of convenience, of course, to benefit the groom primarily. Though not a real marriage, the economic calculations made it seem like an actual Hollywood one, which technically and geographically it was. I gained a stepfather. It's still bizarre that I should call Osvaldo Campos my stepfather. There was affection for him on my part, but it had nothing to do with fatherhood, more with the closeness and intimacy gained from an awkward but inevitable situation, the immigrant need for survival. Osvaldo stood to gain papers, those ever elusive legal documents that millions of immigrants in California lack. Hence, the wedding. A rushed one. Things worked out fairly well until Osvaldo went and got himself viciously murdered.

"Wait, Osvaldo's already married!" I spoke up.

My mother shook her head. "In Chile, yes, of course, but in the United States . . ."

"That marriage still counts."

"They won't find out about it."

"And his wife?"

"Sandra knows."

"Well, if everyone's OK with it, I guess."

"I'm not asking for your approval; I'm just telling you."

"Sorry."

"You called me names only a few months ago . . ."

"Names?"

"You said I was headed for my fifties."

"But that's true."

"It hurt. I'm getting married."

"I didn't mean for you . . ."

"No need to talk about it anymore. We need a witness—you and Sandra."

"I'll be there."

"Wear something Italian."

Osvaldo and his wife Sandra both entered the United States as tourists and then overstayed their visas. Sandra had a brother in the United States, but—while legal himself—he couldn't apply for permanent legal status for his sister. The best he could do was provide moral support while she and her husband established themselves in L.A. They hadn't completed their university degrees in Chile; in the United States without papers, they settled on cleaning offices and homes. Osvaldo boasted a more formal education. He'd married Sandra after leaving a Benedictine monastery where he had been apprenticed to become a monk. He gave that up. He surrendered chastity for marriage to the lively, pretty, and outgoing Sandra. Her father was a Jewish merchant who'd been separated from her mother in Chile. There was something exotic, even "dangerous" about Sandra, at least for a man such as Osvaldo, influenced by a celibate, Catholic lifestyle. In Chile, being even half-Jewish apparently still titillated. It was flirting with a perilous Other.

Osvaldo exuded discomfort around independent women, and he let them know it: "Too many mannish women these days, acting tough, losing their appeal." His marriage to Sandra was hanging by a thread, but he didn't seem to know it.

I went to visit and watched cable television, another minor luxury I couldn't afford. The birth of MTV promoted quick bursts of titillation for those of us with short attention spans. I emulated Madonna's "Like a Virgin" as she writhed on a gondola in Venice or exulted in Laura Branigan joining an orgy with masked strangers in "Self-Control." It was my attempt at sublimated passion left over from my own Catholic upbringing. Osvaldo berated me: American pop culture created eternal adolescents, and I was the reigning example of it.

"You're in your twenties, and you fall for that crap," he said. "Madonna on a gondola; give me a break!"

"Touched for the very first time," I sang back, teasing him, and he rolled his eyes.

I was a consumer of the filmed musical image, absorbing quick flashes of spectacle that overloaded the imagination, making me feel overwhelmed, even dizzy. The camera refused to stand still in the average music video. My reading, which was once calm and linear, is now as jumpy as my 1980s imagination, exploding in megabytes of stimulus. Reading is a form of processing the imagery of language—as if my own thoughts were on a screen in a music video. The music in my head has not entirely stopped. In the 1980s, each song evolved into a short film in my head, a minor narrative. Pat Benatar runs away from home as she belts out, "We are young." Bruce Springsteen bids us to go "dancing in the dark." Michael Jackson begins his scary ride into the darkness with "Thriller." I was enthralled with the illusion for hours on end until Osvaldo turned off the TV and made me concentrate.

He wanted to talk. He continued to complain about the assertiveness of American women. Watching them on television, he lambasted the look of corporate suits worn by professional women.

"That's not feminine," he complained. "Women should look delicate and beautiful, not hide their appeal."

"Hey, it's the modern world," I told him. "Women aren't putting up with your shit."

But Sandra had, until then. In the United States she had become her own woman, something other than the missus. "She's learning that American feminist talk," he complained. "She doesn't want to have children, wants to be equal partners in our business, talks back at me . . ."

Conflict between them—a standard battle of the sexes—had been brewing for a while when Osvaldo decided he needed to marry for papers. I didn't think María would go ahead with it, but she made it clear she would.

María's Wedding

I continued to live in my own world of the imagination, and that summer was spent writing odds and ends, bits and pieces of unfinished plays and novels, or watching Olympic coverage and the lively Democratic Convention in which Jesse Jackson quipped the line I remember best: "I would rather have Roosevelt in a wheelchair than Reagan on a horse." How true, it seemed. How inevitable that a progressive ticket that included a female vice-presidential candidate would defeat Reagan in the fall. The United States seemed more progressive from the blinders of Los Angeles culture than it was. For all my mother's fears that I was becoming a vagrant, I could point to the promise of youth. A vibrant, scintillating life was moving forward, in theory, and in aspiration. I enjoyed the idea of my mother getting married, too. I liked the circus of it all.

Sandra found another friend to marry her, and she and Osvaldo moved forward equally toward legality. It became a competition of sorts. The moment Sandra obtained legal residence before Osvaldo did, she gained power over him. He so resented the idea of female domination that he must have looked for a woman who appeared vulnerable, with no real prospects for marriage. He found my mother.

My mother's private life had stalled. Friendships abounded, but private affairs did not. She had left behind sex and passion for a life of self-abnegation. In her thirties, she retreated from any relationships and started to live the life of the spinster even while looking appealing and vivacious. The few men who courted her learned a lesson. She wasn't interested in men from her own social class. She was an immigrant, her English substandard, but she wasn't about to date men who shared those deficiencies.

"The only choice I might have—if I'm lucky—is a bunch of foreigners," she said. "Forget that."

Mother didn't marry an immigrant for real, but in high pretense. It wasn't difficult for her to transfer hidden yearnings for a personal life into a phony marriage. There were no intimate feelings involved, just friendship, and a need to help, maybe even a touch of adventure, a feeling of underground intrigue.

Sandra, however, claims that her late husband Osvaldo was sexually ambiguous. "Something was going on in that mind of his," she said recently. "I was too young and naive to notice. He spoke ill of gay men, but he insisted on living in West Hollywood within walking distance of all the gay clubs. He abhorred talk about sex, and yet he had a strange ear for picking up sexual noises among the neighbors in our apartment building. He became obsessed with them. He made me go knock on our neighbors' door and tell them to keep it down because he couldn't sleep with all that noise. I was naive enough to obey him and go knocking on the neighbors' door to ask them to quiet down. All that repression he absorbed from the monks stuck with him through our marriage. I suspect sexual repression, whatever his sexual identity was."

Osvaldo and María—two Chileans with profound issues regarding sexuality and intimacy—had found each other in Los Angeles. After Osvaldo's cloistered youth in Chile and my mother's own upbringing by nuns, the two of them made for an ideal asexual couple in a make-believe marriage. It worked somehow, this life thus created, wearing masks like the theatrical people they'd become, taking on roles to substitute for something concrete that was missing in their lives.

The entire arrangement could be summed up as follows: Osvaldo pledged to contribute to her Hollywood rent for a year. This wasn't a demand of hers, just his way of contributing something. Aside from a marriage certificate, nothing was written on paper. A sloppy informality reigned throughout this negotiation. A minor investigator could have blown the lid off the marriage with a few basic questions, but as things would turn out, the INS didn't even have rank amateurs to investigate anyone. It was overwhelmed by numbers of people entering the country and then staying. Mother contributed to this growing national dilemma, but she wasn't trying to make a statement. She was just helping out. That was a simple arrangement between friends, as she saw it. The added bonus was a bit of cash over the course of a year, but even that she would manage to pass up on as well.

Osvaldo and Mother were married by a female Presbyterian pastor in Malibu in the spring of 1984. Religion was the last thing on anyone's mind. The choice of a female priest struck me as odd, given Osvaldo's beliefs in strict roles for women. In making the arrangements, Sandra made the choice for Osvaldo randomly out of the phone book. Osvaldo needed his papers and chose not to make a scene over a female pastor. A lively, middle-aged woman, the pastor opened her doors to this motley crew of foreigners. I was one witness, and Sandra—Osvaldo's actual wife—the other one. Neither my mother nor Osvaldo had practiced for this crucial day. They were dressed appropriately enough, Osvaldo wearing a dark brown suit and a tie, and Mother a loose, spring-weather dress with patterns of red and white roses. Though the bride was in her forties and the groom in his thirties, they constituted a Hollywood marriage as phony as the rest of them. When the minister bid Osvaldo to kiss the bride, they both froze. They hadn't considered the possibility that they would have to do this. The female minister noticed the awkward pause and saw the face of panic in both newlyweds. Osvaldo made a frightened move toward my mother, and she kissed him lightly on the edge of the lips with a look of embarrassment. The minister gave them a look, tried to smile, but seemed to be thinking through this ceremony—as if she were finally figuring it out. There was something suspicious about this union. The two newlyweds looked especially nervous around each other after the kiss. It was a Hollywood wedding all right, and an immigrant one at that. She wasn't new to this, I gathered. Which one's the illegal, she must have wondered.

"I took out a new driver's license with my husband's last name," announced María a few weeks later in the apartment she still shared with Carmen. "And I changed the name on my Social Security number as well. I'm now María Campos."

She sounded proud, as if the marriage were real, as if she'd actually entered a new phase in life.

"When's the honeymoon?" I asked. "I mean, you might as well get yourself a husband with benefits."

"Oh, I don't need *that* anymore," she said.

"When did it stop for you, in your thirties?"

"It never really started," she admitted. "My relationship with men has always been sporadic."

"You've been a saint, and I was the only sin. When was the last time anyway?"

"Last time . . . back in Maryland, it was M———."

"The black janitor. You're very progressive."

"I didn't sleep with him because he was black, but because he was married."

"So they have to be unavailable just like my father."

"I'm only attracted to what I can't have."

"Osvaldo's married—I mean in addition to you, so he qualifies. Time to fuck his brains out."

"No, he and Sandra might break up any day, and I wouldn't want a man to myself; that's a lot of responsibility. I want to be a full-time nanny, not a caretaker for grown-up babies."

"Is that all marriage is? Caretaking?"

"Just about. I can't be his real wife. I married him because he's already married, *y ya.*"

"You're messed up."

"No, *you're* messed up!"

My translation of Spanish-language conversations with my mother only captures part of the obtuse humor. Did I really say "fuck his brains out"? In Spanish (in Chilean Spanish at that), it sounds a bit more jovial, less explicit: "*Ya, po', acuéstese con su marido!*" The word *acostarse* literally means to lie with someone, but the subtext and my specific intent said something else. Chileans often say outrageous things in a casual, matter-of-fact style. I've always had problems translating this intimate family dialogue as a playwright. Characters who should be speaking Spanish—and Chilean Spanish particularly—have to speak in English. As an interpreter, I have to translate the experience for the English-language listener or the reader. It never quite sounds like the original, and I suffer for it. The playwright Joe Orton captured the essence of outrageous conversations among working-class English characters, but he was writing in his native language. I'm not. The immigrant is at a disadvantage when working in an adopted language. This aside is also an attempt to say my entire life has required cultural footnotes to explain both sides of the linguistic divide.

The marriage of María and Osvaldo became our 1980s Ortonesque comedy, a bizarre period in which we began to lead double lives. Orton's own biography would soon be playing in the Cineplex as *Prick Up Your Ears*, starring Gary Oldman. It set the tone. The system never caught on with our deception. It was perfectly possible to lose oneself in the United States, adopt a new name, and go unnoticed. Anti-immigration advocates had not yet turned angry. It was still acceptable to be an immigrant—legal or otherwise—if you contributed to the economy and stayed out of people's way. Americans went on about their business and didn't notice the sorry lot that made up the rest of us. My mother's new license listed Osvaldo's address. There her younger husband theoretically lived with a new wife and his first wife in a bigamous arrangement. My mother stayed with Osvaldo and Sandra for only a couple of months after she impulsively decided to move away from Carmen. At the same time, Mother decided to bring her niece, Catalina, to the United States, in yet another impulsive act. Catalina's tourist visa expired in a matter of months, and that meant yet another *indocumentada* living in the same apartment in West Hollywood.

I had warned my mother about the consequences of bringing her niece into the country at the same time as she was preparing to marry Osvaldo. I had moved out of her apartment and gone to share another one in West Hollywood with a couple of gay friends. One can adjust to family chaos, but my mother's improvisations at this point had become too dizzying even for me.

"You shouldn't be bringing your niece to the U.S. at this particular time when you're trying to make changes in your life—changes to benefit you. This is another mouth to feed, to begin with."

"I got married, gained a child. It's a change of life."

"Let Osvaldo get his papers first, then worry about your niece. Now we've got two people without papers, and you're taking on both."

"Catalina will study, and I will be helping out my brother back in Chile who can't afford too many children."

"Catalina's not a little girl. She's fourteen and may not be easily disciplined. Will Carmen adjust to her?"

"Oh, yes, Carmen. We'll see about that."

Carmen had been her roommate for ten years. Yet, she was never consulted about the decision. Carmen was opinionated and obstinate, and when she heard about the upcoming arrival of the niece, she did not take to the teenage burden lightly. Carmen may have been an immigrant Chilean, like my mother, but she boasted an upper-class upbringing in Santiago. She didn't have to put up with this arrangement, having to share a small apartment in Los Angeles with low-class types from Mother's family. Catalina landed at LAX with the marked barrio slang of a working-class neighborhood in Santiago. It was evident that the two women were not meant to share living space. Catalina proved to be an uncontrollable *atrevida*, and that's not the type of crap Carmen would have to put up with.

"So I told Carmen we'll separate," Mother told me over the phone.

"All for your niece?"

"We can't all live together. And it's time to go our separate ways. Oh, we had a little cry," she added, repressing tears. "We couldn't say goodbye.

We'd still live in the same city and see each other from time to time. But I have to take Catalina away from that. I stopped trying to referee between those two. Catalina makes comments about black men, how hot they are, and Carmen comes from a different background, where you don't say those types of things out loud, and it's time anyway—time to get away from Carmen. I'm a married woman now."

María was on the go.

"I'm one step closer," she announced on another one of my visits. She served a fresh batch of the steamy *pastel de choclo*, the corn-and-meat pie that had become her specialty through the years, and provided insights into her world in between glasses of Chilean cabernet. Catalina and she shared a foldout bed in Osvaldo's apartment. The arrangement was meant to be temporary. She was saving money and soon they'd have their own apartment. I often think Mother thrived on this type of inconvenience. A crowded, inconvenient place mirrored life back in Santiago, as if she couldn't be without noise and people coming in and out. She felt desolate alone and yearned for a bigger substitute family than she could ever collect in the United States.

"I quit working for Galanos, too," she added that day. "I'll have my own day care center. I've started with two children right now." Two different sets of parents up in Laurel Canyon had agreed to have María care for their two children in their homes, alternating the houses at the parents' convenience. She was happy among children. She had an ease and a love for them that inspired her to have more of them—not by begetting them, but by assigning herself their caretaker.

"Galanos has been a great boss," she explained, and caring for his house in the Hills had been an incredible opportunity for nearly six years, but that had to end, too. "He wasn't going to give me a raise any more. His personal assistant found out I was earning more money than she was, and it offended her deeply. Apparently she told her boss, 'Your maid earns more than I do!' When I asked for a raise, it outraged her even more. He couldn't give me a raise at that point. His assistant would have considered it an insult. Not my fault she went off to college and only got some measly assistant job that paid less than the help. I also called her up and told her I wasn't a maid. My new title was a 'key lady.'"

"A 'key lady'? I thought you were a 'household manager.'"

"That was a new one—I liked 'key lady' better. I took care of his house, I wielded the power, and, yes, I carried the keys. When he was in Italy doing some fashion show, I was back here in Los Angeles, making sure the workers came in to do repairs, or paint or build, and I supervised things, not just cleaned. I made sure it all ran smoothly. So now that I'm married, I have to move on. I have my lovely niece staying with me, and I have new responsibilities as her godmother. Things are moving forward."

"But then you have to come down the hill, and deal with a phony marriage, and a niece without papers—that's so much to take on when you don't have to."

"And I have a son who wants to be writer," she reminded me. "That worries me even more, really."

"You shouldn't worry about me," I said. "I am a writer, whether or not I get paid for it."

"This lawyer I saw on a talk show, he wrote a best seller, and he was able to do both. He's rich now."

"Good for him. Would employment do?"

"I guess, full time preferably."

"Part time is good when I'm still in school," I said. When September had rolled around, and a new quarter started at UCLA, I got back my cashier job. I was taking more Italian and French. That seemed exciting to me, even if my mother smelled another delay.

"You know what I mean, real work, something that leads to something."

"But the choices you make don't lead to great riches either."

"I don't speak English like you do," she said. "I came to work, not to learn languages. I communicate with my boss, but my sentences don't have to have perfect grammar, and that's the type of work I can get. But you have so many options. I'm waiting for you to do something."

She became a U.S. citizen in 1983, and while this fact made her feel she had made progress, it also paradoxically convinced her she was falling behind. Other friends who had migrated around the same time were buying homes, partnering up, and having children.

"That lady who lived next to us all those years at the Formosa apartment? She was an 'illegal,' too! Well, her husband bought her a house. They got to move out. They've fixed their papers and have a new baby. Her two grown-up sons are going to USC, and one is talking about marriage . . . oh, I don't know, they're just doing so well, I hate them."

"Well, you're a married woman now, so there's no need to envy them."

"Yes, but they're really married, they're a family, and they're normal in every aspect, and I don't live like that, and I don't know . . . I have to wonder why they have it all, and I live in make-believe. I hope one day you'll have something closer to the truth."

I wanted to ask what she had in mind exactly, but I didn't want to envision something I knew I couldn't yearn for, a traditional marriage or an idealized version of it. How odd, it seemed, that my mother, who never settled into anything like a conventional life, seemed to think there was something missing in ours. The adventurous choice of migrating to the United States had excited her imagination and led her to break from a more sedate life back in Santiago. Yet, the neighbor had emigrated from Mexico, illegally at that, and found herself married, her papers fixed, her children looking "normal." Then my mother would turn around, and there I was. There was something missing in her family, and particularly in me. Once in the mid-1980s she was astounded to hear Rock Hudson publicly admit he was dying of AIDS, but she never expressed any particular fear that I would be exposed to it. She saw me as her asexual son. I didn't make time for sexuality, or companionship, or even for friendship. I thought of weekends as writing time, and that worried her just as much as any extravagant lifestyle. She worried more that I would be alone, and sensed that I wasn't socially active, let alone sexually. She feared she, as an unmarried woman, had provided a bad example.

"One day you'll marry and do better than I ever did with that," she said. I was too busy discussing the plays I was writing, and my plans for graduate school. "I just hope you'll find what you're looking for, and I won't mention it again because I know what it's like to have parents rub it in your face. My mother worried about me, too, but instead I left the country."

Marriage to Osvaldo afforded her the satisfaction of being able to talk about a husband at least and to think ahead toward the day when he'd help her buy a home. If she had her own personal needs, she couldn't bring herself to express them. She never told me she wanted a husband, or even a lover. She could make crude jokes about sex, particularly around other women, such as the one about the Spanish Civil War and the nuns who are disappointed that Franco's soldiers ravaged the town's women but didn't get to them. A sick joke about mass rape. That was my mom and her Chilean friends after a few glasses of wine. But she could never seriously discuss with me any issues of desire. She revealed that she felt woozy, nearly fainted in a screening of *Picnic* in Santiago. That's because the actors

William Holden and Kim Novak do a slow bossa nova as they stare at one another with a scandalous look of yearning. The younger sister played by Susan Strasberg nearly throws up, crying that she feels sick. We watched it during the late show in Hollywood some time in the late 1970s. "I was such a young girl myself," María said. "I felt sick, too, just like Susan Strasberg. I almost fainted. Isn't that silly now?"

Yes, it was silly even in the 1950s, but she never seemed to speak of desire again. It made her uncomfortable during the rest of her life; that's apparently why jokes about nuns wanting to be raped struck her as hilarious.

It mattered little that, in Hollywood, we lived in an environment of open sexuality. The disco 1970s, the Hollywood scene, and the neighborhood of Hollywood with its Sunset, Santa Monica, and Hollywood Boulevards and its prostitution, sex shops—these were not places one could easily avoid or ignore. We did just that. My mother and I were both innocents in a sea of decadence. If that made us chaste in the eyes of some, it also created a strange dissonance in our lives. I was able eventually to act out on some sexual needs, but my mother—I believe—expressed none whatsoever for most of her life after her mid-thirties. As a family we had redefined normality. There was something strangely quaint about it all, this strange innocence in the midst of the sexually abundant world around us.

"I'm moving back with Carmen," she announced no more than six months since she had left. "And Carmen's all right with that. She needs someone to share the rent, and none of the roommates have worked out." She hauled her niece back in with her. If the younger woman didn't get along with the older one, too bad. They'd have to cope with it this time, and she would work to keep them apart.

"I don't understand," I complained. "You talk about progress, and then you go back to living with Carmen?"

"Oh, it's OK," she said. "Carmen and I are friends."

"But you said . . ."

"I said a lot of things, I'm sure. We weren't getting along. We weren't making any progress at that point."

"And now?"

"The old rules don't apply. We have to stick together, pay bills, do what we must to make ends meet, and progress . . . well, I have to make progress my own way. I can't just leave my friends behind. I have to take responsibility for my niece, too. I'll be a role model for Catalina: I'm enrolling in community college," she added.

After she reinstalled herself in her apartment on Formosa and Sunset, she enrolled in courses that would lead toward certification as a day care provider.

"Osvaldo says we'll look into qualifying for a loan for a house eventually, and I'll use it as my home day care center. His business is doing well, after all, and he is legally my husband. See? That works. What about you?"

It was a day for comparisons.

I was rejected by UCLA for graduate school, but it made no sense that I should have applied to film school. My sample writing was a play, not a screenplay, and my playwriting professor, Carol Sorgenfrei, let me know my chances of getting into the MFA program in playwriting would be good, if I bothered to apply. So, I didn't apply. I thought film school would be a greater challenge and allow me into that charmed world of Hollywood moviemakers, except that the MFA in screenwriting got hundreds of applications, and I hadn't even written a screenplay.

"Why don't you just follow your teacher's advice? She seems like such a nice lady."

"You don't even know her."

"I mean, she took time to counsel you, and you're not even following her advice."

"I wanted something else! Film school! Why can't I do that?"

"Then you'll need to write a screenplay."

"I can do that. But *anybody* can do that."

"Anybody? You can't afford to be a snob."

I had taken one class, written a short screenplay, but it wasn't particularly effective. I thought of the screenplay as a lower form of expression, and that my playwriting allowed for a more poetic sensibility. I sought entrance to a screenwriting program in which the admissions committee would recognize my loftier artistic goals. My supposed refinement would bring greater sophistication to the screenplay form, poisoned by the Hollywood mentality that I would expose in graduate school. I was stubborn enough to think I could get into UCLA film school with a sentimental play called *Flute of the Andes*, with Chileans turned into Peruvians, as a form of national cover up. It was my way of putting distance between my background and the characters, creating an alternate family, dramatized, idealized, entirely gracious and winning. Once rejected, I applied the following year with the same play and was again turned down. My stubbornness backfired. My attitude as a fake-Armani-wearing, step-haired, gel-heavy, college-educated, condescending snot of a kid had slapped me in the face just as the producer of the *Joker's Wild* had for other reasons. I started writing short stories. I completely changed my tune and followed a literary path. This was one reversal too many for my mother.

"You're all over the place!" María cried over the phone when she heard about what I was doing. "You're writing plays and short stories, and yet you say you want to write screenplays, but don't have a sample script to show. You're avoiding the main problem."

"I'm not!" I denied the assertion, although I was proving it every day with erratic choices.

"That's it," she said, giving up. "Talk to your stepfather, for once, now that you have one. Maybe he'll give you some advice. You need it; you're crazy."

Advice? He was a foreigner, he didn't understand the university system in the United States, and he worked in maintenance, far from the literary world I thought I needed, or deserved, to inhabit. Anaïs Nin's world made sense. In her diary, she was living on a houseboat and hosting—having fabulous sex with—Henry Miller. Now that was a grand literary life. This was the first time I remember my mother using the word *stepfather. Tu padrastro.* I had trouble getting used to it, but I began to suspect this marriage might mean more to her than circumstances called for. In our strangely farcical existence, this marriage could become genuine.

If he never became a de facto father, let alone consummated the marriage, Osvaldo became at least a good friend during this period. Closer to me at least. He became more my friend, I believe, than he was to Mother. He was physically attractive, thin, short, petite, but his sexist beliefs made me wince. I often wondered what might have been. Given his wife's later suspicions, I wonder what might have happened had he worked through the sexual repression allegedly guiding his life. What if he had "come out"? "An affair with my stepfather?" My youthful imagination invented erotically charged, if irreverent, scenarios, better accommodated in fiction and in drama. A new rule imposed itself upon my land of propriety: *thou shall not fuck your stepfather.* Osvaldo did develop the protectiveness of a stepfather. He would come to offer me financial help as his fortunes improved.

Osvaldo and Sandra moved into my neighborhood, West Hollywood, and started a maintenance company of their own. Incorporation meant taking on a professional role. They were no longer simple immigrant workers. They were the owners of a business. They put together a brochure of their services, printed business cards, opened up a phone line, placed a listing in the yellow pages, and ran several ads in the free weeklies that were delivered to every home in the neighborhood. As the business began to grow, they needed somebody who spoke—and wrote—English. They turned to me. I was graduating from UCLA with a humanities degree in Italian literature. I had no immediate offers of work. Other kids graduate from college with business contacts, parents eager to place them in entry-level positions with, say, prominent talent agencies. My "contacts" were all in maintenance, not in the film industry. I was not sociable. I did not network. I avoided the idea of soliciting people for anything. When Osvaldo needed help with basic editing in English, he wasn't shy about asking for help. My first job out of school was translating and then fleshing out Osvaldo's copy for promotional materials. I added some flair and style, a colorful adjective or two to make "environmentally friendly cleaning materials" sound appealing to a liberal Hollywood crowd of customers. American employers preferred to deal with intermediaries. They were one step removed from the unpleasant task of hiring illegal folks who actually did the cleaning. Osvaldo and Sandra contracted the workers, and the employers dealt only with the owners of the service. The middleman provided all the maintenance to the companies without their managers having to sully their hands with phony papers. Osvaldo's business thrived. Reagan was president, and the Camposes—one husband, two wives, one stepson—found a form of prosperity in this epoch.

My mother was livid at my involvement. "I didn't emigrate from Chile for you to be working in maintenance," she said over dinner. "That's for immigrants; we're citizens now. You're supposed to be educated. You have a bachelor's degree. You should be doing something else with your life."

"I'm only writing his promotional copy," I said. "It's writing of some kind; I'm getting paid for writing, see? Finally."

Mother gave me her look of exasperation, perfected over many years of dealing with me. "You know what I mean!" She added, "And I wouldn't call that writing. Do you understand the importance of this?"

"Do you feel betrayed?"

"It's not progress."

"Well, maybe *progress* is not the right word. He's paying me, and I don't think it's wrong to provide a service."

"Talk to me when you've got something to make me proud."

"What exactly would make you proud?"

"A full-time job—almost anywhere, as long as it's legal."

"But if I took a job with Osvaldo's company . . ."

"There is no such job! He hires illegals; they do the work. There's no full-time job with his company."

"He'll need a promotions manager."

"You know what I mean! You know precisely what I mean! You can't work for Osvaldo's company, and I don't want you wasting time even writing his brochures. It's not real writing; it's not creative writing. It's not what you were meant to do in this world, and I am not going to argue with you anymore about this. Just stop doing it; don't go near him! Find something else to do with your time."

Osvaldo believed he could get "a better class" of workers, and he offered to take me cleaning. He didn't always like the people he hired and was under the illusion that he could find people with a more cultured, educated attitude. Customers who never stopped to talk to workers would have the opportunity to converse, even bond with these English-speaking workers. It was a new angle in his attempt to sell.

"English-speaking workers will make the customer feel more at ease. They'll pay more for the service."

I had trouble cleaning for myself. I wouldn't go near a mop, even if Osvaldo offered to pay me well for it. His business began to have problems with employees, often people who were hired without references, and certainly without background checks. One of his workers, a young woman, lifted expensive jewelry from the home of an FBI man. The FBI officer told Osvaldo his worker had twenty-four hours to return the jewels or suffer the consequences. The worker delivered the diamonds to Osvaldo, who returned them with humble apologies. Osvaldo had no choice but to fire her. He called me to tell me what had happened, and asked if I would go with him to clean offices and empty trash cans as an emergency—for this time only. I turned him down, but my mother heard about it and delivered another harangue.

Living in my own apartment with a couple of friends in West Holly-wood, I became a temp for UCLA's personnel services. Within a couple of months, the Latin American Center, which hired me via the temp services, employed me for good, and I became an official clerk for their publication department. I took orders from universities across the country, including orders for the Hispanic Periodicals Index, and other research materials. It was a better or more "prestigious" job than working for Osvaldo's cleaning services, though it's possible I would have earned better money working for him. I had a concerned mother looking out for me, and her sense of immigrant progress did not include her son doing maintenance, let alone the promotional material for it. Working for the university was at least a step away from mops and brooms. This mattered to her deeply.

I continued to write, even finishing my share of "first" novels (I wrote five of them during my undergraduate years), along with countless short stories and plays. I wasn't submitting much of the work, but a semifinalist letter came from the Sergel Prize for the saga of Peruvians in L.A. called *Flute of the Andes*, the same play that had not impressed the UCLA Film School. This was enough validation to keep me going. In sixteen years, the Sergels would publish my play *Men on the Verge of a His-Panic Breakdown* through their Dramatic Publishing Company.

I wrote endlessly, without understanding the entire process. I felt inspiration and hard labor would get me somewhere, but logorrhea isn't the same as inspiration, as I discovered. I toyed with Serious Lit concepts, existential scenarios, the anxieties of a young repressed Catholic man growing up in Hollywood in the midst of heathens, among other such contrasts, and writing about sex made me as uncomfortable as the real thing. However, my most gregarious short story, "A Pope, a Mom, and a Peter," was risqué, and I feared submitting it altogether. As John Paul II drove into Los Angeles waving from the bullet-proof bubble in his Pope-mobile, I conceived of the story of a closeted gay man who has an affair with a Protestant boy the night before the Pope's arrival. He wakes up with the Protestant boy's penis stuck inside him. They attend the pope's welcoming committee dressed as a two-headed altar boy until they can get the erect penis out. It was probably the funniest, bawdiest tale I had written up until then—and I shirked away from publishing it. I read it out loud to friends at a party—mostly gay men—and my words managed to draw loud, spasmodic guffaws. With my delivery, I discovered a performative skill. I didn't know that humor was physically forceful, and that it had the ability to lift people from their seats. I no longer felt as short, or as quiet. Armed with the right language, I could have an effect on people. But given the bawdiness of the tale and the satirical angle, I feared my own capacity for sarcasm. My friends found it funny, but I didn't have the confidence to share it with others. I stashed away the story yet again, reinforcing my highly developed skill for overall repression.

My first one-act play had been produced at UCLA upon my return from Italy. I landed at L.A. airport with a rewritten version of the Cubans on a raft play that I'd developed before leaving. When I went to UCLA to catch up with the theater department, I found a notice posted on a bulletin board by a student director, saying he was eager to read new work for the student one-act series. Two days after I left him my script, he called to tell me he'd chosen to direct my play. I became hooked on the process—of putting on a play with actors, a director, lights, costumes, and sound. That first play, *The Sickle and the Hammer*, was my attempt to copy, perhaps even outdo, Jean Paul Sartre's *No Exit* in portraying a Latin American existentialist world. My main character was a woman, an ex–Communist Party official in Havana who'd had an affair with a married man and who was now leaving Cuba behind for good. On the boat she was stuck with her ex-lover's wife, who reminds her of her past sins. She thought she was running away by getting on a raft to Florida, but she was really committing suicide for being a ruthless government henchwoman. The boat is actually a ride on a moving, purgatorial land that floats through existence. This bizarre mix of elements created an entertaining dark comedy for the audience, but some people were not amused. One particular UCLA professor, who'd been blacklisted during the McCarthy era, stopped me in the hallway of Melnitz Hall (where the theater department was housed) and told me that my play promoted an anti-Communist view of the world that Ronald Reagan couldn't have expressed better. I smiled and told him I was sorry if he took it that way; I didn't mean any harm. But perhaps I did. Surely a satirist seeks to provoke some sort of reaction from people, but I didn't want to argue with a professor who's seen his share of persecution. The Cuban boatlift had been on my mind since 1980, when it first began. Reading *No Exit* had helped me coalesce two images, the entrapment of people in their respective destinies in hell and under dictatorship. I was fast and loose in my denouncements of dictatorships. My play in 1996, *Chilean Holiday*, which denounced the right-wing Pinochet dictatorship, got me tagged as a "left-wing radical" by a few patrons of Actors' Theater of Louisville, who filled anonymous feedback forms after the performance. "Why don't Communists like Reyes write about oppression in Socialist countries?" one of them asked.

At UCLA, another evaluation came from one of the creepier film school students—a young man who attended all the critiques and didn't seem to have much of a life otherwise. His take on *Sickle/Hammer* addressed the market value of the work: "It was mildly entertaining, but not commercial. Politics, philosophy, homosexuals and Hispanic characters— nothing that'll make money." He spoke with a calm, cool demeanor during our one-act forum when we dissected the productions and the performances, as well as the writing. A couple of Reaganite students complimented me for drawing a negative portrait of communism, which made me want to write *Chilean Holiday*, since I didn't think of myself as partisan so much as "pro-human rights." I didn't want partisan people hijacking the play to promote their politics. Yet, being told my work was not commercial seemed like the ultimate form of rejection in a mercantile society such as ours. I had brought together on stage elements of politics, sexuality, and Latin American history that interested me, and already the film people were telling me I needed to learn to entertain without those elements. I am still being told the same thing by people who judge my work: too many ideas, politics that offend both left and right, Hispanic people, and clearly not enough commerce.

That I had stirred some debate among my peers and managed to entertain them made my mother and her friends look at me in another light. María, Carmen, and other friends drove over to UCLA to see *The Sickle and the Hammer*. They didn't understand all the dialogue, but they heard the applause. I was the promising young writer at last, although my mother continued to harass me about proving it with money. Years before I could do anything with my promise, *The Sickle* helped establish my mother's support, no matter how tentative and concerned (and even condescending).

My mother decided that she didn't need Osvaldo's help with her rent, as had been part of their arrangement. Osvaldo had been saving up to start monthly payments in 1984. My mother said she wasn't in a rush; he could take his time. When he finally decided to start paying her to fulfill part of the deal, in early 1985, she decided that a more appropriate beneficiary would be me. Osvaldo surprised me by coming over to my apartment in West Hollywood. I thought he needed help with a translation of another document. He was paying a social call.

"And by the way," he said, "your mother thinks I should give you this."

He handed me an envelope with $250 in cash inside.

I was astounded to be holding that much money in my hand.

"From now on, I will deliver my monthly payments to you until next year," he said, describing the arrangement casually.

"Oh, OK," I said. What else could I say? I had forgotten the shame of being called a welfare addict by the producer of *Joker's Wild*. I was working for UCLA, and I never would be on welfare. Student aid was not welfare, I wanted to shout at the few people who would listen at a time when all government subsidies (except to the wealthiest sectors of society) were under attack.

Over the next year, Osvaldo gave me money owed to my mother to pay part of my own rent. This became my unofficial subsidy as a writer. No government arts grant—which I did not get at that age—could compare to this minor miracle. I had no qualms about accepting it. I just wanted to make sure I put the money to good use, to buy myself time to write. It helped to have a father after all. Now I knew how that thing called father-hood works. It's about support and favors, even guidance. The money freed up my time, the most precious thing a writer could ask for.

I continued to work at UCLA, but I negotiated a day off. I would work only four days a week for thirty-two hours. This extra day bought me a much needed respite and a three-day weekend in which I didn't do much else except write. It was the first break I got in my life as an artist. My mother had made her marriage of convenience work for the benefit of her son. "I never gave you a father," she once told me. "Osvaldo is the closest thing to it." Osvaldo seemed to agree about being my benefactor at least. I had the responsibility now of actually becoming a writer.

Osvaldo's business continued to prosper. It was time to start spending money after years of deprivation. He wasn't a particularly showy man, and he wasn't about to buy diamonds and furs for any of his wives. But along with my arts subsidy, he helped my mother qualify for a home loan.

"It looks like I'll be buying myself a house in the Valley," announced my mother. She quit working for the designer Galanos and enrolled at Los Angeles Community College to pursue a certificate in child care.

"What do you mean, you're buying a house? You're no longer working full time, and now you've gone back to school!" I said.

"It's a house owned by Sandra's brother in North Hollywood. He's going to rent it to me first so that I can start my day care center, but after that, I want to buy it. With Carmen's help, we'll have two incomes. Osvaldo's name will help secure the loan, but I'll pay the mortgage. Part of our arrangement."

"You're the one who told me to stay away from him."

"I meant from working for him. He had no business trying to offer you a job."

"But you have no qualms about using his name to qualify for a loan."

"And why should I? He's technically my husband. And Sandra's leaving him."

"Is she really?"

I shouldn't have been surprised. Constant phone calls from Sandra kept me abreast of their struggles. Sandra had enrolled in a computer course at a private college where she'd been working on a business degree. She invited Osvaldo to a get-together of the students, where they clashed over Osvaldo's anxiety disorder around strangers.

"He didn't want to talk to anybody," said Sandra. "He broke out in a sweat. He just couldn't handle being around my new friends. He didn't know anybody there, and words wouldn't come out. His English deteriorated, and he was suddenly shy. Since when is he shy?"

I hadn't imagined Osvaldo at a loss for words, but I understood the dilemma of certain immigrants. Loud and rambunctious in their native language, in English they will crawl in embarrassment into their little shell, often unable to speak at all. I had experienced a similar phenomenon in my summer alone in Paris when I was taking French lessons, and it took two months to form coherent sentences in French. I would withdraw from conversation, even run back to the tiny apartment I had sublet. There is a certain panic when words fail, and I was able to understand what had happened to the big shot, Osvaldo, at a party in which Sandra gathered with her friends and conducted herself with great skill. Sandra spoke English with an accent, but nonetheless nobody stopped her from expressing herself. The party was one more sign that the time had come to leave Osvaldo and strike out on her own. Maybe she'd figured to leave him to his new wife, my mother, except nobody seriously thought those two would actually get together as husband and wife.

In spring 1985 Osvaldo and Mother received the letter giving them an appointment at the downtown L.A. offices of the INS for their final interview.

"This is it!" Mother called. "The final step—I need to look young and sexy! I'm going shopping."

I stood outside Osvaldo's West Hollywood apartment on San Vicente Boulevard, leaning over his old Chevy, waiting for my mother to emerge. Osvaldo came to join me to wait for his wife to finish her final touches of makeup. There was some small talk about future plans. I spoke about grad school, in spite of two rejections in a row to film school, and Osvaldo looked amazed. How much more education do you need? he seemed to ask. It had taken so long to finish up as an undergrad; now I was thinking of applying for yet another degree, this time in playwriting. He looked supportive, but skeptical.

"You have that American drive, of always wanting more."

"Well, you're not doing so badly now; you obviously got it, too."

"Another degree may not be the answer for you, though."

"No, but it's precious time to practice what you really want to do. And time is precious, isn't it? You ever thought you'd be in your mid-thirties married to some middle-aged woman and deceiving the INS just to stay in a materialist country making more and more money?"

"True, it wasn't that long ago, I was in a monastery thinking I would practice celibacy the rest of my life and devote myself to nourishing the spirit. So, anyway, let's get this over with."

"How much time does your mother need?" he added.

"She's almost fifteen years older than you. You need her to look convincing."

"I could have been a monk by now."

"Not as much fun, I'm sure," I said.

"Instead, I sell maintenance and I have a fake marriage because I can't get papers any other way. There's something unholy about our lives. It's about money, and making it, and not much else."

"Well, you need papers; you'll figure out the spiritual shit later."

"If I ever get the time to read my old books again, St. Thomas of Aquinas, St. Augustine, I might be able to recapture what I had once. I spend the day shuttling illegal immigrants around."

"We all make choices," I said. "And staying in the U.S. is better than going back to a dictatorship you hate."

"True, Reagan's an asshole, but not a dictator. I have made a choice. I'm not complaining about living in the U.S., just that at one time, I thought . . . well, I believed celibacy would be the answer. To what? I'll never know."

María emerged from her hiding place wearing a flattering purple dress, her decent legs exposed slightly above her knees.

"Wow!" marveled Osvaldo. "Hot legs!"

High heels lifted her up to her husband's height and rejuvenated her look. She wore make-up, a rare thing, and her face radiated luminescence and vigor. Next to the rather boyish Osvaldo, who looked youthful, thin, and pretty in his own right, she stood as the sensual, slightly older woman. They made a handsome couple, highly convincing as the real thing. There was no reason why a straight man wouldn't have made moves on his lawfully wedded wife then and there. They drove off like honeymooners, Mother waving back at me as if she were heading for a Mexican resort.

"There she goes, Foxy Lady," I thought. Obviously, the folks at the INS did, too. In spite of a fifteen-year gap, the couple looked great together. There was no point asking serious questions. Their papers were immediately approved. The interview was over. Hollywood illusion worked.

The letter came from the Admissions Office of UC San Diego. I was one of two students accepted into their MFA playwriting program.

"Hey, your mother told me!" Osvaldo called a few days later. "We have to go out and celebrate!" Osvaldo had met a young woman from El Salvador. She was moving in. The man now had two wives and a live-in girlfriend. Sandra and he hadn't finalized their divorce papers, but how exactly did that work? Would a record of the second marriage show up? How would the Chilean marriage be dissolved? Would the state ignore his marriage to my mother? Apparently, it did. They were living apart, and Osvaldo was moving in with a new young woman. The arrangements had become routine, hardly news for us. The only papers I needed were from admissions. "How should we celebrate?" he insisted. "You tell me."

"I don't know. You've done enough," I said. The monthly payments had stopped. I no longer needed them. But one year had been helpful enough and a boost to my confidence. I had written enough new plays for one of them to get me accepted into graduate school. This was the earlier version of a play that became in the 1990s *The Seductions of Johnny Diego*, to be developed at UC San Diego and then later in the Mark Taper Forum New Plays Festival. It wasn't a masterpiece, but it showed early signs of raw wit with its emulation of Joe Orton in a Latino, Mexican American world. Grad school, I hoped, would help me concentrate exclusively on my writing, and that's all I wanted at that point.

Osvaldo bought a pickup truck, a red tanklike creature that intimidated its way down the street like a snarling bull. He drove to my apartment to show it off.

"Get in, let me give you a ride," he said as he pulled up outside my building. "We really need to have a drink, not only because of your acceptance to grad school, but because of . . . *everything*."

"Everything!" I said. "That's impressive."

I wasn't impressed by cars. I still didn't drive. In Los Angeles, I walked or took the bus. Osvaldo's former spiritual values had turned, big time, into family values—home, business, a gas-guzzling pickup truck, and a girlfriend and wives galore.

"It's too big," I told him, but for some people, there was no such thing when it came to cars and trucks, and Osvaldo was becoming this type of American. Bigger, better, mightier. I enjoyed the height and the elevation of the truck and could look down onto the smaller cars beneath. The driver felt empowered and proud. Osvaldo was eager to go somewhere and celebrate. I suggested the reliable Café Figaro, still my favorite West Hollywood hangout, for a bite and a cappuccino. He agreed; it was his treat. He was in a joyous mood.

"Without your mother, I wouldn't have made it this far," he said. "Without you either."

"Oh, please," I said, getting grumpy about this, even cynical. "You would have found somebody else to marry you for papers."

"I wanted it to be your mother," he said. "She's a pretty lady who deserves better. I'm not sure why she never married for real, but that's how it goes sometimes. I really wanted to help her get her home loan. She told me she wanted *you* to have a home, something she could never give you on her own. And to give you, of course, a father, too."

"She actually said that, that she wanted to give me a father?"

"She talks a lot about you. Face it; you are her whole reason for living."

"Ah, well, I wish she'd find herself another reason because I'm getting a little tired of being somebody's sole reason for living. It comes with strings attached. I'm not allowed to fail, for instance."

"You're not failing."

"I'm almost twenty-six and a part-time clerk. Mother has seen me as a failure for a long time. Grad school may not fix that. She knows that it's more education. She doesn't trust that. She knows it's not what Americans would call success, and more education may well be a delay tactic from confronting the market place of ideas."

"Just write popular movies. Why can't you do that?"

"I don't know. I end up writing about history, politics, Latinos."

"Boring. Write about detectives, and car chases and smash-ups. You know, stupid movies that make money. Why can't you do that?"

"I bet I could, but it's not in my genes."

A UCLA classmate of mine, Shane Black, had recently written a chase thriller called *Lethal Weapon*, filmed and released with Mel Gibson. I had quietly and shyly admired Shane from a distance as a promising, handsome actor (about as handsome as Gibson himself), but he found his calling in life with a humorous take on the chase thriller. I've been asked so many times (not just by my stepfather but by any concerned friends) why I couldn't follow that lead. I wondered if it was in the genes, the urge to tell that type of rambunctiously loud story with conviction, with manly guts. I knew "manliness" had something to do with it, and, again, the lack of it in me was one more fault in my literary makeup. I had no convincing language for sissiness and feared the ability to express it on paper except through highly indirect means. I couldn't share or explain this to Osvaldo, or anybody else. I did not discuss my personal life, notwithstanding the fact that I had trouble getting one to begin with. Whatever went into my writing was an observation of other people's lives; I had little interest in delving into my own. Shane had found a commercial venue for expressing something that apparently masculine men felt, a need to express their hormones through rage, guns, adventure, and lethality. I couldn't explode on the page.

"Your mother is worried about you—and I hope I have been able to help somehow."

"Oh, sure, you've been helpful."

"She loves you. She wants you to do better, and she feels she hasn't done enough for you. That's why she wants you to have a father."

"We survived without one, and my mother's always been an independent woman. We didn't need a father."

"Everybody needs a father."

"Maybe, but guess what? You're not my father."

This wasn't about him, he made clear. He insisted my mother was trying to constantly move us in a direction toward progress—or an illusion of it. She wanted me to enjoy the blessings of home and fatherhood; Osvaldo was part of that new mission. He knew precisely what she was up to and even embraced it as noble.

"She always talks about her regrets, about how not giving you a father helped make you so . . ."

"So different?" We never talked about sexuality, his or mine, but the subtext was clear: fatherlessness equals homosexuality for a young man. The pop analysts on television still repeated that old mantra.

"Well, as if there were something important lacking in your life," he finally said, avoiding the real topic. "When she suggested I should turn the money I owed her over to you, it made sense. You've never had a father give you money, but now you do."

"My actual father—Guillermo Reyes—gave me his name," I said, lest we forget that my late father had never denied his paternity. "He also kept up child support until we left for the U.S."

"I didn't mean anything against your father."

"I just want to make sure my real father doesn't get pushed over in this equation." Not that I had thought much recently about my actual father, but I felt the need to fend off this intrusive stepdad.

"But I'm the one who's taking responsibility now," he claimed, and this seemed like too much of an impertinence.

"But it's not real!" I reprimanded him. "It's not a real marriage. You're not my actual stepfather; it's all make-believe. It's my mother's way of creating a family she could never quite give me for real."

"Don't be an asshole. It isn't easy for a single mother to marry. We men abandon women. We always end up with younger ones. We don't like them aging even when we get old ourselves. And single women with kids—they have trouble remarrying, I read somewhere."

"I don't believe this," I told him, amazed. It just didn't sound like the old Osvaldo I'd gotten to know, the one whose political views once annoyed me. "You're sounding like a feminist. I'm just not used to that."

"I'm clearly not a feminist, but I think I understand a little better what women have been through, especially the immigrant ones. Most women that age have enough trouble getting married, but when they can't speak English well, and everything begins to sag . . . well, you know how it goes. I have tried at least to show my appreciation and gratefulness to your mother for helping me by helping you."

"OK, that's fine, that'll do," I said, embarrassed, my eyes buried in the foam of the cappuccino. My mind was cluttered by so many things—the future, the aspiration to write, the need to get away to grad school, to leave these people behind. How pathetic they all seemed. To me, this was a phony marriage, and a phony Hollywood lifestyle. We had failed to make a real life for ourselves in the United States. Our lives had become an arrangement. I didn't think of it as a triumph. I thanked Osvaldo for coffee and desserts. One thing at a time: the real gratefulness that I felt would have to be expressed somehow much later, after his brutal death.

"Well, time to go," I said cutting things short. I could have stayed longer, talked about other things, but I was impatient, as if I needed to get on with my life then and there. I was bothered by him and my mother and all the immigrants in Los Angeles hedging their bets on something like a marriage of convenience.

"I'll drive you home," he said, resigned to my brattishness, as I behaved like a teenage stepson he was impelled to care for. He dropped me off in front of my apartment, and I barely waved goodbye. I'd never see him again.

The confrontations with my cousin escalated. My mother managed to arrange an abortion after her first pregnancy, but after that she refused to fly back to Chile and ran away from home. She was a strange presence that first Thanksgiving of my graduate school years when she arrived at my mother's apartment while we were eating dinner with Carmen's family. My mother made Catalina stay at the door, and once she walked back inside, prepared a paper plate with turkey, mashed potatoes, yam, and cranberry sauce and then stepped out to hand it over. Dressed in a black dress with high heels and frizzy hair, Catalina looked like a woman on her way to a cocktail party rather than the seventeen-year-old ingénue that I still remembered. She smiled and waved back through the window at the rest of us with a sincerity I found askew. She was living on her own with a boyfriend we didn't know, and although she had come asking for food, she was capable of smiling as if she were leading the life she had chosen in high spirit. It was sad that she could walk away with this carefree quality about her, carrying a paper plate covered with aluminum foil, pretending nothing was wrong with that picture.

"I only brought her to the United States to study," María said that night to Carmen's sisters, Carmen, and myself in the afterglow of the Thanksgiving binge. We drank coffee and tried to eat pumpkin pie despite being satiated. "But she didn't want to live around too many old ladies."

"And we're supposed to be the old ladies?" asked Carmen. "Who does she think she is? *Es una atrevida. No digo yo?*"

"Young people want excitement," Mother went on. "But she didn't know how to get it out of school . . ."

"She got it after school obviously!" said Carmen.

"She's young; she chose the wrong company."

"She got pregnant!"

"I know that! And there I am, a Catholic woman who has to pay for her abortion, but I figured I was to blame for bringing her here, so what else was I supposed to do?"

"Have her deported."

"I tried." My mother revealed that she had gone to the INS to consult about her niece. She was hoping they would deport her, since she had failed to put her on a plane back to Santiago. "They said they can't be chasing after runaways. Can you imagine that? I bring them a tip about an illegal immigrant, and they can't do anything about it. In fact, they asked me about my papers. I told them I was a U.S. citizen. In this stupid world, they wanted to deport *me*, a hard-working taxpayer, instead of the troublemaker."

I began a short play, "Deporting Perla," in which a woman tries to get her niece Perla deported, but the INS agent falls in love with the niece and has the aunt deported instead. I never finished it, but I was slowly beginning to get the point that our strange lives were worthy of interpretation.

"I'm responsible," my mother continued. "I didn't realize some young people don't really want to study even when we try to make it possible for them to do so. I assumed everyone was like my son here."

The women turned to stare at me. That angelic smile on my face hid the strange alienation I felt. Sometimes you do have to run away, but I interpreted that as a need to rebel against one's elders in a symbolic way. It's a rite of passage to grow up and assert one's own independence, but it's also disastrous if it's all about frustration and the venting of rage, and you don't have the skills to back them up. My severing ties started with a need to go to UCLA and then to UC San Diego as a graduate student. I didn't hold that need against my mother. She had encouraged it. But that type of thinking also made me seem so conventional and "straight," part of the equation against which Catalina rebelled. I was the cousin who studied, read books, behaved properly, and was ultimately the bore. I didn't envy my cousin's fate. She eventually broke all ties, not only with us but also with her family in Chile. She gave birth to two children whom she abandoned on my mother's doorstep. My mother drove those children to their father and left them with him. Catalina's actions became an unsolved mystery for us. Her family in Chile has never heard from her. My mother did not understand this type of failure.

I went into a new stage as a playwright grappling with the need to interpret, and then "translate" for an American audience, an immigrant experience they otherwise didn't witness through television, film, or theater. It seemed like a good mission, but it came with its own struggle. Anglo Americans aren't always compelled to enter into our world; they see the immigrant as someone who adapts himself or herself into their world. Unlike my UCLA classmate Shane Black, I didn't know how to interpret this reality with a car chase and massive weapons. My experience had been defined by the feminine, by women struggling for survival in a foreign country. I went back to San Diego that Sunday after Thanksgiving with the understanding that I would make my experience somehow accessible. I had some ideas, but it would take years to do anything with them.

I graduated from UC San Diego with a degree in playwriting in 1990. I had lost track of my arts patron, my stepfather, who had helped buy my mother's house. In three years, I had spoken on the phone with him barely a couple of times, but another trip to Europe, a summer internship in San

Francisco, a heavy load of course work, and a tendency on my part to limit extended visits to my mother's home prevented me from seeing him. Then Mother called from Los Angeles.

"Osvaldo is missing," María said.

On the night of September 14, 1990, his girlfriend, the Salvadoran young woman whom I hadn't met, waited for Osvaldo at the apartment she co-habited with him. She had received a phone call from him as he was about to leave one of the office buildings that he and his workers cleaned, not too far from where he lived. Half an hour went by, forty minutes, an hour. She fell asleep on the couch and woke up past midnight. There was no sign of Osvaldo. She decided to give it more time and woke up with the light of dawn. He hadn't come home that night.

She called up the people she knew, such as Sandra and Sandra's brother. They called the police.

"They say he's missing," my mother told me. "He probably took off on a trip to show off his money," she added. My mother was trying to find the humor in the situation, so certain that it would end with a funny anecdote, some last-minute adventure, a flight to Mazatlan, beaches, girls, another girlfriend perhaps, a need to get away from the current one. You know, Osvaldo and the ladies. "*Se hace el interesado*—he's making himself seem so important." A nervous laugh accompanied the statement. That Osvaldo, such a clown. "He'll show up a week later with hickies on his neck."

A week later his body was found inside a trash can in an office building. He had been severely beaten, his head bashed in. His pickup truck was gone. A search through credit card records revealed a charge for gas at a station in Arizona. The Arizona police arrested the group of teenagers driving his truck.

The sordid details of what happened came from Sandra, who heard it from the police. But the police got their story from the killers, a suspect source. No one could tell the victim's side of the story. Osvaldo allegedly picked up a teenage girl on some Hollywood corner and drove to a parking lot to have sex with her. Two male teenagers followed and pulled him out of the car before he touched the girl. They attacked him with baseball bats. The girl was their accomplice. The three of them absconded with the truck and drove out of state.

The Osvaldo I knew had almost become a Benedictine monk and wasn't in the habit of picking up teenage prostitutes. Yet I'm not sure any of us questioned the police report. We accepted the alleged facts and decided not to discuss what, if anything, they meant. We believed the story and found it too embarrassing to discuss. The Osvaldo I knew was sexually repressed and despondent about prostitutes, gays, and "loose" women. Perhaps because of that, he may have crossed a line to taste his share of temptation, to be a "john." Without the facts, I don't believe what the police told the family. I don't believe the young killers who took his life, and I don't consider them reliable witnesses to Osvaldo's final moments in life. If there's a secret life, we're all entitled to one, as I see it. But having to hear it from those who killed him . . . that's not my idea of proper closure. I fear he never got one.

"Don't come for the funeral," said my mother over the phone. "I'm staying away."

"Now what?" I asked. "Why can't I go?"

"The INS will deport me!" she said.

"Where did you get that?"

"I talked to the father of these children I care for. He's a lawyer. He said marrying somebody for papers like Osvaldo did is a federal offense. They could deport me!"

"Mother, you're a U.S. citizen; they can't deport you."

"They could revoke my citizenship or they could send me to jail."

"Mother, you're not being rational."

"Stay in San Diego. I'm not going to the funeral. We can't be involved with Osvaldo any longer; it's dangerous."

Mother implored me to stay away, and so I did. I regret it now. It was a safe choice, but the wrong one. Sandra was still his first wife, and the only valid one. She had been a partner in the business, and she claimed the property. The new girlfriend might have been entitled to a share of it, but my mother didn't feel the need to get involved. Two wives and a girlfriend—who knows how the law would have judged that? As long as people left alone her house in North Hollywood, still partly in Osvaldo's name, that's all Mother was concerned with. Sandra took his ashes to Chile, where they were delivered to his mother.

The panic over a phony marriage prevented me from paying my respects. I didn't find out about my actual father's death because the family in Chile either didn't want to contact me or didn't know how. Again, I missed the opportunity to mourn a father—or a father figure, my first "arts supporter," whether he realized it or not. Mother and I had achieved the American Dream through a phony arrangement, and we'd managed to create some sort of family unit out of it. I shared more time with Osvaldo than I did with my real father. For theatrical people such as myself, the illusion worked. I mourn him now.

A Memory: Closing Time, Last Chance for Romance on the Border

The millennium draws near.

"Only a few more hours and all the computers will stop," my ebullient, adventurous ex-roommate Manuel cries out. He's kidding around. He doesn't believe the millennial hysteria about the malfunctioning of computers, provoking a shutdown of the world's infrastructure. He makes plans to party instead. He has invited me to spend New Year's Eve in San Diego, where he's doing a postdoc in ethnomusicology at my alma mater, UC San Diego. A few months later, Manuel will leave for India to join a Buddhist monastery where he'll embrace vegetarianism and celibacy. Meanwhile, I made the drive from Phoenix to San Diego in a quick five hours. We'll cross the border into Mexico to celebrate the dawning of the new millennium in a Tijuana gay nightclub.

"I'm the one who should be joining a chastity cult," I tell him when I hear about his plans for abstinence in the Himalayans. But he won't have me tease him about his future plans. He's interested in meditation, in a life away from the temptations of the flesh, but only after the new millennium.

"Well, I believe in debauchery," I say, "that is, if you can get it. So let's get it in Tijuana before the Y2K strikes, or before closing time at least."

"Agreed, let's go."

Manuel drives to San Ysidro and leaves his car on the U.S. side of the border to avoid paying for Mexican insurance. We walk from the parking lot into the gated, fortified border through a turnstile. Not far from the border awaits el Extasis, the rambunctious nightclub teeming with Mexican men who aren't shy about befriending a stranger. I welcome a smile, but I'm not used to it. In bars and nightclubs in Los Angeles or San Diego, I've always sensed more hostility from gay men than anything resembling flirtation. I affect a cool facade. I take on the air of the single bachelor out on the town, but it's not a convincing act. I live on a defensive mode, influenced by an anxiety disorder that tells me my act's not working. I blame aspects of myself such as my immigrant background. In the United States I'm still a foreigner. If that was ever exotic and hot, it's now belittled. The anti-immigrant rallies have made us suspect. Even legal immigrants were bashed in the California hysteria of the 1990s. In Arizona that issue has become even more contentious, and it surely must affect the dating prospects of someone like me. If that's not the issue, is my personality the problem?

"Relax," says Manuel.

"Oh, I'm relaxed. Don't I look it?"

"No. Have a drink."

In Tijuana, men talk to me. I'm ever more defensive: what on earth do they want? My wallet? My passport and social security card? But it usually turns out the young man in question just wants to talk, perhaps flirt, and dance. I am surprised by the friendliness of Mexican men. Lights flare, men dance on the floor to a techno-disco beat that pounds at my eardrums, and liquor makes the experience visceral and tactile, open to the senses. I am dancing with a young Mexican man, maybe even more than one. The experience is exotic, strange, and utterly foreign to me.

That night, a man of about forty approaches me, and says, "My friend wants to meet you."

"Huh?" I have trouble talking all of a sudden. This is where my suspicions begin; what friend? Is he sure he means me? Is there a mistake? I turn around to look for the person he really meant to talk to. No, he insists, he is talking to me. "My friend, over there."

He points him out on the dance floor, a short young man, dark, surprisingly handsome with a vivid smile. Why would he want to meet me? I'm not convinced this is on the up and up. Who is this older man? A pimp, trying to sell me one of his boys? How long will it be before he asks for money? The young man, Armando, approaches. He's not as young as he looks at a distance, perhaps mid-twenties, which is a relief. He smiles, but looks mature and stable. Nothing boyish or giggly about him. He works at a travel agency. He's short, comes up to my shoulders (I'm 5′6″), and he is friendly, with a touch of diffidence about him, no arrogance in sight. Armando sounds genuine, surprisingly real, without the ulterior motives I had imagined.

"I saw you come in earlier, and I waited . . . your friend didn't seem like a lover. He went dancing with someone else. That's when I asked my friend to go talk to you."

María's Wedding

"Why your friend and not you directly?"

"Oh, I'm not good at that. It worked, didn't it?"

"Yes, it did."

I'm delighted to hear him admit shyness, but my sense of survival is keen. I'm still suspicious. I've seen *Hold Back the Dawn*; I know how it works. In this 1940s film, Charles Boyer plays a French man stuck in Tijuana who is desperate to enter the United States. He seeks a lonely American teacher, played by the unassuming, naive Olivia de Havilland. He feigns interest in her, motivated by the need to find an American wife to get U.S. papers. By the end of the film, to the delight of war-time moviegoers, they fall in love, and the lonesome teacher—at first suspicious of the man's ulterior motives—finally has a claim on genuine romance. The movie, for all its charms, reminds me to be cautious.

We begin kissing on a couch. I haven't kissed anyone in three years. I haven't had "real" sex in about as many years as well. The first years of my appointment as a professor of theater at Arizona State University have been spent mostly on accomplishing steps toward tenure—production and publication. I've been good at it. I've been less proficient as a lover. Well, I admit, there was that one encounter in the dark room in Mexico City, but I don't remember any kissing. It seems to matter to me that what counts as a love life should include lips and tongue. Partners who want access to genitals need to work for it—well, I'm not always consistent with the policy, but the ideal reigns in my imagination.

Armando's skin is dark and smooth, and his lips are like a magnet. They cling to me. He stops and feels compelled to tell me the oddest of compliments: "I like men who are whiter than I am."

"What? *Qué dices?*"

It dawns on me that in Mexico, I am a light-skinned man. In the United States, I am part of a "nonwhite minority." I was also brought up to think of myself as white by my mother's Spanish half of my family, while my father's darker side expelled me altogether for being illegitimate, so I never had a claim on mestizo consciousness, let alone Indian identity. But now I live in the United States, and white Americans define "whiteness" very differently than Latin Americans do. What you see you don't get from me—I am apparently a white person trapped in the body of a mestizo, but white Americans don't know it, and it took this young Mexican for me to remember what I am, depending on the borders I have crossed in any given day. I am white for now, at least to him. In Mexico, plenty of darker people such as Armando also live out the internalized racism that makes them admire whiteness, and they say so explicitly. He would not be the only Mexican man to ever say that to me, but that was the first time I heard it, and it made an impression.

I don't question the motives. I take what I can get. To somebody out there, I will, for once, be considered "appealing" or "attractive," never mind the reasons. This had never happened before, that all these issues should crystallize in one night in the arms of a young man as handsome as Armando, who thought of himself as "too dark" and, therefore, "not as attractive." Finally, my ethnicity works in my favor. I have found the heart of the borderland that so many poets have tried to define for themselves like Gloria Anzaldúa, who wrote about the bleeding wound of *la frontera*. Some of us are smack in the middle of it, our hearts exposed to its perilous divides. White enough for Mexicans, not white enough for Americans.

"Why do you say that?" I asked, not meaning to question or interrogate him. He's not ready to say more.

"It's true . . . *eres güero.* You're white."

I embrace him and kiss him again, and hope he won't take it back. I know that once I walk back through the border turnstile, I return to being "non-white." I am *el güero* for this night, and don't anybody tell me otherwise. What's next? Being called *el gringo*? It could come to that.

Prince's song "1999" comes on.

"This is it," I tell him. "It's the only chance we'll get in this lifetime to bid farewell to a millennium and welcome a new one with Prince's tune."

"Ah, that's what it's about," he said. He had grown up listening to the song, and as with most English-language hits on the radio, he simply absorbed it for its rhythm. "Now it makes sense."

After the dance, we sit down again, and I find the words to counter his. "You are dark, and you are beautiful," I say. I sound awkward, but I'm glad I didn't say, "You are beautiful anyway." I almost did. He looks at me skeptically as if he has rarely, if ever, heard beauty and darkness together in the same sentence. What can I do to convince him of his own appeal when cultural standards in Latin America conspire against him? Indigenous blood darkens his olive skin, which feels smooth to the touch. I am enthralled by it, and the only way to prove it is to act upon it, with more kissing and groping.

María's Wedding

Hours go by like this. It's nearly four a.m., quite early into the New Year and a new life. Gore will be elected president the following November, I project ahead, and the new millennium promises great new beginnings for us all as a country and for me as a lover.

Manuel wants to drive back to San Diego. Nightclubs close somewhere between five and six a.m. in Tijuana. He wants to avoid the rush back to the border. The teenagers who cross over to Mexico in order to legally party in nightclubs will create a traffic jam that will have us waiting till dawn. I explain the situation to Armando.

"I'm sorry we have to go, but I will drive back all the way from Arizona to see you, I promise," I say. "You're the best thing that's happened to me lately. I have to start the year right."

"The best thing?"

"Yes, yes, the very best."

He looks skeptical but gives me his number on a piece of paper.

"I try not to fall in love with those who live *al otro lado*," he says. "But you never know; I might take a chance on you."

Love? He's already talking about falling in love? I'm the one who started it after all, with the boundless enthusiasm I've shown through the course of the night, and with my offer to drive across the desert to see him, but my mind has begun its usual inclinations toward suspicions. Who is Armando, and why is he talking about love if he isn't part of a conspiracy to kidnap American professors, preferably short wimpy ones, and turn them into some sort of money-making scheme in, say, the illicit trafficking of organs? Perhaps I will never return to Tijuana, I tell myself. Gay men do not talk about love—not often enough to me—so there's got to be something wrong with this picture.

Manuel and I make it across the border before sunrise. I am celebrating the new era, crooning "Let's Get Loud," in which Jennifer Lopez sings a duet with her future husband, Marc Anthony. I am enthralled by the possibility of romance, by the sudden outbreak of it. How will I bring Armando to the United States?

"You think I could I smuggle him in?" I ask.

"You're drunk."

"I am not," I say. "Come on, three beers?"

"You'll sleep it off," he says.

María's Wedding

But I wasn't so sure.

I call Armando from Phoenix for the next two months. I miss you, says Armando. He sends me cards; "for my love," they say. How can he use that type of language: *para mi amor*? Based on a few measly hours of kissing? I want to believe it, but I don't. I gather my friends Trino and Daniel in Phoenix. They've seen me stumble with men and make a fool of myself many times before. But this time, they think it's great, if it's real and genuine, and they urge me to go for it, to drive across the desert, then across the border, and see if it's real. But my doubts continue. The man who introduced us—I still insist—could be the head of some crime ring, and he uses those boys to attract romantic, easily deluded fools like me from *el otro lado*. They will take my car and my wallet, perhaps a kidney or two. It's a carefully concocted plot. Trino looks at me like he's heard all the scary stories about Mexico and still doesn't believe that people living in the United States, with one of the highest murder rates in the world, still find Mexico scary. As a Mexican-born immigrant himself, he resents it. Is this what I think of Mexico and of Mexicans? he asks. Is this what I think of a young man who took a liking to me and made me feel special? I've heard all the stories, I tell him, feeling guilty and embarrassed to have brought it up. Trino tells me to stop thinking like a gringo.

"I'm not thinking like a gringo, but like a spinster," I say. Like that's any better. My friends shake their heads. They find me lacking in something. Some people are naive when they travel abroad; others are so suspicious that they forgo all sense of spontaneity. I show perplexing elements of both: naive enough to fall in love, but suspicious of the lover's intent. Dare to take a risk is the general consensus.

During spring break, in March 2000, I drive myself with my faltering 1995 Toyota Tercel all the way to San Diego, where Manuel has left the keys to his apartment with a friend. Armando has renewed his day permit that allows him to cross the border legally. I drive for more than five hours to the San Ysidro border crossing, where I nearly collide with the San Diego light rail train. If the conductor hadn't chimed his bell, I would have ploughed into it. A complete stranger saves me from a serious crash, and then I go obliviously on my way to the pick-up/drop-off spot outside the customs office. Armando awaits me with a smile on his face and an overnight bag. He gets in, and I hug him. I kiss him lightly on the cheek, and a cop shines his lights at us. We're not allowed to dawdle at this stop. "Let's get out of here," I say, pressing on the pedal. I drive him off to the city of San Diego, where I have reservations at a Spanish restaurant. I treat Armando to tapas and sangria, and then afterward, I take him to Manuel's apartment.

An entire night and then another day of lovemaking ensue. We wake up early, around nine a.m., and go out to breakfast, but then we come back and continue our bedroom antics for the rest of the day until it's time to go out to dinner. We go back to Hillcrest for a quick meal and then later watch *All about My Mother* at the Hillcrest Cineplex. A Spanish film by Almodóvar, the film's tragic consequences for its HIV-positive characters don't register immediately. I am only in the right mood to absorb the film's sharp, often dark humor. I pick up Almodóvar's references to *All about Eve* and *A Streetcar Named Desire*, and I know that the queer director and I are on the same page. The mother and son are an inseparable team, watching *All about Eve* on television, debating why the literal translation *Todo Sobre Eva* sounds awkward in Spanish ("*Me suena muy raro*"), and then the two go watch *Streetcar* at a local theater, where the young writer will meet his tragic fate trying to chase after the play's notorious star, Huma, through the rain for an autograph when a car ploughs him down. The mother is left to wonder what might have been, for her and her son, product of a liaison with a transgender man who has since impregnated a nun (Penelope Cruz), who has contracted HIV from him. At the end, after Cecilia Roth's character has learned to live with her various losses in the film, Huma recites lines from *Blood Wedding* in which she enacts the stern Spanish matriarch's lament for her dead son. It's a touching reminder of how theater mirrors these people's tragic yet strangely humorous lives and transforms them into art.

I am holding Armando's hand, and the warmth permeates my senses. Armando's presence keeps me grounded in my reality, within my flesh, sweaty and altered, and yet vibrant and alive. I respond to his breathing and to the feel of his skin. The film's message will hit me later when I have to bid farewell to him and drive back across that long, hot desert.

I don't know this young man well. For an entire day we've spent most of our time in bed, clinging to one another until we get to the part of sexual consummation, but our bodies respond better to the intimacy and indeed the romance of kissing. I know he's Mexican. I know he's lived in Tijuana most of his life and works as a travel agent, except he can rarely afford to travel, earning enough to get by. His mother seems accepting, but they don't talk about it, his sexual identity, the unspoken element of their lives. He lived once with his godfather, who took him in when he needed to be away from home and explore his identity. The two men became lovers. The relationship with this older man, his father's age, made him comfortable enough with his sexuality to take off and be on his own for a while. But he couldn't afford independence for long.

He's back to living with his mother, but still, he's romantically on his own now, working at his travel agency and hoping to find somebody with whom to share his life. He's a young man with a plan. I'm barely fourteen years older than he, and still young enough not to fall into that trap of the older man/younger man syndrome. I am not looking to maintain anybody. I am not interested in a "kept boy." But I still quiz him over dinner; why did he make that remark about liking men who are white or light-skinned like me? Because it's true, he says, he's not attracted to darker men like himself. Now I've made him feel uncomfortable, and he even sounds defensive. I want to analyze, but he clearly doesn't. He doesn't think of himself as self-hating. That's just his preference: whiter men and slightly older. That's me. So why question it?

I ask him something else: "What about this new movement toward gay marriage?"

"What about it?" he wants to know.

"Would you marry a man?"

"I don't know; under the right circumstances, maybe," he says.

"If we lived in the same country, you and I, and if the circumstances were right, would you marry me?" It's a bold question on my part. But he got started with all that love stuff only a few hours after we met.

He stops, thinks, and answers, "Yes, I probably would."

If the border lends itself to impulsive heterosexual lovers who go to Tijuana to marry overnight, it simply won't do the same for gay lovers to do the same, not tonight, not that year. A marriage certificate, recognized by the federal government, would have made Armando eligible to cross the border as my spouse, like Charles Boyer in *Hold Back the Dawn*. Without this motive, I begin to conclude, calmly now, that Armando can't be trying to set me up. Maybe he actually really does like me, but why? I am not convinced he finds me attractive, as I find my looks deficient. I am mesmerized by the experience, perplexed at the strangeness of this affair, not altogether believing it. I've also read Henry James's *Washington Square*. The film version, *The Heiress*, also stars Olivia de Havilland fending off a young man, a handsome

María's Wedding

Montgomery Clift, conniving to marry her in order to inherit her father's wealth. But, in my case, there is no inheritance for the illegitimate son of a teacher in Santiago. My professorship is middle class at best, and I am not tenured yet. He has made the wrong move, if indeed it was a "move." Even my credit card is maxed out, and I pay for our dinner with cash. Surely, he's noticed.

It's time to head back to the border. We've been at it for over twenty-four hours without much sleep, packing a lifetime of sensation into one day of sensual delight. I drive him back to Tijuana and leave the car on the border again. We are together at the Extasis, this time as a couple. I meet his friends, young men also seeking their share of romance and passion. They seem quite proud of Armando, with his weekend fling with a professor from Arizona.

It's past midnight, closer to one a.m., and I am feeling the panic. I need to return to the United States. I can't bring Armando with me, to live with me, to share my life. Armando walks me back to the border and asks when I will return. "I don't know," I say. "But soon, certainly during the summer." Perhaps I could rent a place in San Diego and spend most of my summer crossing back and forth to see him. "That would be nice," he says. "That would be great. I love you," he adds. He kisses me in the middle of the bridge that leads back toward the crossing point. It's a public kiss, and I am not afraid, for once.

I let go of him and walk back. I am distraught. I feel the loss already. The border divides us, keeps him *al otro lado*. I live across it, in my little world made up of dramatic fantasy. There's no cure for this divide, nothing that will bring us together. I walk forward through a line without wanting to move toward the guards. I am not thinking clearly. Ahead of me, young, blond boys who've been out in Tijuana drinking the night away are laughing at their lame jokes, calling each other "dude," and making a ruckus. They are going through a turnstile, and nobody's even checking their papers. The border patrolmen are letting them cross because they "look American." I am right behind them. Then I go ahead against my better judgment and cross the turnstile, and suddenly—as if an alarm for a border crosser has gone off—a patrolman screams loudly, startling me. "Hey! Where the fuck do you think you're going?"

He and two other beefy, tall men run over to control me. The white blond boys have just gone through the same turnstile without being checked, but I'm the one who gets stopped, in a rude, even violent manner. They put their hands on my shoulders to constrain me.

"I've got papers!" I tell him in perfect English, but I realize "papers" is the wrong word. I'm a citizen; I don't need "papers," but I don't have time to say this.

"Well, you get back in line! You hear me?" he screams.

I'm about to speak up, say something, ask why the white boys were allowed in without their papers being checked. But in the United States you don't ask such questions. The border patrolman who shouted at me himself looked like a "Latino," so the issue went further than racism. He himself had bought that the blond boys "looked American" and didn't descend upon them with the ferociousness and anger that he heaped upon me. I got back in line and pulled out my U.S. passport. I had to prove my Americanness to these people, and I'm perfectly fine with that, if all crossers were required to do so. After September 11th, that type of episode—I would assume— would be less likely. Still, I knew a young Chilean woman living without papers in L.A. who went regularly to Tijuana to party with her friends. She was a blonde from a Chilean white family and spoke unaccented American English. Nobody required her to show her papers, as if Americans could never put two and two together: that you could be white and "look American" and still be an "illegal alien." By now, I've learned that the real lesson of being an American who "doesn't look American" and living on the border is to learn to run for your life—to be savvy and aware at all times when you cross a crucial turnstile about how you'll be perceived. Our borderland bleeds, and for a frustrated lover like me, it bled all over my private life that winter of my discontent.

I never saw Armando again. My summer plans went in a completely different direction. By then, he wasn't accepting my phone calls. Earlier, during a long phone tryst, he promised to come see me, and he called me once saying he wanted to take a flight from San Diego and visit me in Phoenix. I told him I'd love to have him visit, that I would even pay for the plane fare, which he said wasn't necessary, but I insisted. When I revealed that my mother had been diagnosed with breast cancer, he expressed sincere regrets and then made a sweetly comic statement: "My poor mother-in-law is sick!" When I called him back to make the arrangements for his visit, he didn't return my call.

8

Pterodactyls

I was sleeping in a house of dying people.

It was August 31, 2001. Mother had been diagnosed with cancer and sent to Hopewell House, a hospice in Portland, Oregon, where people deemed terminal live out their final days. The hospice included a guest room upstairs for relatives or loved ones. One room out of twenty or so. I was the occupant for that night and the only one officially not dying.

Breast cancer had spread undetected until tumors grew on her spinal cord, sending paralyzing waves of pain up and down her back. She collapsed one morning in January. I got a call in my office at Arizona State University. One of her employers found her stretched out on the floor of her apartment, afraid to move. She had left a note for me, apologizing that she wasn't leaving me money. "Your mother is irresponsible," she had scribbled on a piece of paper after her collapse. "I cried last night, not because I'm going to die, since after all I'm going to rest. I cry because I won't be seeing you again." It was a nightmarish week. Carmen had collapsed a few days before with appendicitis, and then Mother succumbed to the pain wreaking havoc on her body. In her note she adds, "I'm alone. Carmen's in the hospital, although she's recovering." The two women were in separate rooms in the same hospital, and their friends got an opportunity to see both on one visit. My mother found that funny and cracked a joke or two about it. "I chose the wrong week to get cancer," she said. There she goes again, I thought, referencing Ronald Reagan in his assassination attempt comment, "I forgot to duck."

Pterodactyls

Carmen recovered. Mother was sent to radiation and chemotherapy treatments. Rounds of chemo prolonged the unpleasantness. Since the doctors had told her she was terminal, she decided not to continue with either radiation or chemo. Pain medication sedated her. She was given a few months to live.

Eight months later, under medication, her condition stabilized. The chemo had worn off, and she began to thrive again. A period of adjustment, and unexpected calm, ensued. My mother, a Chilean immigrant, sixty-four, was expected to die any day. The doctors kept her at the idyllic Hopewell House, a home ensconced in a wooded area of the urban jungle, a place of tall pine trees, bird houses populated by yellow-headed blackbirds, squirrels in trees, and kind-hearted caretakers—a place in which one might choose to die. The pleasant ambiance allowed my mother to feel alive. One goes to a hospice to die, not to live in relative comfort. More than six months had passed since she'd arrived at Hopewell, and she wasn't dead yet. The authorities expelled her from the hospice. The director announced the decision with a caring smile on her face. María was welcome to come back any day when *she was truly dying*. I had to find a dying woman another place to live. I flew to Portland with this singularly bizarre task in mind. I got in late that evening, barely had a chance to say good night to my mother, who'd gone to bed, and went upstairs to the hospice guest room to rest up for a long day of house searching.

It felt soothing up there on the second floor of the hospice right above all those dying people, with the peacefulness of both the cradle and the grave. The weather was perfect: cool, breezy, Oregonian comfort. But at night, the demons are easily unleashed from the feverish imagination of a writer who thinks about civilization and death (Herbert Marcuse paired eros with civilization, but I for some reason—not well trained in eros perhaps—seemed to study the cataclysmic end of it instead). In a deep sleep, my mind drew up an infernal, foggy world with a noisy, violent scenario: The nation was under attack from the air. The aliens had captured Senators Hillary Clinton and Nancy Reagan (she had been elected to the Senate in my dream; Hillary's election didn't need my playwright's enhancement). The invaders used pterodactyls dropping bombs from the sky. A state of emergency was declared. I was huddled in a basement with other strangers, listening to news on the radio. The pterodactyls kept coming, pummeling the city with their bombs in the shape of prehistoric boulders.

Pterodactyls

The wave of kidnappings meant that our legislators were disappearing one by one, leaving us without a system of government. What was to be done? We, the citizens, were trapped in our hiding places. The radio broadcasts came to a sudden halt, but the bombing continued. There were no signs that anyone would come to our rescue. An epic struggle, the war of the worlds, had begun.

I woke up suddenly. My eyes opened to the peaceful night in Portland, a window overlooking the woods, cool air-continuing to provide comfort and pleasure in the midst of summer. It wasn't just a dream, I thought. Every civilization becomes threatened sooner or later. Pterodactyls themselves became extinct. So why were they being used by this new enemy? Who was the enemy? An attack from the sky that leaves us without a functioning form of government—that seemed paranoid. It couldn't happen here. I went back to sleep.

In the morning, I did a reality check: I was a Chilean native. Planes had roared onto the capital of Santiago on September 11, 1973. Planes bombed the presidential palace, and the military shut down Congress and all other aspects of government. Every Chilean I met, even abroad, associated the day with attacks from the sky. At every anniversary, some riot would break out, as demonstrators clashed with police, and even U.S. papers—usually oblivious to Latin America—would cover it as long as the riot proved deadly or bloody enough. For weeks, it had been in the back of my mind; another anniversary of September 11th approached, and I wondered what type of riot would break out this time. I had no idea that somewhere in Washington, counter-terrorism czar Richard Clarke had raised the alarm to President Bush, Condoleezza Rice, General Colin Powell, and the rest of the administration, many times that same summer, that a terrorist attack was imminent. Given my annual reminder of the Chilean September 11, I still insist I dreamed the catastrophe that awaited us in the United States within a few weeks.

An anecdote after 9/11 struck me as the type of dark humor I often end up incorporating into my work and my life: the U.S. Coast Guard hired Hollywood screenwriters to conjure up scenarios of future terrorist attacks. Imaginative people were asked to project ahead and figure out how a terrorist might plan new attacks. I felt left out. I am imaginative and possess enough historical baggage with the Chilean past to know how twisted minds work. I, like the bizarre pre-cogs of Steven Spielberg's *The Minority*

Pterodactyls

Report (based on the short story by Philip K. Dick) felt convinced that I was developing an ability to dream this stuff. That's my Minority Report, another Latino dramatist getting left out of a national debate.

I can smile now at the strange coincidences of history that coalesced that summer to make me dream of the future by way of the Chilean past, but that summer while my mother was dying, my dreams felt strangely real to me. My heart was beating fast when I woke up inside the hospice in Portland.

"There is no emergency," I told myself that morning. "It's a peaceful day in Portland where people are quietly dying. My mother is alive and relatively healthy; that's why she's being kicked out, the best possible reason."

I had to get up and prepare my mother for her house search. She could move well, and walk slowly, holding on to my arm. The rich cocktail of medicine, which included marijuana pills, kept her stable, almost fully functional. She wished to drive, but I insisted she shouldn't. Her pain had faded. The tumors had responded to radiation therapy. She had defied diagnosis. The doctors had made a turnaround and determined she would live much longer. The same doctors had told us she only had a couple of months to live. So we packed up her things back in April and held a garage sale. Her belongings were mostly gone. She no longer had a place to call home. The hospice gave me addresses of rest homes or foster homes where she could live.

"I could die tomorrow, and all this effort would be for nothing," she said, cheerfully.

"But you could also live another three years, so it's best to plan and think ahead."

"My son is practical."

"And my mother is so alert and cheerful. No wonder they're kicking you out of the hospice. You're supposed to be dying."

"I am, but the marijuana keeps me going."

"A real life saver, that marijuana."

"Maybe it's the Paxil."

"Whatever they're giving you, it's a winning combination. It keeps you happy!"

"I've never smiled so much in my life."

"That's nice: a smiling, dope head of a mother."

Pterodactyls

The first home brought out the worst in her. Too much cheerfulness was no longer an issue. Set in the northwestern end of Portland, it was a home for financially challenged people. My mother didn't want to think of herself that way. She didn't like the "look" of the people living there. "Too many poor people," she complained.

"It's well kept," I told her to at least give it a positive spin. My attempt to sound too cheerful didn't sit well with her.

"You just want to dump me off anywhere and take the first plane back home."

This hit a nerve. It was partially true. I wanted to get this over with, but I didn't want to dump her anywhere. The first place we went to see didn't strike me as being altogether bad. She called it a dump. I didn't know what we could afford, and although Oregon along with Medicare would pay for most of it, it wasn't clear to me what "most" of it meant.

Two more homes; no better choices. One place looked like a madhouse, with lonely cubicles for rooms where older people were kept and heavy doors to lock them in for the night. In another home nuns lived among the elderly and the dying. Mother did not have pleasant memories of the nuns who cared for her during childhood. She still didn't trust them. We went back to the hospice marveling at the safety, the cleanliness, and orderliness of it. Why couldn't I stay there? she whined. Hopewell House was a tranquil, attractive place for anyone. I had to remind her it was meant for the dying, not the living. We called it a night.

I lay awake for hours. I did not want to get back to dreams of alien invasions, or historical or futuristic cataclysms of any kind. I thought about taking my mother to the movies the next day. That put me in the right mood. She had been asking to do so, but first we needed the time to look for homes. The movies were the perfect escape. That helped me sleep. The next day, however, we chose *Pearl Harbor*. The historical, romantic epic had opened earlier that year on Memorial Day and was now running in the cheaper, neighborhood theaters over in the Hawthorne District. Ben Affleck and Josh Harnett fight for the love of Kate Beckinsale. That was the selling point. The Japanese invasion only crowded up my mind with more images of assault.

"Why were they asleep? Why weren't they prepared?" asked my mother. I didn't have an easy answer. The United States was officially neutral, and the isolationist movement fought to keep the country out of the war. The Japanese staged a surprise attack, but conspiracy theorists still believe the Roosevelt administration tempted the Japanese in order to justify U.S. involvement. I couldn't whisper all this into her ear.

"I'll explain later," I said, but I never did. My only aim that afternoon was escape, not further immersion into the nightmare of the past. September 11th was only a few weeks away then.

Mother and I found a place in northern Portland by the airport, essentially a senior living center. It was modeled after a modern hotel, with all sorts of amenities, a pool, a sauna, and, more importantly, medical care on the premises. A nurse would check on her once a day. It was an attractive place without the stigma of poverty as in the previous home we'd seen, and the manager reassured me that Mother's social security check would be considered payment and that Medicare would pay the rest of the bills. Mother was satisfied. No poor people, except for herself. I felt relieved. She was at ease and seemed eager to live again with a semblance of normality. Her friend Carmen even got her—of all things—a part-time job. Carmen would pick her up, and the two would go care for children at a local church's day care center. This new period of relative calm, when her life would get a second wind of hope and physical energy, lasted less than a month.

Only a few weeks after my strangest of dreams, the attack came, like a bad plot twist on the twenty-eighth anniversary of the Chilean military coup. The pterodactyls, like the stars, aligned to deliver the blow. The fossilized minds of religious fanatics led them to assault us with the equipment of the modern transportation system—and used it with sophisticated precision. The World Trade Center, symbol of our modern economy, was pulverized, along with one of the wings in the Pentagon. Other targets included the White House and the Capitol where, as in my dream, Hillary Clinton (but not Nancy Reagan) would be found. If successful, the enemy would have wiped out our legislature.

That morning, after hearing the news, I rang my mother from Phoenix to check up on her, but first I called one of the nurses at the rest home to see if she could curtail my mother's television viewing for that day. I knew she watched television night and day. It was too late.

"They're having a revolution in New York," she said, trying to form some sort of coherent thought after her morning medicine. "I'm scared."

Pterodactyls

"Mother, nothing's happening in Portland. You're safe there," I told her. Her Chilean friends rushed in to be with her. I was in Phoenix, thinking ahead to my next flight to Portland. All flights had been cancelled, and there was no word yet when the airports would re-open.

In the Phoenix area a group of friends decided to hold a town meeting at a well-connected friend's house, a woman who usually opened her home for fundraisers and receptions. It was as if we were holding a wake for the death of our complacence. The Sunday after the attack we talked about our fears and anxieties.

I seemed to be the least surprised. Since January I had been living under the shadow of death, my time organized around trips to Portland to check up on my mother's condition and to witness a process of gradual deterioration for myself. Some of the members in the gathering speculated about future terrorist attacks. Would they start bombing airports or train stations? What about supermarkets and malls? Would we live from now on as the people of Israel did, with the expectation of a domestic attack any day? An older man showed up who harked back to Pearl Harbor. "Been there, done that," he said, and warned us we should expect war.

A month later, Bush invaded Afghanistan. Anthrax was selectively sent to news media outlets such as the *National Enquirer* and also to postal workers, some of whom died after exposure to the substance. Our world was under siege. Attack of the pterodactyls. It was no longer a dream.

Three weeks later, a nurse found my mother in her room babbling incoherently. She had soiled herself and then lost consciousness. She was rushed to the hospital. The doctors declared her dying once again. I was summoned back to Portland to put Mother's affairs in order and to arrange funerary services. She was given a few days to live and ended up back in the same hospice—and the same bed—she had previously vacated. This time, they told me over the phone, it was for real.

My mother lived one more year at the hospice, breaking records for longevity in a place where you're not supposed to be doing well. The nurses at Hopewell became friends and adopted her as a resident straggler. She began to get up again. Friends came by to take her out to lunch or to the mall. She returned at the end of the day to sleep. The hospice had become a hotel. But her roommates kept dying. Nearly a dozen of them must have expired in the bed across from hers during her time there. She thrived on that strange capacity to observe the dying.

Pterodactyls

"I sometimes go up to them and hold their hand," she told me over the phone. "That way somebody's there at the exact moment when they take their last breath. Usually, their family comes in too late for that. I don't want them to be alone when that happens. I certainly don't want to be alone when it happens to me."

She lost the fear of death, she claimed, and the feeling transferred to me. Hers had become a rather peaceful, gradual deterioration. The Oregon nurses gave her pot in small doses. Perhaps medicinal marijuana allows for hope—and hallucinations of eternity. No wonder the Supreme Court banned it. Conservatives suspect that someone, somewhere, even while dying, is having fun. I didn't dare borrow any of her medicine, but I admired the process. I could do this, I told myself. You might say I look forward to it. If I had to choose my death, that's the one.

In summer 2002 Mother was expelled from the hospice for the second time and went to live in a smaller foster home where a Brazilian woman took care of elderly and disabled people with that warm, Maria von Trapp–like sweetness my mother could appreciate.

Mother showed timing, even precision, in the last moments of her life. She called me from Portland that week and asked me when I'd be coming to visit. I reminded her that I was flying out that Saturday, July 20, 2002. "I think I can hold on till then," she said, sounding slower than ever, her voice beginning to break up, but still making sense. "I want somebody to hold my hand."

That night, she went into a semi-permanent deep sleep. The caretaker told me she woke up only once a night during those last couple of days to ask for some tea. Then, she'd go back to dreaming and talking in her sleep.

I arrived that Saturday afternoon to find my mother snoring soundly and deeply. I had nothing to do but sit by her side. A television set played reruns of *Happy Days* and *Laverne and Shirley*, but time had come to a standstill. I held her hand. She would stir and would mutter something about her mother. "Mama, mama . . ." Those were the only words that were comprehensible, the rest sounded like some profound statement in the language of the dying.

A friend of hers arrived, a Chilean woman, an immigrant, conversant in Spanish only. She relieved me, asking me to take a break. I'll hold her hand for you, she said. Mother would know the difference, I insisted. She looked at me with understanding. Then, she'll wait for you, the friend said.

Pterodactyls

On Sunday, I repeated the routine. I arrived by noon, held her hand for a couple of hours as I watched more television. The Brazilian woman entered that afternoon and told me, "She woke up briefly last night. It was past midnight. I told her you were here in Portland. She smiled and seemed to understand. She knows you're here."

A couple of hours passed, and out of boredom I left her again to a couple of her friends who had arrived to keep a watch on her. I went off to Starbucks, to read a book, *The Noonday Demon: An Atlas of Depression* by Andrew Solomon, a personal account of the author's own struggles with the disease. I usually chose books like this, with an eye out for challenges and for hints on how someone else had faced up to his fears. A book about nuclear terrorism was forthcoming from Amazon.com. I'd rather know about it now than be surprised later. That's how the Cassandra syndrome works. It nourishes my strange fears and inspires dreams. But something told me it was time to leave Starbucks and go back to the foster home.

When I returned, her friends had left. Mother was alone. Her breathing was deeper, a hoarse, belabored snore. I held her hand while watching television. I had begun to doze off when I heard a strange breath, a quick intake of air, then a sudden, final release. Everything stopped. I drew up to her, felt her pulse, put my hand beneath her nose to test for breathing. Nothing. I had witnessed her last moments. Mother said she'd wait for me. She had even waited for my return from Starbucks. Then she was gone, on the early evening of July 21, 2002. *Happy Days* continued in full, living canned laughter, and the Fonz gave the thumbs up.

A procession of cars made its way to a local Catholic parish. Mother's friends included a good segment of the Chilean community of Portland. Dozens of people who formed a small but tight-knit group of immigrants, a subgroup of the Latin American diaspora, paid respect. The undertaker had dressed Mother in a purple business suit, colored and recast her hair into a fashionable combed-over look, applied blush to her cheeks, and transformed her into a dead woman who wouldn't frighten the living. The radiance of her look struck me as fetishistic and bizarre. I did not care for the ghoulish spectacle of viewing the dead, but her Chilean friends insisted that's how we do things back in Chile. I can at least cherish memories of a pretty woman, her arms crossed, a red rose on her hands, at rest at last.

Pterodactyls

When the time came, I delivered a memory of my mother in English and in Spanish. The words have been incorporated into this memoir: Mother arrives in the United States on her own, we drive across the country to the West Coast, she survives a potential drowning; Mother loves the children she cares for, she moves to Portland, she begins her battle against cancer. It's the end of an American journey, an overall peaceful transformation into eternity. I did not find the tears in me to cry publicly. Mother said she herself rarely did. She only wept at movies: the end of *Casablanca*, or Captain von Trapp's transformation into a singing trouper in *The Sound of Music*, or the death of Jack in *Titanic*. In order to cry, I need a narrative as well. Perhaps by finally writing down a narrative of my mother's immigration to the United States, I might find the strength in me to cry. But don't count on it. I cry at the movies, but rarely outside of them. It's one of the strange habits I inherited.

I was now on my own in the United States. In 1980 Mother saved herself from drowning because she feared I would be left alone in the United States as a teenager, but that life seemed so distant. She knew she would be leaving behind a grown-up man, in a functional capacity, not entirely at home in his own body, but nonetheless employed and fully creative, as his talents would attest. In the 1980s Mother feared that nebulous state of mind I lived in, the young writer making notes in a journal while avoiding the effort of settling down into a full-time job and a traditional marriage. She finally told me in her usual blunt tone, half-kidding and yet serious in intent, "I hope when I die, you will at least have a job."

I realized that day in July in Portland that I had fulfilled that hope, somewhat, if barely. I had finished six years of full-time work as a professor. Up until then, my résumé had included a hodgepodge of part-time gigs mostly because I had been a student and a freelance writer, dramatist, and, at times, performer. My way of life had alarmed her and made her fear for my future. I also wasn't married or in a relationship, and she found that to be her own personal defeat.

"I did the same," she once told me in the 1990s, as if ending all future prospects for romance and marriage, for herself and for me. "I can't be self-righteous. It's in the blood. We don't marry."

"Well, never say never," I said.

"Prove me wrong then, but I say . . . there's something about us."

"And what would that be? A curse?"

Pterodactyls

"No . . . just the blood."

"But that sounds like a curse."

"It's something . . . but not a curse. It's our own ability to turn away from people, to choose solitude."

"Is that what you do?"

"It's what you do."

"Do I?"

"But it's because of me. I did the same, see?"

I flew to Santiago, Chile, in May 2003. The U.S. invasion of Iraq was winding down in what was called "a quick victory." President Bush declared "Mission Accomplished." I laid Mother's ashes to rest in the Pacific. My mother's relatives gathered in the small port of San Antonio, where tourists rent sailing boats and go off into the ocean. As we were about to board, a rig stationed not far from the port became unmoored and dropped into the ocean, creating a wave that splattered over us like some school kid playing a joke. It lent the ceremony an odd, even comic uncertainty as winds picked up and the water below created a rocking motion. Mother's ashes were compressed in a sturdy plastic bag, which I couldn't open, not even with my teeth. A friend pulled out a Swiss knife and helped me tear it. The airport authorities had opened the container to check for explosives, but they found only the remains of a modest Chilean woman who'd gone to work in the United States as a nanny for professional American moms. The bag gave way, and as I spread the ashes into the waters of the Pacific, the wind kept shaking the boat, blowing ashes into my eyes. It was messy and undignified. Family members prayed, and some wept. My aunt Gladys accompanied me along with Aunt Chata and her daughter, who had long ago made up with my mother over their unfortunate visit to California. My godmother Cecilia arrived. She had been my mother's best friend in her years in Catholic Youth; she now belonged to a swim team and looked fit and pretty. Her brother, Fernando, invited me to talk to his students at a private school where he taught. Also present was Teresa, my late grandfather's second wife, looking as lively as she was penitent. Other friends and relatives crowded themselves into the rickety boat that swayed into uncertain waters. I looked awkward with ashes on my face; I wiped them away with my sleeve. We headed back to the port, with our stomachs in a knot.

Pterodactyls

I had arrived in Chile a younger man, to paraphrase the lyrics of Bob Dylan: "I was older then, I'm younger than that now." My body, with all its perceived flaws, and a likely future victim of cancer (since both my parents died of it), had defied its own odds. The Front Runners, which I had joined in 2000, had traveled as a group to run the San Diego Half-Marathon in late April, and I tagged along. I completed my first half-marathon in two hours. I was in better shape than I was as a teenager. I was more likely to be out of the house at the Bridle Path in downtown Phoenix at six a.m. to avoid the desert heat, running six miles for the pure thrill of it.

I slept on my childhood bed that spring of 2003 in the neighborhood of La Palmilla in Conchalí, north of Santiago. The magazine trading shop had been converted back to the bedroom it had once been. Bricks and cement sealed the opening and turned the place into a private space again. Childhood was gone, but youth clung to the middle-aged body by a thread. I surprised my family by appearing thinner than I'd been as a teenager and relatively youthful.

"I already did a half, so now I'm preparing for a marathon," I announced on a whim. I thought the half was hard enough. I didn't know if I had the stamina for a full one.

One of my aunts wondered out loud, "Aren't you too old to be doing such things?"

That was the assumption of my relatives, who seemed to think there were limits to what a forty-year-old could do, as if implying that at that age, I should be settling into middle-aged stasis, not preparing for marathons. But I was defiant. It was my mother's habit to let the family know what you will do next, and then to actually do it, the same way she announced she would go to the United States and then had to live up to that dare. I slept in a bedroom I hadn't seen since my teenage years and felt I had come full circle, a much more capable, audacious man invigorated by my own journey and the memory of the sturdy immigrant woman who had once taken me with her on her adventures into the United States. My mother's venturesome energy, her enthusiasm, and her ability to inspire children to have fun suffused the memories of my Santiago childhood. I took, again, the same bus to downtown Santiago, to face a world of strangers crisscrossing the city on their way to work or back to their sleeper communities, streets that led to the movie theaters where Mother had exposed me to the obligatory Disney offerings or the hit films such as *The Sound of*

Pterodactyls

Music, The Wizard of Oz, Cleopatra, The Ten Commandments, and many others. A long hike on the Santa Lucía Hill reveals a fort once built by the Spaniards, with a phallically inclined cannon pointing toward the city that commemorates the Spanish colony, overlooking the snow-capped Andes Mountains, which glow into a radiant, reddish tint as the sun sets. A mural commemorates the poetess Gabriela Mistral. "We were going to be queens," reads one of her poems, among my mother's favorites, though I don't know why. The spirit of it is poignant, but defeatist. In the poem, a woman reminisces about her past. She and her childhood friends spoke of growing up to become royalty and reach the sea. The years pass, and the disappointments of life have run them down. They never got to do a damn thing with their lives. What is left is the childhood aspiration: "*Ibamos a ser reinas.*" Mother yearned for greater things, but she never stood still. She rebelled against a stagnant life. She picked up and left. She touched the sea, and nearly drowned in it, yet she saved herself to give her son a home and a life. In the end, she returned to the sea, where her ashes remain. The unfulfilled promises of the poem strike me as anomalous to a time when women did stand still, like Chekhov's heroines in *Three Sisters* who talk about going to Moscow and never do anything to get there. *Ibamos a ser reinas*, my ass, my mother told this stagnant world; I've got a plane ticket to Washington, and you're only going to get me back to Santiago to bury me for good.

A trip to Mulchén in southern Chile also helped me complete the journey, back to where I was born, and back to where Aunt Nelly now lived with Parkinson's. The lively, plump aunt Nelly, who had once sang her songs with the rough, throaty voice of Nell Carter, sat around helplessly as a thin elderly woman in the house Aunt Tecla had left behind, the same Tecla (my grandmother's half-sister) who had revealed the secrets of our bastard lives to me in 1971. Thirty-two years later, her stepdaughter, Aunt Nelly, had returned from the United States to her hometown to live out her days in Tecla's house, knowing she could count on her family to care for her. Her U.S. Social Security was deposited automatically in her account, and it paid for a nurse, and her general maintenance.

Aunt Ruthy, another cousin and Nelly's stepsister, lived in the main house and supervised her care. She led me to a guest house on one of those cool June nights in which rain enveloped the city in this usually torrential part of Chile. A small wooden plank prevented me from slipping into mud and I balanced my way toward the little house to reach her. She saw me enter and smiled wanly.

"A special guest is here," said Aunt Ruthy. "All the way from the United States . . . it's *el Willy*."

My aunt's face barely lit up. She stared toward me, not knowing what to think.

"From where?" she asked. "*De dónde?*"

"From *los Estados Unidos*. You know, Nelly, it's el Willy."

"Oh, the little boy," she said. "He's still little."

True, I'm vertically challenged, and I haven't grown from my 5′ 6″ frame since 1977 or so. I've struggled, through marathoning gigs, to prevent myself from growing sideways, but I often managed until I turned forty to come across as "boyish" or "little." I assume she recognized me through that feature.

The magnetic Nelly, who posed with me once when I arrived in Washington D.C. on the steps of the Lincoln Monument overlooking the Washington one, now sat inside the little guest house all day, slowly, gradually watching the winter rains. I was headed south for Puerto Montt. A website for gay tourists promised the southernmost "alternate" nightclub in South America. I needed the titillation at a time when the occasion had turned somber. I wasn't there to "party" but Nelly would have been the first to go clubbing in D.C. She was the one who introduced my mother to the nation's capital, and she wasn't shy about dancing with the eligible bachelors. She had managed once to keep up an affair with a hot Portuguese man whose sturdy looks made me blush in my teenage years—that lucky aunt Nelly, I thought, until my mother ran into him at the supermarket with his wife and children that he had just brought from Portugal. My mother broke the news to her, and *la pobre* aunt Nelly stayed in her room for several days until she put on a more calm face again and could confront the world with it. This dance is for you, I thought, partying in Puerto Montt in the middle of a cold, rainy winter. The women who had cared for me had either died or aged or become incapacitated—and I decided to let myself run to Puerto Montt and stay up late into the night to give this life one more whirl before I aged any further myself.

One last stop at Aunt Gladys's in Santiago, and a couple of glasses of wine later, Gladys finally told me the story that had once been too personal to tell while Mother lived. Gladys was also grateful I was leaving her the urn in which I had carried María's ashes before I spread them into the Pacific. She felt privileged, could bond with me then, and she didn't think she had to hold back much longer about the secret. First, it wasn't a complete secret: I knew that my mother had been married briefly once, to a man called Cipriano, a couple of years before she met my father. But the reasons for the quick dissolution of their marriage weren't at all clear to me. My mother said it hadn't worked out, that's all. Gladys knew more. Within six months of the wedding, María acted quickly to get an annulment from the church. My aunt Gladys visited her in the southern city of Concepción during the difficult period when María was seeking the annulment, to provide some much-needed moral support, and my mother revealed to her the main reason.

"We have never had relations," she told her cousin.

"What?" My aunt smiled, amicably, not knowing what to make of this. "What exactly do you mean, no relations?"

"You know . . . we've never . . ."

"You've never had sexual relations with your own husband since you married?"

"I can't do it. Don't ask me why; I don't know. I just can't. He must hate me, this poor man. No wonder he didn't make a big fuss over the annulment. He must think I'm a horrible person for putting him through this."

Her local diocese required her to undergo a chastity test. A doctor approved by the church confirmed her virginity and wrote her a certificate she could show at her local parish the next time she married. She felt adamant about getting it—and today I wonder, where did that certificate of chastity go? I can't find it in her files she left behind in Portland, and, most likely, she didn't travel with such a thing to the United States. What an odd thing that might be to behold.

"Your mother wanted to marry through the church again, and she needed that certificate to prove her virginity. Of course, after going to all that bother, your mother met Guillermo, your father, who was a married man, and virginity went out the window. So much for chastity and purity!"

That was the paradox of our Catholic repression. My mother was incapable or unwilling to have sex with her own legally wedded husband, but found the courage to lose her virginity to a married man not her own. I followed in similar steps: I was for the longest time a technical virgin in, of all places, Hollywood, on Santa Monica Boulevard itself, into my twenties, until I arrived in Italy, where I lost mine to a double set of Communists. From chastity to debauchery. My mother never revealed the mystery of her unwillingness to consummate her marriage, and Aunt Gladys guesses she was simply "disgusted" by the thought of it. But my father quickly came along to help her overcome that.

At Santiago's international airport, a few family members came to see me off at three a.m. Why do Chilean authorities schedule departures at that time? Is it to test the will of the traveler's family to see how important the farewell is? I left behind a motley crew of sleepy relatives, people not connected to me by blood, the substitute family we'd managed to create as bastard children since the beginning of our lives. Teresa, *la otra*, came to bid me farewell along with her son Pablo, his daughter Charlotte, and a neighbor, Nana, who'd been a childhood playmate of mine. Now a grown-up woman, Nana spoke in fiery detail of her separation from her husband and her inability to divorce him under the Chilean law (a couple of years later, the Chilean Congress would finally legalize divorce). They stayed with me until the time to go through security. I bought them drinks. They marveled at the airport's prices, which by U.S. standards didn't seem excessive. I paid ten dollars for the entire bill, and they thought it was overpriced. These relatives have never traveled abroad. They can barely afford to travel within Chile. Economics keep them beyond that door. They can't afford to visit me; I must always visit them. In Chile, the airport is the one place where you will be physically cut off from your family members. They remain there, you are on the other side of the divide, and those walls may never be breached. It doesn't take a Berlin Wall to keep you separated. All it takes is a paycheck that buys you only a few groceries that keep you going till the next check. And my relatives are not starving, they are actually "middle class," by Chilean standards, but nonetheless they usually stay, with few exceptions, on that other side of the fence. I can't do anything about it. My mother tried to bring her niece to the United States and failed miserably. Aunt Chata decided she wouldn't be happy in L.A. and chose to go back to Chile. Others can't just pick up and go; most can't just come visit either. The plane fares are astronomical. One can get a better deal with a European package, including plane fare and hotel, than a roundtrip fare from the United States to Santiago. My Mexican friends visit their families constantly, and some members visit them in the United States in turn. The proximity allows for some interaction and sharing. My family does not see the home in which I live, or ride in my car, or meet my friends. The movies give them glimpses, most of them distorted by fantasy. They do not see me. They do not know me.

Our world is separate and unequal. I, the writer, want to draw us closer, knowing I can't make it so by wishing it into being. There's still the hope that words can bring us together, as actions brought us apart. It may happen some day. I can't live waiting for that to happen. I lead a separate life, but I am not forgetful.

I get up every other morning and take my six-mile run in Phoenix. Sometimes I cheat and take off a mile or two, or start the day with a visit to Starbucks nearby, followed by a steady run. I'm not deluded, I hope, but I sense that I have become stronger with age. I fulfilled my dare by completing the P.F. Chang's Rock 'n' Roll Marathon in Phoenix, my first, in January 2006 in a slow but steady five hours and twelve minutes. I broke no records, but that was not the point. I was able to train, employ my body at its fullest, and get to the finish line. That is one of the things María would have wished for, and I hope I have come to a point where she wouldn't have worried about whether she did the right thing to bring me so far away into a foreign country or whether she failed to strike it rich, or whether she could have done something else to provide me with a real father. She held on for as long as she could, and that was enough for me to keep alive the boundlessly life-affirming memory of her.

Epilogue

As I approached completion of the first draft of this book, in March 2007, I received an e-mail from a half-brother in Santiago, Chile, that opened up the floodgates of new information and revelations. I decided not to pursue them in this book, which would remain true to the spirit of the mood in which I started it and to the worldview—the bastard's raison d'être—that explains or justifies my various prejudices, hangups, and anxieties. The new information would have to queue up and, properly, wait its own place and time in the scheme of things.

Gonzalo Reyes, my half-brother, wrote in Spanish: "*Estimado Guillermo,* . . . we think you are our brother, and we would like to get to know you better and be in contact on a more permanent basis. . . . For me, it's extremely important to meet you since we only found out the facts about you when our father was very ill, and he told us of your existence. We, *your family* [emphasis mine], are united, and we love each other as brothers and sisters, and hope that one day we'll be able to embrace you and give your our familial affection."

Gonzalo revealed I have three brothers and two sisters, one of whom (Ximena Reyes) lives in Islip, New York. Shortly thereafter, I spoke on the phone with Ximena, who revealed that she tried for years going through the Los Angeles phone directory and calling every Guillermo Reyes listed in the area, to no avail. Only my mother's name was listed whenever I lived with her, but even now, in Arizona, I make a point of not listing myself, and who knows why exactly? The university's the appropriate place to find me, I suppose, which is where Gonzalo Reyes finally did reach me with the help of his Internet-savvy daughter, Javiera.

That spring as well, a student director, Fernando Contreras, of New York University, decided to produce my play *Deporting the Divas*, in a student-driven forum for October 2007.

"Edward Albee refused to give us the rights to do one of his plays," the young director told me over the phone. I felt obliged instead to give my consent. I even announced I would gladly go see it. "I might even meet my sister," I added, sounding casual, leaving the young director a bit perplexed. My double-tasking must seem annoying to people who want my undivided attention. But the thought had dawned on me: the double feature of watching my play and meeting with my sister seemed like the right form of drama for one short weekend.

In this book, I have chronicled what I knew about the two families that reared me, the Cáceres and Bravo families, but I remained mostly ignorant of the Reyes family that gave me its name. I am clearly not ready to accept legitimacy and to embrace the idea of belonging somewhere. To do so would spoil a worldview that embraces marginality and outsiderness. Gonzalo's e-mail certainly didn't change that view of my growing up. When I decided to write about my family, I thought I might find through the act of writing some sense of purgation shaped by language. I didn't expect the words alone to make me feel legitimate, or to expunge the solitude I felt as an only child. My half-brother's e-mail didn't reveal how the family would embrace me, or regard the many unsavory revelations in this book. When I wrote them, I didn't think it would matter to them, but this e-mail and later my phone call to Ximena made me realize that it probably will.

The one thing my brother's unexpected communiqué helped me do in this book is soften the language in the first chapter where I had referred to the Reyes family as distant people who didn't want to know me. A brief conversation with Ximena over the phone and my subsequent e-mails about my visit to New York erased that impression.

During the Halloween weekend of 2007, I flew out to New York City to see *Deporting the Divas* at New York University. I flew out there as the generous playwright who had given permission to have my work performed. Life, luck, and fortune had not given me the airs of Edward Albee, who could shut down any production because he disapproved of the interpretation. I was not quite the "legit" playwright in the American theater, and I was the bastard son in the Reyes family—altogether, I was quite consistent in the scheme of things. Not embraced entirely by the theater community, or by my family, it all made sense. But to actually experience acceptance at some level would change the scheme of things. I found myself feeling resistance toward change.

There is only one established Chilean restaurant in all of Manhattan, and that's Pomaire on Restaurant Row on West 46th Street. I chose to eat early because I knew I had a play to get to at NYU, and I found myself as the only customer at four that afternoon. I waited with a glass of Chilean wine and my favorite Chilean appetizer, the beef empanada, and wrote upon a journal about this visit to the city, even though there was nothing new to report yet. The waiter had no one else to spy upon, and I briefly told him I was meeting my sister for the first time. The only thing I had known about her once was that she was named after the love interest for El Cid, in the epic poem my father cherished and had taught to his adult school student, my mother. The waiter looked impressed, but perhaps a bit intimidated about the revelation of family drama, and left me to tend to my journal, where such things belonged. About twenty minutes later a woman more or less my age coursed in a bit out of breath, having walked all the way from the train station in cool weather, parting her hair from her eyes. She was visibly nervous.

The agreeable waiter stepped forward and knew just how to welcome her, pointing at me, the only customer there. "*Mire, señora, su hermano está ahí.* Your brother's right there."

Ximena walked over, sat down to share a glass of Chilean wine, and then began a lifetime of conversation that had to be rushed into a couple of hours. I told her not to despair. We had nothing but time, and whatever we missed on this occasion, the talks would continue for years to come. I was even writing a book, I told her. Why, our father was a writer, too, she said; he even wrote plays. I didn't know that. She picked up a glass of the Chilean cabernet, and we knew there were more surprises ahead. The pre-Broadway dinner crowd had only just begun to come in. Our voices began to fade into the crowd.